Double Truth

SUNY Series in
Contemporary Continental Philosophy
Dennis J. Schmidt, editor

Double Truth

by
JOHN SALLIS

STATE UNIVERSITY OF NEW YORK PRESS

Published by
State University of New York Press, Albany

For information, address State University of New York Press,
State University Plaza, Albany, N.Y., 12246

Production by Cathleen Collins
Marketing by Bernadette LaManna

Library of Congress Cataloging in Publication Data

Sallis, John, 1938–
    Double truth / John Sallis.
        p.   cm. — (SUNY series in contemporary continental
philosophy)
    Includes bibliographical references and index.
    ISBN 0-7914-2267-4. — ISBN 0-7914-2268-2   (pbk.)
    1. Truth.   2. Deconstruction.   I. Title.   II. Series.
BD171.S234   1995
121—dc20   94-5768
                                                      CIP

10 9 8 7 6 5 4 3 2 1

" 'Alle Wahrheit ist einfach.'—Ist
das nicht zweifach eine Lüge?—

Nietzsche, Götzen-Dämmerung

Contents

Acknowledgments

The double-face head fragment shown on the front cover comes from ancient Mesoamerica, from the Remojadas culture; it is dated 300–600 A.D. The genesis of the image is also double, indeed multiply so: the photograph redoubles the sculpted image of the ancient double-face. I am grateful to Jerry Sallis for the photograph and to Marta Cosenza Krell for the re-creation of the ancient fragment.

Thanks to the Alexander von Humboldt-Stiftung for continuing support and especially for the grant that made it possible for me to spend several months in Germany completing the present project.

For permission to draw on previously published papers I would like to thank the following publishers: Blackwell Publishers for material from *Derrida: A Critical Reader*, edited by David Wood; Indiana University Press for material from *Reading Heidegger: Commemorations*; The Johns Hopkins University Press for material appearing in *Diacritics*; Kluwer Academic Publishers for material (pp. 201–15) from *Eros and Eris: Contributions to a Hermeneutical Phenomenology. Liber Amicorum for Adriaan Peperzak*, edited by Paul van Tongeren, Paul Sars, Chris Bremmers, and Koen Boey; and *The Southern Journal of Philosophy*.

Thanks also to Nancy Fedrow and Jeffrey Taylor for their generous assistance.

Nashville
December 1993

Χαλεπόν

When, well along in his discourse on the cosmos, Timaeus proposes to make a new beginning because of the need to declare and make manifest another, third kind, he repeatedly expresses the character that such an undertaking will have by the word χαλεπόν: severe, difficult, troublesome, dangerous. He could indeed have said the same about declaring and making manifest the second kind. He does in effect say it of the second in saying it of the third, for what proves to be at stake in the question of the third is precisely the possibility of the second, the possibility of being other than one. It is a question not only of the second kind but of the second as such, of the possibility of a two that would not simply duplicate and coincide with the one. Such a two, the double, will always be χαλεπόν. As at the outset of the second hypothesis in the *Parmenides*: If one being is such that one and being are not the same, if therefore it is two, then it proves unlimited in number. A severe consequence, difficult and troublesome for one who would circumscribe being, dangerous for one who staked his security on such enclosure.

The double has always remained χαλεπόν. Doubly so, since philosophy has not been able—or only rarely—to forego the second sailing by which it would double what appears, doubling back to it only from the double, counting backwards so that what was one becomes two, so that what at first appeared becomes *après coup* the double.

The double is χαλεπόν because it never simply remains the double but, undoing the definiteness that the article would ascribe to it, always broaches redoubling, doubling the double. As in the case of mimesis, at least certain cases of mimesis: to submit an original to an image through which it would appear, perhaps even to itself, can always have the effect of also dividing the original from itself, rendering it itself double, so that, as Derrida says, one plus one makes at least three. Or equally: the second is already (at least) the third, two is already three. In other words, the double is false.

And yet, in its most classical and enduring determination truth is a double. It is that which doubles that which is, that is, truth is the double of being. If a proposition or judgment is said to be true, this is taken to mean that it accords with, corresponds to, duplicates, doubles, the matter itself about which the proposition or judgment is asserted. If, in turn, truth is ascribed also to things so that one may say, for instance, that one stands on the true earth, this is taken to mean that the thing, in this case the earth, accords with, corresponds to, duplicates, doubles, the very idea of such a thing, the essence by which is determined what it is. Both forms of *adequatio rei et intellectus*, both doublings of being, are gathered most intimately in speech about the true earth, which is, as Hegel said, the universal individual.

Precisely because truth is the double of that which is, because it is the double of being, truth is one, is unique; it is *the* double of being, the double that truly doubles being, the true double. Truth is the one true double, even though—troublesomely—there is a double doubling of being, the truth of propositions and the truth of things—hence a doubling of the one true double. One would need, then, to control carefully this doubling, to distinguish and keep rigorously separated the two orders of truth so that, within each, truth would remain unique. They would be allowed exchange only at the limit, in the one thing they have in common. Except, perhaps, in such troublesome cases as that of the earth.

One would be able, then, to speak—and to speak of—the sole truth. In this situation *double truth*—not truth as itself a double (of being) but rather a double of such truth, a double of the double—could only refer to untruth, falsity, error. If truth is unique—at least within each of its seemingly distinct orders—then a double of truth can only be something that masquerades as truth but is not indeed truth at all. In the order of speech, double truth, a double of truth, will always have been produced by one who, while in truth lying, ventriloquizes the truth. Thus, a double (of) truth would not be just untruth, falsity, error, of the sort that would be evident as such, that one would recognize as such and set aside from the sole truth. Such a sort of untruth might be troublesome, but it could never be dangerous. A double (of) truth is dangerous precisely because it is not exposed as such, because it conceals its character as a mere untrue double of the sole truth, because it is deceptive, self-concealing as such, an untruth in which one can become severely entangled, a falsity that one can expose only with the utmost difficulty, an errancy into which one can be drawn unawares. No word is more fitting for double truth than χαλεπόν.

The situation and its difficulties are only compounded if, as with Heidegger, concealment is shown to belong essentially to truth, to the essence of truth. For not only will truth then have been doubled in an essence—more precisely, an originary truth set forth as making truth possible, *Erschlossenheit* as the existential-ontological foundation of *Entdeckend-sein*—but also the concealment belonging to truth will prove to conceal itself as such. The concealment intrinsic to truth can come even to double back upon itself, this concealment of concealment making it seem, then, that there is no concealment at all, that, in doubling being, truth simply holds it open to unhampered vision. A concealing, therefore, of truth as such, of its very essence.

There are other doubles of being that are in a certain respect double truths. Among these none have proved more troublesome to philosophy than the doubles produced by mimesis and by imagination. From the beginning philosophy has sought to put mimetic images at a distance, banishing the poets from the polis and consigning their mimetic products to the inferior order of being to which they are taken to belong. For they are not even doubles of being, as are true things, but only doubles of the doubles, doubly removed from being itself and, because of their double removal, all the more capable of deceiving and corrupting those who fall under their spell. Philosophy never entirely ceases chanting the incantation by which protection would be provided against falling under that spell. The incantation will give voice to an insistence on keeping the orders not only rigorously separated but also in their true order, forestalling every effort by the poet (or by the philosopher fallen under his spell) to circumvent the intervening order and to ascend toward being itself on the wings of imagination. There are few evils that have not been attributed to imagination (in his treatise *On the Imagination* Pico della Mirandola writes an entire chapter "On the numerous Evils which come from the Imagination"). Even madness and every other manner of monstrosity can be linked to the doubles that phantasy, for instance, brings forth as if from airy nothing, the phantoms that come to haunt the scene of every presence, doubling the living spirit itself. And yet, philosophy has its wings too, as well as its madness. Keeping its doubles rigorously separated from those of mimesis and imagination will always prove difficult, troublesome.

For instance: if perception, to which mimesis and imagination would be rigorously subordinated, should prove incapable of dispensing with the image, the double. Especially if the image, in turn, should prove it-self irreducibly double, something both of the object and yet one's own.

For instance: if the philosophical ascent should prove inseparable from the indeterminately dyadic, from the play of the double. As in the absence of the true one. As in the flight that circles between earth and sky.

In all instances double truth will prove severe, difficult, troublesome, even dangerous. Yet also, if one follows its manifold doublings, prac-ticing an unheard-of kind of geometry, it may also prove capable of provoking a wonder not unlike that with which philosophy begins.

1

Doublings

"Erst der Mensch verdoppelt
sich so, das Allgemeine für
das Allgemeine zu sein."

Hegel, *Enzyklopädie*
Zusatz 1 to §24

One cannot (therefore) have begun.

For one will always only have begun again, redoubling what will always already have commenced.

Redoubling—the word is itself double, saying again in its prefix the repetition, reproduction, that is said in *doubling*. Its sense too is double: it means both to double and to double again—hence, a doubling itself subject to doubling, reiterable without a controlling limit, doublings. As in the exhortation that Shakespeare has Gaunt deliver to Bolingbroke:

And let thy blows doubly redoubled
Fall like amazing thunder. . . .[1]

Doubly redoubled: the phrase itself doubles what *redoubled* alone (in its double sense) already says, thus both saying and enacting doublings.

To begin will always be (or prove to have been) redoubling—which is to say no beginning at all.

Even for Socrates, paradigmatic figure of the beginning of philosophy. He (too) must redouble his effort and can begin only by beginning again, by setting out on a δεύτερος πλοῦς. His final discourse, spoken in the face of death, recounts his redoubling turn to discourse, his re-

---

1. Shakespeare, *Richard II*, act 1, sc. 3, lines 80–81.

1

course to λόγοι. The turn traces out the scene on which the history of metaphysics will be played out. For it is a turn away from the blinding vision of origin: Socrates will "be careful not to suffer the misfortune that befalls people who look at and study the sun during an eclipse. For some of them ruin their eyesight unless they look at its image [εἰκών] in water or something of the sort." A turn, then, to images. And yet, also a turn to λόγοι: "I thought of that danger, and I was afraid my soul would be blinded if I looked at things [τὰ πράγματα] with my eyes and tried to grasp them with any of my senses. So I thought I must have recourse to λόγοι and examine in them the truth of beings [τῶν ὄντων τὴν ἀλήθειαν]."[2] Both the discourse that follows in the *Phaedo* (which interprets the recourse as issuing in ὑπόθεσις) as well as those around the center of the *Republic* that are linked most closely with the pivotal discourse of the *Phaedo* serve to demonstrate that the recourse to λόγοι is nothing but a way of redoubling the drive to origin, of posing in every instance the thing itself (τὸ πρᾶγμα αὐτό)[3] as εἶδος and thus (re)launching the advance toward the originals. It is thus anything but simply a recourse to images, and one soon realizes that a redoubling haunts that very turn with which philosophy would begin. The turn is, at the same time—in Greek one would say, more appropriately, ἅμα— both originary, releasing an advance toward the origin, *and* regressive, directing one back to the images through which, if not among which, one would advance only by a kind of double vision. Thus, the double turn both directs one toward the origin and opens the space of the difference between the εἴδη and the things of sense. In turn, the εἴδη will only double in a sense, in sense itself, in sense as such, the things of sense, doubling thus the very sense of sense, establishing the limits that delimit (almost) the most gigantic of spaces, the scene of every γιγαντομαχία περὶ τῆς οὐσίας.

After Nietzsche—if not already in the Platonic inscription of the ἐπέκεινα τῆς οὐσίας (which fathers images—doubles—of itself), to say nothing of the χώρα (the mother of images, the virtually unspeakable condition of doublings)—one can no longer—that is, it turns out that one never could—be assured of controlling this doubling, of limiting it by referral to the delimiting origin. For when the true world finally becomes a fable, it is not only the (no longer) true origin that is set adrift but also the very doubling of sense. Now writing, whose very sense is in

---

2. Plato, *Phaedo*, 99d–e.
3. Plato, *Epistle* VII, 341c.

a sense to double sense, cannot but drift as on the open sea, on beyond "the land of truth," on beyond that "island, enclosed by nature itself within unalterable limits," out upon "the wide and stormy ocean."[4]

As if, again, on a δεύτερος πλοῦς. But now still more openly exposed to doublings. A writing amidst doublings.

Which is to say (also) a writing of—in the double sense of the genitive—a certain release of mimesis, a writing that would exceed the interpretation of mimesis that, inscribed in the Platonic texts, has governed, among other things, the history of the relationship between philosophy and literature. Even in the Platonic interpretation, mimetic doubling involves a mechanism that foils any effort at a controlling inscription, except perhaps one that would itself double textually (as in certain dialogues) the very logic that the mechanism releases. In its very simplest schema this "sort of logical machine"—as Derrida calls it in "The Double Session"—consists in the following: mimesis both furthers and hinders the disclosure of the thing itself, disclosing the thing by resembling it but obscuring it by substituting a double in place of it.[5]

Another, related mechanism is outlined in one of Derrida's discussions of Saussure in *Of Grammatology*.[6] The discussion belongs to that moment of double reading in which one undertakes to expose a certain doubling interior to the text itself, a doubling by which the metaphysical solidarities that are marked undergo a certain destabilization. The solidarity in question is phonocentrism, the subordination of writing to speech. For Saussure this subordination is secured within the order of mimesis as representation: "Language [*Langage*] and writing are two distinct systems of signs: the second *exists for the sole purpose* of representing [*représenter*] the first" (*G* 46; *C* 45—Derrida's emphasis). Writing would thus be related to human speech in the global sense (*langage*)

---

4. Kant, *Kritik der reinen Vernunft*, in vol. 3 of *Werke: Akademie Textausgabe* (Berlin: Walter de Gruyter, 1968), A 235/ B 294–95.

5. Derrida writes that "the whole history of the interpretation of the literary arts has moved and been transformed within the diverse logical possibilities opened by the concept of *mimesis*. These are numerous, paradoxical, and disconcerting enough to have released a very rich combinatorial system." Derrida adds a note outlining this logic in two propositions and six possible consequences and concluding: "this schema . . . forms a sort of logical machine; it programs the prototypes of all the propositions inscribed in Plato's discourse as well as in that of the tradition" (*La Dissémination* [Paris: Éditions du Seuil, 1972], 213). The simple schema that I suggest here is discussed in *Delimitations: Phenomenology and the End of Metaphysics* (Bloomington: Indiana University Press, 1986), chap. 1.

6. *De la Grammatologie* (Paris: Les Éditions de Minuit, 1967)—references indicated in text by *G*. Saussure, *Cours de linguistique générale* (Paris: Payot, 1980)—references indicated in text by *C*.

as outside to inside. Since writing is "foreign to the internal system" (*G* 50; *C* 44), it is to be excluded from the field of linguistics, spoken language alone constituting the object of that science. Thus would linguistics be rigorously delimited: "External/internal, image/reality, representation/presence, such is the old grid to which is given the task of outlining the field of a science" (*G* 50). Thus, in turn, is marked the solidarity of Saussurian linguistics with one of the oldest chains of metaphysical concepts. What produces a certain doubling back over this mark is Saussure's inability simply to disregard writing: "Thus, although writing is foreign to the internal system, it is impossible to disregard a process by which language is continually represented [*figurée*]" (*C* 44). Writing cannot be disregarded because, even if properly outside, it is not in fact simply outside but has always already contaminated spoken language, invading the interior and usurping the role that belongs properly to spoken language. Saussure cannot but denounce this inversion of the natural relationship and propose to protect speech from the violent intrusion of writing, to restore thus the natural relationship. What is especially to be denounced is the usurpation: writing (a mere representation, an image, of speech) becomes so intertwined with speech (the presence, the reality, the original) that there is an inversion, a perversion, in which it comes to seem that speech is an image of writing. In place of the rigorous distinction between the original reality and the representational image, there is a mingling of image with original, a confusion that Saussure can only denounce as a dangerous promiscuity—dangerous because it obscures the origin, dividing it from itself. Hence the mechanism:

> There is no longer a simple origin. For what is reflected is split *in itself* [*se dédouble en soi-même*] and not only as an addition to itself of its image. The reflection, the image, the double, splits what it doubles [*Le reflet, l'image, le double dédouble ce qu'il redouble*]. The origin of the speculation becomes a difference. What can look at itself is not one; and the law of the addition of the origin to its representation, of the thing to its image, is that one plus one makes at least three. The historical usurpation and theoretical bizarreness that install the image within the rights of reality are determined as the *forgetting* of a simple origin. (*G* 55)

Determined as (merely) a forgetting of a simple origin, this mechanism by which the double splits, and thus redoubles, that of which it is the double—this doubling operation is also determined by Saussure as catastrophe or monstrosity. Derrida cites from the *Course in General Linguistics*: "Language [*La langue*] is independent of writing" (*C* 45); and then, assuming (one of) the voice(s) of Saussure, he continues: "such is the truth of nature. And yet nature is affected—from without— by an overturning that modifies it in its interior, denatures it, and obliges it to deviate from itself. Nature denaturing itself, deviating *from itself*, naturally gathering its outside into its inside, is *catastrophe*, a natural event that overturns nature, or *monstrosity*, a natural deviation within nature" (*G* 61).[7] Thus catastrophe, monstrosity, within the very order of mimesis, released by the very logic of such doubling. Or rather, what— within a certain interpretation of mimesis, within *the* interpretation of mimesis that both governs and is governed by metaphysics and its history—can only appear as catastrophic, as monstrous.

Writing as catastrophic doubling. Writing of monstrous doubling— again in the double sense of the genitive.

How, then, is a δεύτερος πλοῦς to be undertaken again? How is the turn that is inscribed in the Platonic texts (most succinctly in the pivotal discourse of the *Phaedo*) to be reinscribed in a writing of monstrous doubling? No doubt, by remarking the metaphysical inscriptions, submitting those texts to a double mark, a double reading and writing.[8]

---

7. Saussure offers several examples of such inversion, such monstrosity: "But the tyranny of the letter goes even further. By imposing itself upon the masses, it influences and modifies language. This happens only in very literary languages where written texts play an important role. Then visual images lead to wrong pronunciations; such mistakes are really [*proprement*] pathological. This happens often in French. Thus for the surname *Lefèvre* (from Latin *faber*) there were two spellings, one popular and simple, *Lefèvre*, the other learned and etymological, *Lefèbvre*. Because *v* and *u* were not distinct in the old system of writing, *Lefèbvre* was read as *Lefèbure*, with a *b* that had never really existed in the word and a *u* that was the result of ambiguity. Now the latter form is actually pronounced" (*C* 53–54). Citing this passage, Derrida asks: "Where is the evil? . . . And what has been invested in the 'living word' that makes such 'aggressions' of writing intolerable? What investment begins by determining the constant action of writing as a deformation and an aggression? What prohibition has thus been transgressed? Where is the sacrilege? Why should the mother tongue be protected from the operation of writing?" (*G* 61). Saussure predicts that such violence exercised by writing upon speech will only increase in the future: "It is probable that these deformations will become ever more frequent and that the silent letters [*les lettres inutiles*] will come more and more to be pronounced. In Paris one already pronounces the *t* in *sept femmes*; Darmesteter foresees the day when one will pronounce even the last two letters of *vingt*—truly an orthographic monstrosity" (*C* 54).

8. "This structure of the *double mark* . . . works the entire field within which these texts move. This structure itself is worked in turn: the rule according to which every concept necessarily receives two similar marks—repetition without identity—one mark inside and the other outside the deconstructed system, should give rise to a double reading and a double writing" (*La Dissémination*, 10).

Among those inscriptions there is one that enjoys a certain privilege: a privilege, to be sure, with respect to Derrida's own itinerary, but also a certain limited privilege in principle. For in his readings of the Husserlian texts[9] what Derrida undertakes to demonstrate—or at least to begin to confirm—is "that the recourse to phenomenological critique is the metaphysical project itself, in its historical achievement and in the purity, yet now restored [*seulement restaurée*], of its origin" (*V* 3). What Derrida submits to double reading in *Voice and Phenomenon* is a decisive reinscription of the beginning of metaphysics, a redoubling that would restore the original precisely in the double. Thus it is that, while proposing to relate his texts by way of a strange geometry that would allow them to be, for instance, stapled in the middle of each other, he grants nonetheless that "in a classical philosophical architecture *Voice* [*and Phenomenon*] would come first [*en premier lieu*]."[10]

The voice is the pivot on which Derrida's text turns. It is what would empower speech, what would grant to expression the capacity to become transparent, self-effacing, in such a way as to allow the expressed meaning to present itself in its pure ideality. Thus would expression be differentiated from mere indication, which would always remain outside this sphere of pure diaphaneity. Thus would Husserl, within the limits of the affinity of this differentiation to the Aristotelian differentiation between speech and writing, also authorize the classical concept of writing as the visible-spatial doubling of speech—even if less dogmatically than Saussure, even if also finally, in "The Origin of Geometry," uncovering a decisive (and disruptive) connection between writing and ideality.[11] On the other side, Husserl would protect the ideality of meaning from all empirical contamination, rigorously differentiating expression from sense experience, marking them as distinct strata and precisely thereby undertaking to control the doubling that now comes to double the Platonic turn.

Everything depends, then, on the reduction that Husserl attempts to carry out in the first chapter of the First Logical Investigation. Here it is a matter of the reduction of indication: beginning—though in a sense also

9. Primarily *La Voix et le phénomène: Introduction au problème du signe dans la phénoménologie de Husserl* (Paris: Presses Universitaires de France, 1967)—references indicated in text by *V*. Edmund Husserl, *Logische Untersuchungen* (Tübingen: Max Niemeyer, 1968)—references indicated in text by *LU*.

10. *Positions* (Paris: Les Éditions de Minuit, 1972), 13.

11. See Introduction to Husserl's *L'Origin de la géométrie* (Paris: Presses Universitaires de France, 1962), 83ff.

not beginning, in more than one sense—with the general concept of sign, Husserl's analysis generates a series of "essential distinctions" by which what is nonessential, merely indicative, is separated off from the concept of meaningful sign, from expression, which through the reduction thus comes to be circumscribed in its essence. The reduction is in effect—or rather, in its intended effect—an eidetic reduction of language.

And yet, Husserl evades the beginning; he begins, not at the beginning, but only at a point where a doubling has already come into play and produced a differentiation. Derrida notes that Husserl forgoes taking up the question of the sign *in general*, that he limits himself to the observation that every sign is a sign for something, without inquiring about what it means to be a sign for something. Instead of beginning at the beginning by asking "What is a sign in general?" Husserl proceeds almost immediately to the radical dissociation between two kinds of signs, to the heterogeneity between expression and indication (*Ausdruck, Anzeige*). Derrida notes too that this move may be regarded as an operation of that same logocentric orientation that in general leads Husserl to subordinate the reflection on signs to logic and to undertake such reflection only within his *Logical Investigations*: Husserl's logocentrism would divert his analysis too quickly, dogmatically, in the direction of logical, meaningful signs, i.e., expressions. Yet, on the other hand, Derrida hastens to add, Husserl's strategy can also be regarded as the very opposite of dogmatism, as a kind of critical vigilance. Specifically, it can be regarded as his refusal to introduce some presumptive—that is, presupposed—comprehension of the concept of sign in general. Thus, Husserl would in effect have foregone assuming that there is *a* concept of sign, capable then of being divided into two different kinds of signs; he would in effect have left open the possibility of there being two irreducible concepts improperly attached to the same word. Thus, there would prove to have been a curious complicity between Husserl's logocentrism and his critical vigilance: led by his logocentric orientation to seek the essence of sign in expression and meaning, he would precisely thereby have been drawn away from positing a presumptive general concept of sign. An even more critical vigilance could then also have been brought into play, one that would put the very question into question. For if one were to ask "*What is* a sign in general?" one would have presumed by the very form of the question that it is a matter of asking about the truth or essence of the sign—that is, one would not have asked whether a sign is such a thing as can have an essence. Is it perhaps the case, on the contrary, that essence and truth are first made possible by signs and language? In this case the classical question ("What is . . . ?" "τί ἐστι . . . ?") could not but be interrupted: "For if the sign in some way preceded what one calls truth or essence, there would be no sense in speaking of the truth or the essence of the sign" (V 26).

Derrida's reading retraces the Husserlian text, attempting—in the words of a contemporaneous interview—" to think the structured genealogy of its concepts in a manner most faithful, most interior";[12] yet, at the same time, drawing out what is implicit in those concepts, it would submit that text to the double mark, marking those points at which the text diverges from itself, at which one may use "against the edifice the instruments or stones available in the house."[13] Of Grammatology provides a more precise, more nuanced statement of what deconstruction would venture: "Within the closure, by an oblique and always perilous movement, constantly risking falling back within what is being deconstructed, it is necessary to surround the critical concepts with a careful and thorough discourse, to mark the conditions, the medium, and the limits of their effectiveness, to designate rigorously their relationship [appartenance] to the machine whose deconstruction they permit; and, by the same stroke, designate the crevice through which the yet unnameable glimmer beyond the closure can be glimpsed" (G 25).

Let me recall—ever so briefly—the course of the reading in which Derrida doubles deconstructively the Husserlian reduction of indication.

The first stage of the reduction corresponds to the distinction between meaningful signs and indicative signs, between expression and indication. Husserl grants that normally meaningful signs are bound up (interwoven, entangled—verflochten) with indicative signs; or rather, since the difference proves quickly to be more functional than substantial (V 20), it turns out that most signs function in both ways, that in most signs the two functions are interwoven. Nonetheless, Husserl insists that the entanglement (Verflechtung) of meaningful signs in an indicative function is not essential: in solitary mental life (im einsamen Seelenleben) meaningful signs function without indicating anything. It is clear initially that with this distinction Husserl intends to mark the difference between linguistic signs (speech—Rede) and non-linguistic signs. And yet, as Derrida's reading underlines, the boundary shifts in the course of

---

12. *Positions*, 15.
13. *Marges de la philosophie* (Paris: Les Éditions de Minuit, 1972), 162.

Husserl's development of the distinction, indeed to such an extent that the very sense of the distinction changes. The shift is most conspicuous in Husserl's relegation of certain aspects of speech to the side of indication, for example, in his formulation, "facial expressions [*Mienenspiel*] and the gestures that involuntarily accompany speech without communicative intent" (*LU* II/1: 31). To an extent the exclusion of these aspects from the sphere of expression is determined by their lack of fusion with the meaning-intention. What for Husserl seems most decisive is their involuntary character, their lack of intention; and indeed whatever falls outside the voluntary, animating intention he will exclude from the sphere of expression. Derrida marks the scope of this exclusion: it includes "facial expressions, gestures, the whole of the body and of mundane inscription, in a word the whole of the visible and spatial as such." For: "Visibility and spatiality as such could only lose the self-presence of will and of the spiritual animation that opens up discourse" (*V* 37). Clearly, then, it is no longer a matter of a distinction between the linguistic and the non-linguistic but rather of a distinction within language: "For all these reasons, the distinction between indication and expression cannot rightfully be made as one between a non-linguistic and a linguistic sign. Husserl traces a boundary that passes, not between language and non-language, but within language in general, between the explicit and the non-explicit (with all their connotations)" (*V* 39). The distinction is, within language, between the voluntary, transparent, self-present and the involuntary, external, non–self-present, that is, between the pure spiritual intention (*la pure intention spirituelle*), the pure animation by *Geist*, and those aspects of speech that involve visibility and spatiality, the bodily aspects, as it were, of speech.

Thus, the reduction of indication would enforce an assimilation of language to voluntary, self-present intentional *Leben*. It would place the essence of language on the side of the spiritual, enclosing it in the citadel of *Geist*, securing it from intrusion from without. However problematic both *Leben* and *Geist* remain in Husserl's text.

The second stage of the reduction is addressed to what Husserl circumscribes as the most pervasive indicative function. This function, the intimating function (*die kundgebende Funktion*) or simply intimation (*Kundgabe*—Derrida translates: *manifestation*), is so pervasive as to be interwoven in all communicative speech: it is that function that serves to indicate to the hearer the "thoughts" of the speaker; that is, in Husserl's formulation, intimation provides a sign "for the sense-giving psychic experiences of the speaker, as well as for the other psychic experiences that belong to his communicative intention" (*LU* II/1: 33). For Husserl it is of utmost consequence to distinguish this intimating function from the meaning function. It is, then, precisely this distinction that the second stage of the reduction would enforce.

The turn to intimation serves to show that the reduction is not a matter simply of excluding whatever belongs to the visible-spatial order. Derrida identifies what it is, instead, that determines the reduction: "One approaches here the root of indication: there is indication whenever the sense-giving act, the animating intention, the living spirituality of the meaning [*vouloir-dire*], is not fully present" (*V* 41). It is just such full presence that is lacking in facial expressions and gestures, which retain a coefficient of externality, of non-presence. The lack is more radical in the case of the meaning-intention of another person: the lived experience of the other is radically non-present. Derrida concludes:

> The notion of *presence* is the nerve of this demonstration. If communication or intimation (*Kundgabe*) is essentially indicative, it is because we have no originary intuition of the presence of the other's lived experience. Whenever the immediate and full presence of the signified is concealed, the signifier will be of an indicative nature. . . . All discourse, or rather, everything in discourse that does not restore the immediate presence of the signified content, is inexpressive. (*V* 43)

What determines the reduction is the privilege accorded to presence: any moment of discourse that does not present the signified content, any moment that is irreducible to the self-present intention, is inexpressive, that is, indicative.

In order to maintain the integrity of expression, its essential distinctness from indication, it is imperative that Husserl demonstrate that speech in solitary mental life is free of intimation. His most decisive argument in this regard is the following: "In a monologue words can perform no function of indicating the existence of psychic acts, since such indication there would be quite purposeless. For the acts in question are themselves experienced by us at that very moment [*im selben Augenblick*]" (*LU* II/1: 36–37; cited in *V* 54). Whatever one might suppose to be intimated in speech in solitary mental life would in fact be experienced at that very moment, in the same moment, so that intimation would be superfluous, utterly without purpose (*ganz zwecklos*). Within the moment there would be no difference to be mediated by intimation, within the *Augenblick* no alterity to be bridged by an indicative function: "The present of self-presence would be as indivisible as a *blink of the eye*" (*V* 66).

Husserl cannot but exclude also the articulated sound-complex and of course the written sign, thus distinguishing essentially between the sensible sign and those acts by which expression is more than mere uttered sounds, the acts by which something is meant. Such is the third stage of the reduction: Here again the reference to speech in solitary mental life plays a crucial role. For in monologue the sensible sign itself undergoes a kind of reduction: one speaks to oneself *in silence*. Not that words disappear entirely: one could hardly conceive an expression in which words would be utterly lacking. Husserl's recourse puts into play—without further question—a very old opposition: "In phantasy a spoken or printed word floats before us, though in truth it does not at all exist" (*LU* II/1: 36). Thus is the sensible sign reduced: as mere imagined word it is assimilated to the self-present intention, while as sounded it is consigned to indication. Despite Husserl's aim of delimiting pure expression as the very essence of meaningful signification, his analysis leaves intact only the ephemeral images of words, their imaginary doubles, and displaces their originals (what one would call the real signs) to the side, the outside, of indication, thus setting the originals outside what would be the very domain of origin: "For it is clearer and clearer that, despite the initial distinction between an indicative sign and an expressive sign, only an indication is truly a sign for Husserl" (*V* 46).

The deconstructive doubling is thus such that, on the one hand, it (re)traces the Husserlian text from within, thinking the structured genealogy of its concepts in such a way as to show that the production of the essential distinctions is in effect an eidetic reduction of language, a reduction governed by the privilege of presence; while, on the other hand, it underlines that the pure expression to which language would be reduced would be only a silent soliloquy from which all real signs would have been banished, so that the effect of the Husserlian reduction would be finally to repress the sign, redoubling the metaphysical subordination of the sign to a domain of self-presence that would essentially precede all operation of signs.

Here one can begin to discern in the Husserlian project not just a reinscription of the metaphysical project in general but specifically a redoubling of the turn that marks the beginning of metaphysics. For in the reduction to a domain of pure self-present expression prior to all operation of signs, Husserl would in effect have carried out a turn to λόγοι that, as in the beginning, would serve to redouble the drive to origin. The question is whether this domain can remain intact in its prelinguistic integrity; or whether the turn—this moment of logocentrism—will not be (re)diverted to an operation of signification from which *Bedeutung*, thus adrift, would never be free. Such a diversion is broached in deconstruction as a turn to writing, to a writing that would no longer be the mere image of speech but rather its monstrous double.

Yet, the δεύτερος πλοῦς is not only a turn to λόγοι but also a doubling that matches meaning and sense, a doubling of the sense of sense. In its Husserlian reinscription this doubling appears as a parallelism between expression (purified of indication) and sense (experience). To the reduction of signification to pure expression Husserl would add a second reduction: the reduction of pure expression to an unproductive medium that would merely reflect the pre-expressive stratum of sense, of perception. Derrida's reading is concerned to mark the condition that makes this reduction possible, the condition that allows expression to be regarded as merely reflecting the pre-expressive stratum, as merely doubling in the order of ideality the stratum of sense experience. Such doubling requires that expression recreate at its proper level the presence and self-presence allegedly characteristic of the pre-expressive level of sense: "the medium of expression must protect, respect, and restore the *presence* of sense, *both* [*à la fois*] *as the object's being before us*, open to view, and *as proximity to self in interiority*" (*V* 83). What makes such restoration of presence possible is the essential connection of expression to the voice. It is the voice that preserves presence and thus lets the ideal meaning be immediately present:

This immediate presence results from the fact that the phenomenological "body" of the signifier seems to fade away at the very moment it is produced. It seems already to belong to the element of ideality. It phenomenologically reduces itself, transforming the worldly opacity of its body into pure diaphaneity. This effacement of the sensible body and its exteriority is for consciousness the very form of the immediate presence of the signified. (*V* 86)

In the voice the signifier effaces itself for the sake of the presence of the signified meaning; such effacement is possible only because the signifier never really escapes self-presence, because in the voice self-presence is preserved: "When I speak, it belongs to the phenomenological essence of this operation that *I hear myself at the same time* [*je m'entende dans le temps*] that I speak" (*V* 87).

Again—as with the purposelessness of indication in silent monologue—it is a matter of a certain self-coincidence in the order of time, a matter of a sameness of time that would give one back to oneself in the very unity of the moment in which one would reach out. Because the unity of the moment authorizes both reductions, it is also what determines the Husserlian reinscription of the Socratic turn.

Thus, it is on the question of time that the Husserlian project in a sense—in its doublings of sense and of the sense of sense—runs aground and prompts another δεύτερος πλοῦς that would be more openly exposed to doublings, a writing amidst doublings. For what Derrida marks in the Husserlian analysis of time, what he marks as working against the classical orientation of that analysis in a way that turns it against itself, is precisely a doubling that disrupts the unity of the moment.

Derrida's reading of the Husserlian analysis of time is even more explicitly double than his reading of the reduction of indication. On the one hand, he marks the point by which Husserl's entire analysis is inseparably linked to the metaphysical privileging of presence; that point is precisely the now-point, the punctual moment. Though Husserl grants that the now cannot be isolated as a pure stigmatic moment, as a simple point, this admission does not at all prevent its determination as a point from functioning constitutively in the analyses. Though indeed there is a certain spread from the now-point into the immediate, retended past and into the immediate, protended future—

> This spread is nonetheless thought and described on the basis of [*à partir de*] the self-identity of the now as point, as "source-point." In phenomenology the idea of originary presence and in general of "beginning," "absolute beginning," *principium*, always refers back to this "source-point." . . . Despite all the complexity of its structure, temporality has a nondisplaceable center, an eye or living core, the punctuality of the actual now. (*V* 69)

It is to this punctual—and, as such, self-identical—now that Husserl appeals in the phrase "*im selben Augenblick*," by which he would demonstrate the purposelessness of intimating indication in silent monologue. It is to this self-same now that he appeals also in conjoining, by the phrase *dans le temps*, speaking with hearing oneself, conjoining them into that self-presence of the voice that would make of expression an unproductive medium merely reflecting the pre-expressive stratum of sense. Not that Husserl is in error in making this appeal: on the contrary, he is proceeding from the most secure of grounds. He is moving within the very element of philosophy: such coincidence of intuition and presence as would be the originary as such, the originary from which every as such would be determined, the ἀρχή:

> Moreover, within philosophy there is no possible objection concerning this privilege of the present-now. This privilege defines the very element of philosophical thought, it is evidence itself, conscious thought itself, it governs every possible concept of truth and of sense. One cannot cast suspicion upon it without beginning to get at the core of consciousness itself from a region that lies elsewhere than philosophy, a procedure that would remove every possible *security* and *ground* from discourse. (*V* 70)

Derrida proposes that—on the other hand—it is precisely Husserl's own analyses that serve to cast such suspicion and to disrupt the discourse on—the discourse of—the self-identical present. What those descriptions demonstrate is that the present is essentially, constitutively, connected to the immediate past (by retention) and the immediate future (by protention):

> One then sees very quickly that the presence of the perceived present can appear as such only insofar as it is *continuously compounded* with a nonpresence and nonperception, with primary memory and expectation (retention and protention). (*V* 72)

This is to say that a nonpresence is admitted into the sphere of what would be originary presence, expanding the point, which it would come to constitute precisely in disrupting its punctuality. Thus, the self-identity of the present could no longer function as a simple origin (as present origin or originary present) but would rather be *produced* through a certain compounding of presence and nonpresence, of impression and retention, of impression and protention. Hence, the very constitution of the now, the moment, takes place as a doubling of the previous nows (or the nows to come) in the present now, i.e., as retention (or protention); and as a doubling, an unlimited repetition, of the now as such, in its ideality, as the ideal form of presence. This double doubling in which time is constituted, produced—Derrida will call it *différance*—is thus more originary than the present: it is—"if one can use this language without immediately contradicting it and erasing it—more 'originary' than the phenomenologically originary itself" (*V* 75). It will always already have introduced alterity into the moment, disrupting the "*im selben Augenblick*" and the "*dans le temps*," thus disrupting too the parallelism of indication/expression/sense that would be erected on the ground of that unity. When time begins, a monstrous doubling will already have begun; and it is only by repressing such catastrophe that one can be assured of controlling the doubling of sense marked by the Socratic turn. Deconstruction would release the monster from the cave and begin to write amidst doublings.

The stratification will be ruined, its schema disrupted, the schema that comes to govern and structure almost the entire program of phenomenology from *Ideas* on, a schema with a strong affinity to the classical schema stemming from Aristotle's *On Interpretation*, in which writing, like indication for Husserl, is determined as an outside of speech, as doubling it in the visible order. For the Husserlian schema, which would determine the orders of indication, expression, and sense as distinct, parallel strata, requires precisely those reductions—the reduction of indication and the reduction of expression to an unproductive medium—that are shown by Derrida's reading to rely on the unity, the self-identity, of the present. As soon as the appeal to the self-presence of the "*im selben Augenblick*" is interrupted by the deconstruction of the Husserlian time-analysis, the distinctness and parallelism between indication and expression is ruined: indication—especially in the form of intimation—cannot be kept out of expression, not even in silent monologue. Correspondingly, as soon as the appeal to the "*dans le temps*" that would unite speaking with hearing-oneself-speaking is interrupted, the reduction of expression to an unproductive medium that would merely image sense—in a doubling both controllable and thematizable as such (*Experience and Judgment* would broach such a thematization)—is likewise ruined.

What is at issue at both levels is self-affection. There is no disputing the uniqueness of the voice as a form of self-affection: one can hear-oneself-speak "without passing through an external detour, the world, the non-own [*non-propre*] in general" (*V* 88). There is marked contrast, for instance, with seeing oneself or touching oneself, for in these instances the exterior belongs inseparably to the field of the self-affection; whereas the voice in its purity would return one to oneself this side of any exteriority, fashioning a sphere of self-doubling that would open only upon meaning in its ideality, upon the universal (*das Allgemeine*):

> As pure self-affection, the operation of hearing-oneself-speak [*s'entendre-parler*] seems to reduce even the inward surface of one's own body; in its phenomenon it seems capable of dispensing with this exteriority within interiority, this interior space in which our experience or image of our own body is spread forth. This is why hearing-oneself-speak is experienced as an absolutely pure self-affection, in a self-proximity that would be the absolute reduction of space in general. It is this purity that makes it fit for universality. (*V* 88–89)

For Derrida there is no question of retracting the results of Husserl's minute, rigorous, and quite novel analyses: the uniqueness of the voice and its distinctive capacity for universality is to be acknowledged. Derrida insists even that vocal self-affection is "no doubt the possibility for what is called *subjectivity* or the *for-itself*," that, even further, "the voice *is* consciousness" (*V* 89). Yet, because the voice is submitted to time, to the production that cannot but introduce alterity into the moment, vocal self-affection cannot be—despite its capacity to reduce exteriority—a matter of pure undivided hearing-oneself-speak. Alterity will always already have been operative in the production of vocal self-presence, dividing one from oneself in advance of the very production of one-self, of subjectivity, of consciousness. In vocal self-affection it is not as though there is first a being (the self, subjectivity, consciousness), which then comes to affect itself through the circuit of hearing-oneself-speak. There (is) the (movement of) self-affection—the parentheses marking here the erasure that writing amidst doublings must bring into play. It is from the differential operation of self-affection that the self-coherent self, the self itself, would be produced:

> The movement of *différance* is not something that happens to a transcendental subject. It produces the subject. Self-affection is not a modality of experience that characterizes a being that would already be itself (*autos*). It produces the same as self-relation within self-difference, the same as the non-identical. (*V* 92)

The production of time is also a matter of self-affection. Referring to Heidegger's analysis in *Kant and the Problem of Metaphysics*, Derrida writes: "The 'source-point,' the 'originary impression,' from which the movement of temporalization is produced [*à partir de quoi se produit . . .*] is already pure self-affection" (*V* 93). The structure of this self-affection, of the production of time, of temporality, is not only complex but also such as to interrupt the very language that the analysis nonetheless requires, thus also such as to demand, then, a different writing, a writing of difference, a writing amidst doublings. The analysis extends that of the retentional and protentional structures and involves—to proceed very schematically—three points. First: temporality is *pure production*. There is not some being in which temporality would then come to be produced: there (is) simply production of temporality without any being in which it would inhere. Second: the now, the "originary" impression, *engenders itself*. It is not produced by any being, not produced by anything. Such is its "absolute novelty": to be engendered by nothing, to engender itself without having somehow been there in advance of the self-affective engendering. If one steadily erases (unsaying in the very saying) such locutions as "being there" ("there is") and "in advance," one may say: the now produces itself in a doubling in which there is no original in advance of the double it produces. Third: this self-engendering doubling is (also) a self-differing, that is, the now doubles itself in such a way as to become a not-now to be retained in another now. Thus Derrida refers to

> the process by which the living now, producing itself by spontaneous generation, must, in order to be a now, be retained [*se retenir*] in another now. . . . Such a process is indeed a pure self-affection in which the same is the same only in affecting itself from the other [*s'affectant de l'autre*], only by becoming the other of the same. This self-affection must be pure, since the originary impression is here affected by nothing other than itself, by the absolute "novelty" of another originary impression that is another now. (*V* 94–95)

Because the production of time is pure self-affection (the double doubling of self-differing self-engendering), all language, taking its resources from beings, fails to say such doublings otherwise than by metaphor:

> But one has always already drifted into ontic metaphor. . . . The word "time" itself, as it has always been understood in the history

of metaphysics, is a metaphor that *at the same time* [*en même temps*] both indicates and dissimulates the "movement" of this self-affection. (*V* 95)

This peculiar metaphoricity, this transfer between being and time, is decisive for writing amidst doublings.

The double doubling of temporality and its redoubling in the sphere of the voice disrupt, then, the Husserlian schema that would determine the orders of indication, expression, and sense as distinct, parallel strata, that is, as simple, controlled doubling:

> Also, just as expression does not come to be added like a "stratum" to the presence of a pre-expressive sense, so likewise the outside of indication does not come to affect accidentally the inside of expression. Their intertwining (*Verflechtung*) is originary. (*V* 97)

Between the orders of sense, expression, and indication the doublings of time and the voice would release: doublings. Thus would be prompted a δεύτερος πλοῦς as writing amidst doublings, writing those doublings as, for instance, *la différance*, as *le supplément d'origine*, but also as *mimesis* and as *doublings*. Perhaps most notably, as the doublings of *Geist*: the doublings by which spirit is haunted by spirit and ventriloquized by a phantom whose separation from what would be spirit itself cannot be secured and controlled,[14] almost a parody of spirit's return to itself. Such writing amidst doublings one could call ghost writing.

---

14. See Jaques Derrida, *De L'Esprit: Heidegger et la question* (Paris: Galilee 1987), esp. 66.

2

Flight of Spirit

Flight. Almost always of a bird.

Of a bird of prey perhaps. The proud spirit of the eagle in his magisterial coldness and imperturbable seriousness. Emblem of power: both Kant and Hegel mention Jupiter's eagle. He is an emblem, then, of *Führerschaft*, this namesake of the philosopher of spirit, an emblem of: SA.

Of a dove perhaps. The light dove, cleaving the air in her free flight and feeling its resistance, supposing then that flight would be still easier in empty space, venturing the plunge. Or, afterwards, *revenant*: returning from her adventure, returning to hover between heaven and earth. Emblem of the adventure of metaphysics, extended into an emblem of its end, of the end of its epoch. Emblem also of a venture that will never cease to tempt, perhaps most of all when what is called for is *Führerschaft*. A venture from which one will always again have to return.

Also the venture, the flight, of that other animal that would be other than animal, spirit and not just beast—the undetermined animal, Nietzsche called him. Fabricating himself as a bird—so it is told—he was exposed as he ascended toward the sun and fell to earth, destitute. Man has always dreamed of flying, even at the cost of his humanity. Until he no longer had to dream.

But then it will long since have ceased being a flight of spirit emblematized by the flight of a bird, an animal. It will not be a matter of the living and the spiritual but of the coldness, the mechanism, of technology. *Destitution de l'esprit, Entmachtung des Geistes*. Not only Heidegger but also—almost in advance of metaphysics—the New Testament would announce a new spirit, another spirit. All four Gospels tell

19

of how, as Jesus emerged from the waters of baptism, the heavens were opened and the spirit descended upon him as a dove. A flight of spirit from above, to be received by one properly prepared.

As by the apostles on Pentecost: a sound came from heaven like the rush of a mighty wind, and then tongues of fire, so that they were filled with the spirit and began to speak in other tongues, as the spirit gave them utterance. The fire of spirit brings the gift of speech, so that when one speaks one will always already have hearkened to the promise of the voice of spirit and the tongues of its fire.

The exchange imagined between Heidegger and certain Christian theologians could go on interminably. Or, perhaps, it could come to an end only as in fact it does, at the end of the book *Of Spirit* (*De L'Esprit*),[1] as a result of certain limits, certain binds, announced in that book, as a result of the doublings that occur at those limits and that constitute those binds. Also, perhaps, as a result of unsettling certain other limits that *Of Spirit* would announce.

(a)

In *Of Spirit* Derrida retraces with consummate skill and subtlety the flight of spirit in the texts of Heidegger, retraces it through an itinerary that runs from *Being and Time* to the 1953 essay on Trakl, "*Die Sprache im Gedicht.*" This itinerary is one that has not been mapped previously, and it is not without a certain surprise that, reading *Of Spirit*, one recognizes how operative the various forms of *Geist* are in Heidegger's texts, indeed how forcefully this word governs some of the most controversial of those texts. Not that *Geist* is ever a theme for Heidegger in the way that temporality, language, and the work of art may be said to be themes; and yet, precisely on this account its operation in Heidegger's text is more resistant to the *Destruktion* to which Heidegger would submit all words and concepts belonging to the history of ontology. Its operation is also more consequential: Derrida shows how Heidegger's invocation of *Geist* commands extraordinary authority in the German language, returning to this word an extraordinary force; how *Geist* is regularly inscribed in the most highly political contexts; and how it determines

---

1. References are given in the text by page numbers alone.

perhaps the very sense of the political as such, at least the locus of any such delimitation. Its operation is also more complex, more subject to interruptions, to reversals, to the play of multiple and incomplete *sens*. Derrida's reading submits to this textual complexity, patiently and rigorously exposing the flight of spirit as it is outlined and enacted in a dazzling array of forms in Heidegger's texts.

And yet, it is a reading, guided by certain concerns, following certain guiding threads. Derrida mentions some of the lectures and seminars out of which grew the parameters of the reading in *Of Spirit*: a lecture on *Geschlecht* given at Loyola University in March 1985, the sequel to an earlier essay on the same theme;[2] a private seminar given at Yale the following year, from which came the remarks presented at a colloquium "Reading Heidegger" held at the University of Essex in May 1986.[3] *Of Spirit* itself was presented as a lecture at a conference "Heidegger: Questions ouvertes" held at the Collège International de Philosophie in Paris in March 1987.[4] The text of the lecture, supplemented by several notes, was published in October 1987. Among the notes there is one in which Derrida calls attention to a certain private communication following his remarks at the Essex Colloquium (147–54). The communication came from another of the participants in the Colloquium, Françoise Dastur, who pointed out a passage in one of Heidegger's later texts that cannot but disturb that privileging of the question that Derrida will nonetheless continue to attribute to Heidegger. I shall return to this note later in order to underline its remarkable—and disruptive—insertion into Derrida's text.

---

2. "*Geschlecht* II: Heidegger's Hand," in *Deconstruction and Philosophy: The Texts of Jacques Derrida*, ed. J. Sallis (Chicago: University of Chicago Press, 1987). The earlier text is "*Geschlecht*: sexual difference, ontological difference," *Research in Phenomenology* 13 (1983). Both texts are published in French in *Psyché: Inventions de l'autre* (Paris: Galilée, 1987), which was published simultaneously with *De L'Esprit*. A third text ("*Geschlecht* III") was distributed to the other participants in the conference at Loyola but was not read; it has not been published. *De L'Esprit* leaves open the possibility of a continuation of the *Geschlecht* project (137). Indeed, a fourth text was presented in September 1989 at a conference on Heidegger also held at Loyola University in Chicago. It is published as "Heidegger's Ear: Philopolemology (*Geschlecht* IV)," in *Reading Heidegger: Commemorations*, ed. J. Sallis (Bloomington: Indiana University Press, 1993). Still, the project as a whole, if it can be regarded as such, remains incomplete.

3. An outline of these remarks along with the discussion following them has appeared as "On Reading Heidegger: An Outline of Remarks to the Essex Colloquium," *Research in Phenomenology* 17 (1987).

4. The proceedings of the conference were published in March 1988: *Heidegger: Questions ouvertes* (Paris: Osiris). These proceedings contain only the first part of *De L'Esprit*.

Though the four guiding threads that Derrida's reading follows were introduced at the Essex Colloquium, it is only in *Of Spirit* that *Geist* is introduced as determining and as weaving together the four threads, as spinning them out and repeatedly knotting them together. The first of the guiding threads is the question of the question, that is, of the privilege that Heidegger accords to questioning, a privilege that he seems to have accorded to it absolutely and that for a long time he did not call into question. The statement from the Essex Colloquium is most direct and unqualified: "The question is privileged everywhere by Heidegger as *the* mode of thinking."[5] *Of Spirit* is more cautious, leaving the way open ever so slightly for the exception, for the moment when Heidegger would have broken with the assertion of the privilege of the question: "But he has *almost* never ceased, it seems to me, to identify what is highest and best in thinking [*le plus haut et le meilleur de la pensée*] with the question . . . " (24f.). Derrida proposes to show that "*Geist* is perhaps the name that Heidegger gives, beyond all other names, to this unquestioned possibility of the question" (26). *Geist* would name the assurance of the question, of its possibility and its nobility, would shelter its privilege.

The second guiding thread concerns Heidegger's assertion that the essence of technology is not itself anything technological. This assertion, which Derrida calls "traditionally philosophical," would assure the thought of essence by affirming the purity and separateness of the essence; it would shelter the thought and the language of essence from any originary contamination by technology. For Derrida it would be a matter, then, of analyzing this desire for rigorous noncontamination, linked no doubt to the privilege of the question; and of bringing into view a certain necessity of contamination. Derrida would like to suggest, too, that *Geist* names what Heidegger, in the turn to essence, would like to save from the destitution wrought by technology. And yet, even the destitution of spirit cannot but prove to be itself spiritual, and Heidegger will be led to the attempt to secure a certain purity within spirit by way of the difference between *Geistigkeit* and *Geistlichkeit*. Derrida returns again and again to such doubling. It will be necessary to follow the returns for a while before attempting again, as at the Essex Colloquium,[6] to complicate the question of essence from Heidegger's side. For one can be sure

---

5. "Reading Heidegger," 171.
6. See the Discussion that followed Derrida's remarks at the Essex Colloquium, *Research in Phenomenology* 17 (1987), esp. 180f.

that Heidegger will not have enacted the traditional philosophic turn to the essence without setting into motion a radical rethinking of the very determination of essence.

The third guiding thread concerns Heidegger's discourse on animality. In Heidegger's interpretation of the hand as something that can be had as such only by humans and not by animals—an interpretation that Derrida investigated in *"Geschlecht* II"[7]—he poses an opposition between the human Dasein and the animal, an opposition that leaves intact, according to Derrida, the most profound axioms of metaphysical humanism. This thread is knotted together with the others: questioning is the prerogative of Dasein alone, as is the turn to the essence, as is essentially determined technology. The animal—or rather, that which would be gathered under "this so general and confused word animality"[8]—is capable of none of these. Thus has it been decided since the beginning of metaphysics, throughout its epoch(s).

The fourth thread concerns epochality, the concealed teleology or narrative order that Derrida finds haunting the Heideggerian history of Being, running through and organizing the successive movements "in which," as Derrida formulated it at the Essex Colloquium, "Being gives itself by dissimulating itself, holding itself back in reserve even as it shows itself."[9] In this regard it is a matter of suspicion especially about what would be too quickly foreclosed in Heidegger's text, the interpretation of the Platonic χώρα, for example, or the non-subjective thought of Spinoza, which, falling in an epoch taken to be dominated by the subject-object relation, remains largely ignored by Heidegger. In its greatest scope, as the difference between the epoch(s) of ontotheology and that of another thinking, Heidegger's epochal discrimination will, with respect to spirit, be organized around the intraspiritual difference between *geistig* and *geistlich*. It is this discrimination that is broached and that would be enforced by Heidegger's reading of Trakl; and it is this discrimination that is at issue in the scene imagined between Heidegger and certain Christian theologians, the scene with which *Of Spirit* ends.

Derrida's remarks at the Essex Colloquium conclude having introduced the guiding threads: "These are the four threads. The question at the end is whether we can or should knot them together. Perhaps we

---

7. Derrida cites Heidegger's remark in *Was Heisst Denken?* that "apes, for example, have organs that can grasp, but they have no hand" (*"Geschlecht* II," 173).

8. Ibid.

9. "Reading Heidegger," 174.

should, after the manner of Heidegger, try to think these four threads, not as a unity, but as a *Geflecht* or weave. . . ."[10] In *Of Spirit* Derrida sets about knotting them together, weaving them into the fabric of a text that retraces in all its complexity the flight of spirit in Heidegger's work. And yet, *Of Spirit* is set apart from that flight, especially from a certain nationalism that operates within it and that would lay claim to spirit by claiming that German is the only language in which spirit comes to name itself (113). For the very form of the title of *Of Spirit* (*De L'Esprit*) marks it as French, recalling a certain French essayist tradition and, beyond that, the Ciceronian, Latin tradition. It is set apart, too, by the very space of translation separating *esprit* from *Geist*, the Latinate from the Germanic, set apart at a distance that, at a certain moment in the Heideggerian flight of *Geist*, will be dogmatically asserted and invasively absolutized. Derrida will not pass lightly over Heidegger's remark—almost comic, if one could overlook all that is intertwined with it—that when the French begin to think, they speak German (111). Not only will Derrida quote the remark *in French*, mocking its high seriousness with an unmistakably Nietzschean laughter; but also in order "to breathe a little" he will let his text spin off from Central Europe, from the German center, eccentrically invoking the English spirit of Matthew Arnold's "great doctrine of 'Geist,' " citing in English the Prussian advice that one ought to "Get *Geist*," advice untranslatable as much because of *Get* as because of *Geist* (114–116). *Esprit* is also—wit.

(b)

The flight of spirit begins in *Being and Time*. *Geist* is one of several terms that Heidegger warns ought to be avoided. He inscribes it in a chain of concepts belonging distinctively to modern metaphysics (soul, consciousness, spirit, person), all expressing opposition to things and signalling especially an opposition to the reification of the subject. From such a metaphysics of the subject, such subjective determination of spirit, the existential analytic of Dasein is to be disengaged. The terms belonging to the deconstructible ontology have no place in the analytic of Dasein. Heidegger announces, therefore, that in determining the be-

---

10. Ibid.

ing that we ourselves are, he is going to avoid these terms. As a member of the chain, *Geist* is entangled in ontological obscurity, missing the phenomenality of Dasein, continuing to be governed by a very sedimented ontological determination (*subiectum*, ὑποκείμενον). Thus, the existential analytic must exercise the utmost vigilance regarding it (31–36).

The vigilance consists, on the one hand, in avoiding the term. But, on the other hand, it is also a matter of a mode of avoidance that comes down to saying without saying. For in *Being and Time* Heidegger does not always simply avoid the word but sometimes uses it *between quotation marks*, thus using it without using it, avoiding it yet not avoiding it. By placing the word between quotation marks, something of spirit is withdrawn from the modern metaphysics of subjectivity, something of spirit is preserved outside that chain of sedimented concepts, something that the word "*spirit*" names between quotation marks. A certain return of spirit, a reappropriation, thus begins.

The strategy is perhaps most explicit in Heidegger's analysis of space, of Dasein's spatiality. In the first round of the analysis, Heidegger avoids—simply, purely—the traditional concept of spirit: Dasein is not a spiritual interiority that would somehow become spatial. But then, in the second round of the analysis, Heidegger has recourse to quotation marks:

> The word "spirit" returns, it is no longer rejected, avoided, but used in its deconstructed sense to designate something other that resembles it and of which it is like the metaphysical phantom, the spirit of another spirit . . . , a double of spirit. (45)

Dasein's spatiality does not supervene on a metaphysical spirituality, and yet it is because Dasein is "spiritual" in this other sense, set apart from its metaphysical double by the quotation marks, that it is spatial and that its spatiality has a certain originary character.

Six years later the quotation marks disappear. Spirit, unencumbered, takes flight; the spiritual becomes *le plus haut*, which in its very loftiness (as that which would lead the leaders of the *Hochschulen*) hovers above the most profound forces of earth and blood. It is 1933, and the new Rector is to call for spirit to be affirmed through the self-assertion of the German university, led by a *Führer* who would himself be led by the inexorability of a spiritual mission. Now Heidegger will propose a definition: "Spirit is originarily attuned, cognizant openedness to the essence of Being [*Geist ist ursprünglich gestimmte, wissende Entschlossenheit zum Wesen des Seins*]."[11]

Here spirit no longer has the sense determined by the metaphysics of subjectivity; nor is it to be released by a writing that would have to detach it deconstructively from its metaphysical double. And yet, the strategy by which spirit would be deployed in the *Rectoral Address* (*Rektoratsrede*) will not be able to elude a certain doubling that will surprise it. Heidegger's discourse would confer the most reassuring and most elevated spiritual legitimacy on the political movement in which he engages himself; he spiritualizes National Socialism, would save it by marking it with the affirmation of spirituality, of science, of questioning. This very move also limits Heidegger's engagement: his discourse appears simply not to belong to the ideological camp that would appeal to obscure biological forces. And yet, there is a trap that Heidegger's strategy cannot simply evade: for one cannot simply set oneself apart from biologism, naturalism, racism but rather can do so only by reinscribing spirit in an oppositional determination, by making it again onesidedly subjective. Heidegger's affirmation of a new spirit cannot escape the metaphysical double:

> Spirit is always haunted by its spirit: a spirit, in other words, in French as in German, a phantom always surprises by returning to ventriloquize the other. Metaphysics always returns . . . and *Geist* is the most fatal figure of that return. Of the double that one can never separate from the simple. (66)

The kind of bind from which Heidegger's political strategy cannot simply free itself occurs also in relation to the problem of animality, which Heidegger addresses most persistently in the lecture course of 1929–30 (*Die Grundbegriffe der Metaphysik*) and to which Derrida loops back in retracing the flight of spirit. Derrida stresses that Heidegger's analysis of animality has the great advantage of avoiding anthropocentrism, recognizing a difference of structure that renders the animal's rapport to beings *other* than the human's. And yet, alongside the

---

11. *Die Selbstbehauptung der deutschen Universität* (Frankfurt a.M.: Vittorio Klostermann, 1983), 14. Most striking in this definition is the link forged to *Sein und Zeit* by the word *Entschlossenheit*, rendered as resoluteness in the English translation by Macquarrie and Robinson. Derrida cites Granel's French translation: "*l'esprit est être-résolu à l'essence de l'être*" (60).

value thus accorded to alterity, there comes into play another, incomparable value, that of lack. The animal—unlike a stone—has access to beings, but, in distinction from man, it does not have access to beings *as such* and in their Being. The animal's access is thus impoverished; the animal's rapport to beings is determined, limited, by the animal's being *weltarm*; and the poverty of the animal world requires that a certain erasure come into play in *our* language about the animal: when one says that a lizard is stretched out on a rock, one ought, according to Heidegger, to erase (*durchstreichen*) the word *rock* in order to indicate that that on which the lizard is stretched out, though somehow given to the lizard, is not recognized *as* a rock, not given *as such*. The animal's rapport is other *and* is impoverished; and Derrida suggests that the difficulties that accumulate in Heidegger's analyses in the 1929–30 course arise primarily from the incompatibility of these two values (75–84).

Derrida insists that this axiomatics remains constant in Heidegger's texts. Reintroducing the measure of man in the very gesture that was to have withdrawn the animal from that measure, it remains for Heidegger a matter of marking an absolute limit between the (merely) living and human Dasein, a limit that, at the same time, marks an impoverishment and thus implies hierarchization and evaluation, that is, a certain humanist teleology. Derrida denies—most remarkably—that it is his intent to criticize this humanist teleology, as though this return of metaphysics could simply be cancelled and the Heideggerian text rewritten outside all such doubling. Rather, Derrida wants to recall and to underline that the return of—the return to—such humanist teleology is the price that Heidegger had to pay for being able to issue his ethico-political denunciation of the biologism and naturalism of the Nazi ideologues. Not only the price that Heidegger had to pay but the price that one has had to pay up to the present in order to denounce biologism, naturalism, racism. Derrida's analysis of this "logic"—note here, too, a double writing, doubling what would have been called logic itself—is intended, by his own testimony, "to exhibit and then to formalize the terrifying mechanisms of this program, all the double binds that structure it." How is one to face up to this "logic"? There is no easy way:

Is this a fatality? Can one escape it? There is no sign that lets us think so, neither in the "Heideggerian" discourse nor in the "anti-Heideggerian" discourse. Can one transform this program? I do not know. In any case one will not evade it at once [*d'un coup*] and without recognizing it in its most twisted ruses and its most subtle extension. (87f.)

The Heideggerian flight of spirit continues beyond 1933. The 1935 course *Introduction to Metaphysics* repeats the invocation of spirit launched by the *Rectoral Address*, repeats it at a level that would, however, be more decisively prior to any determined politics; it invokes the freedom of spirit in the leap into questioning. At the same time, the 1935 course also begins to make a certain political retreat by proposing a kind of geopolitical diagnosis, all the resources and references of which lead back to spirit. It is a matter of the destitution of spirit, its *Entmachtung*, its *démission*, in which are produced those forms of misinterpretation of spirit that Heidegger most forcefully denounces.

In this regard, too, Derrida's analysis focuses on the doubling that twists Heidegger's text. Here is how he traces the "logic": if a disempowering (*Entmachtung*) deprives spirit of its force, this entails that spirit both *is* and *is not* force, that it both has and does not have power. For if spirit were force in itself, if it were power itself, it would not lose its force and there could be no disempowering. But if it were not force or power, the disempowering would not affect it essentially, the disempowering would not be something of the spirit. One must say both—that it *is* and *is not* force—doubling the concept, letting the concepts of spirit, force, and world (of the spirit) be structured by the relation to a double. There is, correspondingly, a peculiar "logic" of inside/outside to be traced here: if, as Heidegger says, the destitution of spirit is proper to spirit, if it proceeds from within, then the inside must enclose a duplicity, that is, it must envelop an immanent outside, an internal exterior that would haunt the monologue of spirit, ventriloquizing it so as to rob it of itself. The duplicity that, in his interpretation of Schelling, Heidegger will think as the spiritual essence of evil (67–73; 91–105).

Derrida moves rapidly through Heidegger's readings of Schelling, Nietzsche, and Hölderlin, in order to come to Heidegger's final response to the question of spirit, the last flight, the end of the flight. What is spirit, finally? Fire, flame, conflagration. *Der Geist ist Flamme—une flamme qui enflamme ou qui s'enflamme: les deux à la fois* (132f.).

This response comes in the 1953 essay on Trakl. Heidegger's intention is to show that the poetry of Trakl goes beyond the limits of ontotheology. Thus, Heidegger disqualifies the "Platonic" reading of Trakl's line: *Es ist die Seele ein Fremdes auf Erden*. He proposes to change the *sens* of the interpretation, to invert *le sens même*, the direction of the movement of the soul into which it would be drawn by the flight of fiery spirit. The reversal occurs when one hears *fremd* in its Old High German sense as *unterwegs nach*: far from being exiled on earth as a fallen stranger, the soul finds itself under way toward the earth, which it would, but does not yet, inhabit. The last flight, the end of the flight, is back toward the earth, the return earthward. Yet it is also a flight back to spirit as "the earliest," as the promise that would promise more than Platonism and Christianity, that would promise in a way more proper to the promise. It is a promise that speaks; and it is in the opening of this language that the speech of thinker and of poet are gathered into a *Gespräch* (138–46).

Everything will hinge, then, on this originary language of the promise. And yet, as Derrida expresses it directly in "*Geschlecht* II," "the primordiality (pre-Platonic, pre-metaphysical, or pre-Christian) to which Heidegger recalls us and in which he situates the proper site of Trakl *has no other content and even no other language* than that of Platonism and Christianity. This primordiality is simply that starting from which things like metaphysics and Christianity are possible and thinkable."[12] Hence the scene with which *Of Spirit* ends, the scene in which the theologians are made to say to Heidegger: what you call the originary spirit is indeed what is most essential in Christianity. One can imagine these theologians going on to invoke also the dove as which spirit descends to earth and especially the voice and the tongues of fire by which spirit ignites human speech. Derrida has Heidegger reply that it is a matter of thinking that from which (*ce à partir de quoi*) all of which Christianity speaks would be possible, a matter of a repetition that withdraws toward the more originary. This more originary would be completely other, even if not an other content, even if the turn to it resembles most closely a simple ontological and transcendental replication.

Heidegger's last words to the theologians, his last words in *Of Spirit*: "The completely other announces itself in the most rigorous repetition. The latter is also the most vertiginous and the most abysmal" (184).

His theological interlocutors: "We call to this completely other."

---

12. "*Geschlecht* II," 193.

(c)

In the end, it would be a matter of withdrawal from destitution toward a new dawn, of flight toward the promise of spirit. And it would be a matter of whether—Derrida poses the question without posing it—this promise is not what opens all speech, thus rendering possible the question itself, preceding all questioning without belonging to the order of the question. It is a matter of whether this promise is the call to which every question responds, whether it is thus a promise *prior to every question*.

Avant toute question: these words lead Derrida onto a detour, to a long note that would not have been read when *Of Spirit* was presented as a lecture (Derrida mentions explicitly that the notes were added afterwards, *après coup*); the note—a kind of afterword—disfigures the text, running on for eight pages, displacing the main text to such an extent that only a few lines remain on each of these pages (147–54). This is the note that I mentioned earlier, the one dedicated to Françoise Dastur in recognition of her having called Derrida's attention to a passage in *On the Way to Language* (*Unterwegs zur Sprache*) in the course of the Essex Colloquium. The entire note turns on this passage.

Avant toute question: these words would disrupt the privilege that Heidegger is said to accord to the question, a privilege that could not, of course, be disrupted by simply being put into question, since such a move would only reaffirm precisely that which it would disrupt. But in the words *avant toute question*, there arises what one would have to write (doubly) as the "question" of the question; it arises, not as a question but as a drift toward an experience of language "older" than the question, anterior to and presupposed by the question. It is this anterior moment that is marked by the passage in *On the Way to Language*: when one comes to question, even to the most radical questioning of Being, one must already be in the element of language, one must already have been addressed and have said "yes," have given one's pledge (*gage*), engaging speech toward a speech before the word.

Derrida grants, then, that in the passage in *On the Way to Language* (specifically, in the lecture "The Essence of Language" ["*Das Wesen der Sprache*"], first presented in 1957–58) the privilege of the question is decisively disrupted, retracted. He allows also that one could indeed seek out in Heidegger's earlier texts prefigurations of this disruption; Derrida refers even to several relevant analyses, including those of the call of conscience and of *Entschlossenheit* in *Being and Time*. And yet,

Derrida insists on limiting the effect of the passage, of its disruption of the privileged operation of the question. It cannot be, he says, a matter of a new order beginning from this late passage and extending back in an essential way across all the earlier texts. It cannot be a matter of a recommencement, a reconstitution, of Heidegger's way, for that would be to understand nothing of the irreversible necessity of a way; it would be to submit Heidegger to the laws of a system, of an "order of reasons," to which he never submitted his thought. When the disruption comes, it is already too late: the privilege of the question has already been operative and has determined Heidegger's way for at least thirty years; that operation and determination cannot, Derrida insists, be undone retrospectively. Just as, when the note is added to *Of Spirit* it is already too late: the lecture on *Heidegger et la question* has already been presented. The effect of the note would be limited.

Derrida vigorously defends these limits. And yet, it seems to me that another reading can be broached, one that could justify releasing the disruption of the question back across the span of Heidegger's work. Need it be said that the consequences of such a release would be virtually unlimited.

Since his earliest published readings of Heidegger, Derrida has sought to expose in the point of departure of *Being and Time* an element that would limit Heidegger's work, constraining it in this respect within that very conceptuality that in other respects it decisively disrupts.[13] A similar approach is found in *Of Spirit*: The decisive methodological move by which Dasein is chosen as the exemplary being for the question of Being is said to proceed from the *experience of the question*; that is, the point of departure of the existential analytic would be legitimated from the experience, the possibility, the structure, of the *question* (36). The entirety of fundamental ontology would, as it were, have been inserted within the questioning comportment of Dasein to itself. Thus within self-presence perhaps (as Derrida's earlier readings tended to propose); certainly within the privilege of the question, which would thus prove to have determined Heidegger's thought decisively from the beginning.

In this regard, attention should be drawn to Heidegger's own preoccupation with the point of departure of *Being and Time*, with the *Fragestellung, der Ansatz der Frage*. In the late essay "The End of Phi-

---

13. See "Les Fins de l'homme," in *Marges de la philosophie* (Paris: Les Éditions de Minuit, 1972), esp. 148–53.

losophy and the Task of Thinking," he refers retrospectively to his attempts, "undertaken again and again since 1930, to shape the deployment of the question in *Being and Time* in a more originary way [*die
Fragestellung von "Sein und Zeit" anfänglicher zu gestalten*]."[14] One of
the results of this attempt is to put into question just what it is that constitutes *die Sache des Denkens*: a careful reading of the late essay shows
unmistakably that thinking is no longer—if it ever was—to be inserted
in the fold of Dasein's comportment to itself. The structure of the question as the comportment of Dasein to itself is no longer—if it ever was—
to serve as the point of departure. The *Ansatz* is earlier.

Attention should be drawn also to what Heidegger himself identifies as having been the point of departure of *Being and Time*: certainly
not Dasein's comportment to itself, not even its comportment to its own
Being, but rather, as another late text (1962) puts it directly: "The basic
experience of *Being and Time* is thus that of the forgottenness of Being
[*Seinsvergessenheit*]."[15] An earlier text, *Letter on Humanism* (1946)
refers to the basic experience of the forgottenness of Being as the dimension from out of which *Being and Time* was experienced; and in a
note handwritten in his own copy of this text, Heidegger explicates
as follows: "*Vergessenheit—Λήθη—Verbergung—Entzug—Enteignis:
Ereignis*."[16] The question would be deployed only starting from what
would call it forth, not from itself, not with an absolute privilege.

The passage in *On the Way to Language* that prompts Derrida's
long note is, of course, explicit in its revocation of the privilege of
the question:

> The proper bearing of thinking is not questioning but rather listen-
> ing to the promise [*das Hören der Zusage*] of that which is to come
> into question.[17]

Though this may indeed be the most explicit text in this regard, it is certainly not the only one. Others are to be found—for example, the following from the 1949 *Einleitung* to "What Is Metaphysics?":

14. *Zur Sache des Denkens* (Tübingen: Max Niemeyer, 1969), 61.
15. Ibid., 31.
16. *Gesamtausgabe* (Frankfurt a.M.: Vittorio Klostermann, 1975ff.), 9:328. References indicated in text by *GA* followed by volume number and page number.
17. *Unterwegs zur Sprache* (Pfullingen: Günther Neske, 1959), 175.

The thinking attempted in *Sein und Zeit* (1927) sets out on the way to preparing the . . . overcoming of metaphysics. But that which brings such thinking onto its way can only be that which is itself to be thought [*das zu Denkende selbst*]. (*GA* 9: 368)

A note is added, which, resonating with the title of another text, makes the reading of the passage indisputable: "was *heisst* Denken?" [Heidegger's italics].

One may want to say that this, too, is an isolated passage, a bit earlier than the other, but still not governing Heidegger's earlier way, perhaps not even integrated into the other texts of the same period. Thus, one would still reserve a certain stretch of Heidegger's way for the operation of the privilege of questioning.

Rather than trying to accumulate additional texts—Derrida himself points to several of them in the note—let me refer to a single moment in *Being and Time* that, whatever may be said about the privileging of the question at the outset, would seem decisively to undermine that privilege at a point where the work has just gotten under way. I refer to the analysis of *Rede* (§34) that is carried out in the course of analyzing the constituents of Dasein's Being-in, its disclosedness (*Erschlossenheit*). Without attempting to resume the discussions and debates that have raged around this analysis,[18] let me simply note that the analysis exhibits *Rede, die Artikulation der Verständlichkeit*, as the existential-ontological foundation of speech (*Sprache*).[19] Before there is speech, earlier than any question that Dasein may address to itself, there is the articulation of the *Verständlichkeit* that belongs to Dasein's disclosedness, a prearticulation that speech will always assume and express. Questioning will always already have been transposed into the element of *Rede*, by which Heidegger would translate λόγος. Even in 1927 Heidegger is already on the way to thinking as response, as a ὁμολογεῖν preceded by and responsive to the λόγος.[20] The "question" of the question will never have been something isolated.

---

18. See especially F.-W. von Herrmann, *Subjekt und Dasein*, 2nd ed. (Frankfurt a.M.: Vittorio Klostermann, 1985).

19. *Sein und Zeit* (Tübingen: Max Niemeyer, 1960), 160f. References indicated in text by *SZ*.

20. "Logos (Heraklit, Fragment 50)," in *Vorträge und Aufsätze* (Pfullingen: Günther Neske, 1954), 207–29.

In *Of Spirit* Derrida shows, as no one else has, how various, seemingly isolated threads in Heidegger's texts are knotted together. One could not, then, restore the "question" of the question to Heidegger's way without also disturbing the other threads. Indeed, Heidegger himself identifies one of the knots, identifies it in that very passage in *On the Way to Language* to which Derrida's long note is addressed. For, despite Heidegger's reference to his own earlier proclamation that questioning is the piety of thinking, the retraction of the privilege of the question is announced as an interruption of metaphysics, in which, from early on, questioning has been taken as the decisive feature of thinking. As such, by questioning, thinking was to have responded to the imperative that it be radical, that it seek out the *radix*, the final—hence, first—ground. But what is the source of the imperative? Its source lies in the very determination of essence, in the determination of essence *as ground*. Heidegger continues:

> Insofar as all essence has the character of ground, the quest for essence is a fathoming and establishing of ground [*Ergründen und Begründen des Grundes*]. The thinking that thinks toward [*zudenkt*] essence as so determined is in its ground a questioning.[21]

Hence the knotting together of the privilege of the question with the determination of essence as ground. One cannot retract the privilege of the question without also disturbing the metaphysical determination of essence. Without also, of course, disturbing metaphysics as such, its essential determination, the as such "as such."

It is hardly surprising, then, that from *Being and Time* on Heidegger is engaged in a redetermination of essence that one would call radical, were that not to reaffirm precisely the determination that the redetermination would displace. *Being and Time* announces the redetermination as a kind of reversal: the essence of Dasein is existence. But it is primarily in "On the Essence of Truth" (first presented in 1930 but not published until 1943) that the redetermination is rigorously undertaken:[22] in the course of redetermining the essence of truth, this text moves through a series of redeterminations of essence (as κοινόν, as condition of possibility, as

---

21. *Unterwegs zur Sprache*, 175.
22. *GA* 9: 177–202. A handwritten note at the beginning of this text indicates the course of the redetermination: "Wesen: 1. quidditas—das Was—κοιόν; 2. Ermöglichung—Bedingung der Möglichkeit; 3. Grund der Ermöglichung."

ground of possibility) until finally, in its most decisive move, it turns essence against itself, that is, it opens within essence the space of manifold nonessence, while prohibiting any *Aufhebung* that would surmount and reduce the opposition. The essence of truth would thus include—but in opposition, without reduction—its nonessence (the mystery) and its counteressence (errancy). The latter, as a turning away from the mystery (λήθη) toward readily available beings, could not but broach a contamination of an essence already indeed contaminated by mystery, a contamination that would be all the more irreducible by virtue of belonging to the very determination of essence. Indeed, one may want—under a certain provocation—to pose a contamination that would come from even farther afield, that would arise from an even more remote outside. But in order to do so, one will need to begin with the doubly contaminated essence determined in Heidegger's work and to show how this, in all its structural complexity, is nonetheless somehow breached. For example, by technology. Or by evil.

One could imagine, then, another *Of Spirit*, one that would be of its spirit if not exactly following its letter, a double that would grant the unlimited disruption of the privilege of the question, as well as the disturbances that such disruption could not but produce elsewhere, cutting, shifting, requiring that one retie the knots by which the various threads would be connected. One could imagine that in this double of *Of Spirit* the long note dedicated to Françoise Dastur would have been rewritten and that, by having been relocated at the head of the text (no longer as a note but as part of the main text), it would have set in motion a shifting, a redistribution, of the entire text. One could imagine, then, this phantom returning to haunt *Of Spirit*, but to haunt it as a spur to carry on the incomparably incisive reading of Heidegger's texts broached by *Of Spirit*.

3

The Question of Origin

Before beginning, something else is needed. Before I begin by taking up the question of beginning, breaking, as it were, into the circle—before that, something else needs to be sounded. Before I take up the question of origin and of the human bond to origin that makes one indigenous to a region, however remote it may in fact, even necessarily, remain—before raising the question, there is need, here as anywhere, to let language itself speak. But here it will prove manifoldly appropriate for me to let language speak in a native tongue, in an indigenous, regional tone, not just tolling silently but echoing in the sound given it in the work of one who—preeminently in his work—belonged to a region and let that region sound—or rather, resound—in his works. Language that is bound to a region, to a *particular* region of the earth, is what we call dialect, and the words that—before I begin—are to be sounded echo, in and as a work of art, the dialect of a region.

Most of Faulkner's novels are set in the Delta country centered in northern Mississippi and bounded to the north by Memphis, which figures frequently as a significant point of reference, as a peculiar kind of limit. As in *The Unvanquished*, where Snopes repeatedly goes off to Memphis to sell the mules that Granny has in effect stolen from the Union army by use of a forged requisition. As in the chapter entitled "Vendée," which also, however, in the title refers to a region in France that was the scene of several counterrevolutionary peasant uprisings in the decades following the revolution, thus expressing—according to Faulkner's French translator—something had in common by Southerners and Vendeans: being conquered and having their homeland occupied by people who spoke—almost—their own language.[1] "Ven-dée" opens just after Granny, the unvanquished,[2] has met her violent death, opens at the scene of her burial. The voice is that of fifteen-year-old Bayard Sartoris:

> They all came in again when we buried Granny, Brother Fortinbride and all of them—the old men and the women and the children, and the niggers—the twelve who used to come in when word would spread that Ab Snopes was back from Memphis, and the hundred more who had returned to the country since, who had followed the Yankees away and then returned, to find their families and owners gone, to scatter into the hills and live in caves and hollow trees like animals I suppose, not only with no one to depend on but with no one depending on them, caring whether they returned or not or lived or died or not: and that I suppose is the sum, the sharp serpent's fang, of bereavement and loss—all coming in from the hills in the rain.[3]

This scene is of destitution, especially of the destitution of those whose very freedom has issued in utter and irrecoverable loss, a negativity without reserve that leaves them abandoned to live on with no home, with only the bare shelter that the wild earth provides. All these destitute ones are gathered for Granny's burial. Bayard describes how she, claimed—as we say—by absolute negativity, is entombed in the earth, abandoned to it:

> . . . then Ringo and I stood there and watched Granny going down into the earth with the quiet rain splashing on the yellow boards until they quit looking like boards and began to look like water with thin sunlight reflected in it, sinking away into the ground. Then the wet red dirt began to flow into the grave, with the shovels darting and flicking slow and steady and the hill men waiting to take turns with the shovels because Uncle Buck would not let anyone spell

---

1. See Editor's Note in William Faulkner, *The Unvanquished* (New York: Random House, 1990), 259f.

2. " 'The Unvanquished' was the title of the story of Granny's struggle between her morality and her children's needs, which was the theme of that book and which we extended to cover the whole book successfully" (Letter to Robert K. Haas, 8 July 1938, in *Selected Letters of William Faulkner*, ed. Joseph Blotner [London: The Scholar Press, 1977], 106).

3. *The Unvanquished*, 155f.

him with his. . . . The earth was loose and soft now, dark and red with rain, so that the rain didn't splash on Granny at all: it just dissolved slow and gray into the dark red mound, so that after a while the mound began to dissolve too without changing shape, like the soft yellow color of the boards had dissolved and stained up through the earth and mound and boards and rain were all melting into one vague quiet reddish gray. . . . It was changing all the time, with the slow gray rain lancing slow and gray and cold into the red earth, yet it did not change. It would be some time yet, it would be days and weeks and then months before it would be smooth and quiet and level with the other earth.[4]

I shall take up the question of origin. Beginning here and now, I shall take it up by addressing the earth. Note that I do not say: the *question* of the earth. Not that there cannot be questions about the earth: for example, the Copernican question whether the earth moves or is at rest, a question on which so much once hinged or was thought to hinge, even human life, its origin and end, the very sense of birth and death. Certainly, then, unquestionably, there have been questions of utmost import about the earth. To say nothing of all the questions posed today about the future of the earth, questions, still, of salvation, of protection and cleansing from the pollutants produced by a technology oblivious to all limits, questions of the earth's recovery from the contamination to which it has been submitted. But I shall not address the *question* of the earth, not because there are *many* such questions, but because in a sense—as I hope to show—there can be no question of the earth, because the earth is the unquestionable, not only unquestionably taken for granted, but also itself resistant to questioning, radically resistant, as we say, drawing on a metaphorical system itself rooted in the earth.

I shall take up the question of origin by addressing the earth, by directing my words to it, to what is said in the word *earth*. Yet what kind of word is *earth*? Is it a proper noun, a name requiring capitalization yet marked thereby as more or less—if never entirely—senseless, its conventional reference to the named individual lacking the detour through a common sense, through meaning? Or is the word a common noun, a word that means something but that happens to have reference only to

---

4. Ibid., 157–59.

one individual, to what we call—now using the definite article—*the earth*. Here the definite article lets the saying enact the reference by detour through meaning; it lets one say *the* individual to which the common meaning *earth* has reference. And yet, even if the word is a common, not a proper, noun, the definite article will not always be required in order, beyond the meaning, to refer to something that *is*, something present to sense (in that sense of sense determined by the relation to the senses). There are connections in which one says merely *earth*, as one says also *water, fire, air*. As, for example, does Empedocles in the Greek text of fragment 38 and in the following translation of the fragment: "Come, I shall tell you of the origin from which became manifest all the things we now look upon, earth and billowing sea, damp air, and Titan aither who fastens his circle around all things."[5]

One would need to say, then, that the word *earth* is not of a single kind but rather of at least three kinds. It would require too long a detour to draw out the affiliation between these three kinds and the three kinds of being that come to be counted in the decidedly Empedoclean discourse that Plato puts in the mouth of Timaeus. For here there is indeed a problem of time, one that will become pressing before I am finished, that would become even more pressing were I to follow the detour through the *Timaeus*. Let me, then, suspend the question of the togetherness of these kinds, the question of a certain kind of unity of the word *earth*. Let me suspend it both in the sense of leaving it undecided, in abeyance, and in the sense of keeping it in suspense, as an element of suspense in the discourse to follow.

I am to take up the question of origin. There is of course nothing original about such a project. To take up the question of origin is to set out, if questioningly, upon the upward way that has defined philosophy at least since Plato, even if perhaps not quite exclusively; it is to extend oneself, if questioningly, along the line of ascent that leads up "to the origin

---

5. In the form handed down by Clement, fragment 38 begins as follows: εἰ δ᾽ ἄγε τοι λέξω πρῶθ᾽ ἥλιον ἀρχήν, . . . The translation of ἥλιον ἀρχήν is disputed, and quite different proposals are advanced by Burnet (who, admitting "mere makeshift," alters it to ἡλίου ἀρχήν, hence translating "the beginning of the sun" [*Early Greek Philosophy* (New York: Meridian Books, 1957), 212]), by Diels-Kranz (die ersten und gleichursprünglichen Elemente? [*Die Fragmente der Vorsokratiker* (Dublin/Zürich: Weidmann, 1968), 1:328]), and by Kirk and Raven (first of the sun [*The Presocractic Philosophers* (Cambridge: Cambridge University Press, 1957), 332]). Freeman considers ἥλιον a corruption (*Ancilla to the Pre-Socratic Philosophers* [Oxford: Basil Blackwell, 1956], 57). My translation, adapted from Kirk and Raven, omits it.

of everything [ἐπὶ τὴν τοῦ παντὸς ἀρχήν]," in the phrase that occurs near the center of the *Republic*.[6] This is the ascent that philosophy will always have to carry out first of all, that defines first philosophy for Aristotle: elevating one's vision to the πρῶται ἀρχαί, taking up theoretically the first origins, the origins as such. Thus, to take up the question of origin would be simply to take up philosophy in its most classical determination. Unless, in taking it up, one also put it in a certain suspension, rendering the determination inoperative for a time, as, for example, under certain conditions, a magistrate, an archon, can be suspended from office, barred for a certain period or pending the outcome of certain investigations. It would be a matter of letting there be again a *question* of origin, of putting in question the very sense of origin, thus of suspending that sense of origin that has always prescribed that sense in the other sense (sense in the sense allied with the senses) be suspended from the origin. As a swing can be suspended, hung (*suspendere*), from a high, strong branch of a tree allowing one to swing freely above the earth. Putting in question the sense of origin will thus also put no less in question the origin of sense.

The fragment from Empedocles broaches a discourse on both, a discourse that in telling of the origin itself would say also how all the things we now look upon become manifest from the origin. Among those things is the earth, and thus it could be said of Empedocles too that he takes up the question of origin by addressing the earth. And yet, it is not merely a matter of telling how earth originates from its origin, for earth not only is one of those things we now look upon, as we look also upon billowing sea, but also belongs to the origin itself; thus earth is of at least two kinds. As it belongs to the origin, it is not *the* earth but earth, that is, one of the elements (στοιχεῖα), as they will come to be called, from Plato on, by analogy with the elements of speech.[7] The Empedoclean word bespeaks more directly the affiliation with origin: earth is one of the four *roots* (ῥιζώματα) that provide sustenance to all things of nature, enabling things to emerge, to grow, to unfold into the open space delimited by these roots. Empedocles says this origination in the words

---

6. *Rep.* 511b. Later (533c) Socrates describes dialectic, in which the entire upward way would culminate, as the advance to the origin itself (ἐπ' αὐτὴν τὴν ἀρχήν).

7. It seems that the word is first extended in this way in the *Theaetetus* (201e) (see F. M. Cornford, *Plato's Cosmology* [New York: The Liberal Arts Press, 1957], 161 n. 1). But note the serious reservation that is expressed in the *Timaeus* (48b–c) concerning the analogy.

ἐκ τούτων, *from these*: all things are *from* these roots. To follow the Empedoclean injunction given in fragment 3, that one "think of each thing in its way of becoming manifest,"[8] would thus require envisioning the roots, which, concealed beneath the surface of the earth, give sustenance to what grows up out of the earth. But note the curious doubling that such discourse introduces: earth is a root, and yet the very sense that *root* infuses into the discourse (giving sustenance, one might say, to the discourse) is inseparable from the fact that roots occur precisely and almost exclusively in the earth, growing down into it, drawing from it the sustenance that things need in order to come to light. If one were again to apply the articulation of speech to things, though now no longer as in Plato and Aristotle, no longer as a projection of division into elements, then one could say that the earth as root refers back—through what we would call the metaphorics—to another earth, another kind of earth, in which the roots would themselves grow and from which they would draw sustenance for the things growing up into the light. This other kind of earth would perhaps be indistinguishable from the origin, the ἀρχή, as such. One might well take it to be also the earth, that oldest kind of earth, of which the ancient poet sings in the Homeric Hymn "To Earth, Mother of All." Recall the opening lines of this great song of the earth:

> Earth! Allmother will I sing! Revered
> Firmgrounded nourisher of everything on earth.
> Whatever traverses holy earth or the seas
> Or climbs the air enjoys your dispensation.[9]

In the Empedoclean discourses this other kind of earth, this earth, that is, as it were, beneath earth, serves to seal the bond joining origin and earth. Beginning with Plato, however, this bond is, if not simply broken, certainly submitted to a decisive deformation, stretching and attenuating it. For, once ἀρχή is thought as or in relation to εἶδος, there is need to distinguish it from what come to be called the elements; it becomes indeed most imperative to differentiate between the εἶδος, which, shining through things, lets those things be manifest, and the darkest, most self-secluding of the elements. If in certain dialogues the summing up of being still requires—or comes to require—at least detouring by way of the elements, thus even returning to the earth, the history of meta-

---

8. νόει δ' ᾗ δῆλον ἕκαστον (Diels-Kranz).
9. I am grateful to David Krell for this translation.

physics has for the most part intensified the dissociation of origin from earth that obtrudes already in the injunction found in other dialogues and codified in the history of Platonism: that the philosopher is to die away from the earth. Even if—even despite the fact that—his remains will be buried in the earth or his ashes scattered across its surface. It would belong to the very movement constitutive of metaphysics to draw the origin apart from the earth, to draw it away into the distance where it has less and less to do with the earthly things that engage our senses; drifting away into a remote beyond, the origin would finally become utterly impotent, cancelling itself as power of origination. At least this is the fable related by Nietzsche. Little wonder, then, that the reversal proclaimed by Zarathustra comes to be said in the injunction: "Remain true to the earth [*bleibt der Erde treu*]."[10]

For Husserl this truth—this remaining true to the earth—requires another reversal. Let me turn, then, to another fragment, one in which, also, another earth, another kind of earth, comes to be declared. Derrida calls attention to this fragment in his *Introduction to Husserl's Origin of Geometry*, characterizing it precisely as a fragment and devoting to it an extensive and remarkable note. Husserl wrote the fragment in 1934; it has—perhaps in the extreme—the loose, informal style often found in Husserl's research manuscripts, though in this text, much more than in other instances, one senses the sharp contrast—not to say conflict—between the radicalness of the project set in motion and the looseness and incompleteness of the text. Certainly it is, as Derrida notes, a text that is "very spontaneous and not greatly worked out in its writing."[11]

On the envelope in which the manuscript was placed, there are written some words that serve to identify the other reversal, the one set in motion in this text. Husserl writes there: "Overthrow of the Copernican theory in its usual interpretation as worldview." The Copernican theory and its proposed overthrow have of course to do with motion, with what moves and what remains at rest. Husserl continues—we are still reading what is written on the envelope, almost as if it were the address, the des-

---

10. *Also Sprach Zarathustra*, in vol. VI 1 of Nietzsche, *Werke: Kritische Gesamtausgabe*, ed. Giorgio Colli and Mazzino Montinari (Berlin: Walter de Gruyter, 1968), 9.

11. Edmund Husserl, *L'Origine de la Géométrie*, traduction et Introduction par Jacques Derrida (Paris: Presses Universitaires de France, 1962), 79. Subsequent references are indicated by *Int.* followed by the page number.

tination, to which the enclosed letter is supposed to go, where it would finally come to rest in the hands of its reader—one reads on the envelope: "The *Ur-Arche* earth does not move." The word *Ur-Arche* will not yield readily to translation. Husserl's use of it seems indeed to be one instance in which—despite the looseness of much of the text—Husserl did write with exceptional care and subtlety. *Arche* means of course *ark*, as in Noah's ark. The earth bears all living things, all those that live on, as in the biblical instance, and so it can be called an ark, indeed *the* ark, the primal or originary ark (*Ur-Arche*). But *Arche*—as long as it is merely written or if, saying it, one shifts the accent—merely transliterates the Greek ἀρχή. Earth—to which Husserl's text is addressed—is the origin, indeed doubly so, the originary origin (*Ur-Arche*). Everything will be conveyed to this origin, loaded aboard the ark, and the question of origin will be taken up by addressing what is said to the earth.

Some additional words written on the envelope confirm the theme of origin while also giving the fragment its title: "Grundlegende Untersuchungen zum phänomenologischen Ursprung der Räumlichkeit der Natur" ["Foundational Investigations of the Phenomenological Origin of the Spatiality of Nature"].[12] If we now open the envelope and begin reading the text, we find this confirmation virtually repeated in the first sentence, Husserl declaring the text to be "foundational for a phenomenological theory of the origin of spatiality, corporeality, nature in the sense of the natural sciences" (*GU* 307). Reading the text, one needs also to hear the voice speaking in it, especially since there are at least two different voices to be heard speaking here in the guise or disguise of phenomenology, which is explicitly said to have "supported Copernican astrophysics—but also anti-Copernicanism according to which God had fixed the earth at a place in space" (*GU* 321). One needs also to hear, at some junctures, what is said in two other research manuscripts that stem from the same period and link up with the text that is my primary concern. The other texts go, respectively, by the titles: "Notizen zur Raumkonstitution" ["Notes on the Constitution of Space"] and "Die Welt der Lebendigen Gegenwart und die Konstitution der Ausserleib-

12. Husserl, "Grundlegende Untersuchungen zum Phänomenologischen Ursprung der Räumlichkeit der Natur," in *Philosophical Essays in Memory of Edmund Husserl*, ed. Marvin Farber (Cambridge: Harvard University Press, 1940). Subsequent references are indicated by *GU* followed by page numbers. The inscription found on the envelope is cited in a note added by the editor to the first page of the text.

lichen Umwelt" ["The World of the Living Present and the Constitution of the Outer Environing World"].

If we continue with the text we have already begun reading, it is not long before it comes to address the earth. Focusing on the open, horizonal character of the environing world (*Umwelt*), Husserl indicates how an opening beyond this world comes into play, how one extends the horizon beyond one's immediate locale, taking in unfamiliar, unknown regions that, however, one knows others to be acquainted with, pushing on from Germany to Europe and finally to the earth. What occurs in this movement beyond to the earth, the power that drives it, is synthesis, synthesis of one's own various fields of experience and of those of others. "Representation of the earth"—says Husserl—"comes about as a synthetic unity in a way analogous to that in which, in a continuous and connected experience, the experiential fields of an individual person are unified into *an* experiential field" (*GU* 308). Husserl notes that only one thing differentiates the representation of the earth from the synthesis operative in individual experience, namely, that it uses the reports, descriptions, and findings of others, that one appropriates these analogically.

A distinctive voice now intervenes, breaking with the undifferentiated generality of the opening discourse on synthesis. Identifying itself as "we Copernicans, we moderns," it declares that the earth is not the whole of nature but only one star in infinite world-space; as such it is a globe-shaped body, even if not perceptible as such as a whole. At least this is what the Copernican voice declares, insisting once more ("*Doch ein Körper*") before giving way to the other voice. The transition, though unmarked as such, is unmistakable if one listens to what is declared by this other voice: that though the earth is the basis for our experience of all bodies (*der Erfahrungsboden für alle Körper*), functioning thus in the experiential genesis of our representations, this basis is not, in the beginning, experienced as a body. Only at higher stages of constitution does it become a basis-body. All movement occurs on or around the earth, in reference to it—at least in the beginning, at the originary stage of constitution, in the domain of origin. The anti-Copernican thesis is thus prepared, and yet—remarkably—in its very first statement it is already displaced, that is, the very operation of the opposition rest/motion, on which the Copernican debate depends, is interrupted when one returns to the beginning, to this earth that is older than the mere globe-shaped planet of Copernican astrophysics. Here is what the voice of this older earth declares, its thesis: "In its originary form of representation, the earth itself does not move and is not at rest; rest and motion have sense only in relation to it." Then, as if now blending the Copernican and the anti-Copernican voices, the voices of opposition, of *the* opposition, the text adds: "But subsequently earth 'moves' or is at rest" (*GU* 309). For the moderns, "we Copernicans," it is just one star moving among others in world-space; for the others, their symmetrical opposition expressed in the retrospective designation anti-Copernicans, the earth is at rest at the place in space where God himself fixed it.

But, first of all, originarily, earth is a basis, not a body capable of being in motion or at rest. Husserl contrasts this earth-basis with other relative bases, such basis-bodies as, for instance, a railway car. However much such a body can be experienced as a basis in relation to which other things are in motion or at rest, each such relative basis is originarily referred back to the earth-basis in relation to which each proves to be in motion or at rest.

Because of its character as a basis, there is some sense in saying—despite what has already been declared—that the earth is at rest. But this rest, of which the earth, at the originary level, is capable, is not the rest that the anti-Copernicans ascribe to it. A passage in "Notes on the Constitution of Space" clarifies the relevant difference: "The 'rest', which constitutively precedes motion, is still not a bodily rest, that is, rest understood as a mode of motion."[13] It is rather—coming back to the "Foundational Investigations"—the kind of rest characteristic of an ark. In Husserl's words: "The earth is the ark [one could also read: ἀρχή, origin] which first makes possible the sense of all motion and all rest. But its rest is not a mode of motion" (*GU* 324). Thus, even if one says, in this precise sense, that the earth is at rest, one will still have displaced the opposition that governs the Copernican debate. This displacement is further testified by an interruption of the usual homogeneity of whole and parts: the parts of the earth—if they are represented by themselves as they could be separated off—are bodies; but as a whole the earth is not a body at all, hence is a whole that, though consisting of corporeal parts, is nonetheless not itself corporeal.

Everything depends on the earth, on the move back to the earth, to this other, originary earth. One could no doubt introduce here, as does

---

13. Husserl, "Notizen zur Raumkonstitution," *Philosophy and Phenomenological Research*, 1:32.

Derrida, the word *reduction* and speak of a reduction leading from the interstellar earth back to what Derrida—though not Husserl—calls the transcendental earth. This is the essential move that governs this text, the decisive shift around which the entire discourse is organized—this shift to what I shall call simply the older earth. It is a shift that suspends the interstellar earth constituted by Copernican astrophysics as well as the earlier representation of earth that the Copernican view comes to replace; it is a shift that suspends, that puts in abeyance, the earth as a body so as to return to the earth as basis, the originary earth, the older earth.[14] This reduction or suspension offers in turn the possibility of a certain phenomenological confirmation of the scientific representation of the earth in which it would be shown how and within what limits such a representation comes to be constituted on the basis of more originary experience.

Beyond the opening pages of Husserl's text, the voice heard is for the most part one speaking from out of the suspension, the reduction to the older earth—even though the voice of Copernican science does not entirely cease intervening and especially toward the end comes to challenge the phenomenologist, charging him not only with error but even with madness and hubris. But let me concentrate now on the phenomenological voice and on what is said—what can be said—once the return to the originary earth has been carried out. Specifically, I shall outline four somewhat distinct discourses belonging to the domain of origin.

The first discourse attaches the domain of origin to the earth, situates it on the older earth that remains after the suspension of the interstellar earth. Husserl refers to the way in which the various horizons unfolded in experience are spread out in spaces, which, as the open fields in which bodies have their proximity or remoteness, are encompassed by the earth. As a result, bodies (things) have the sense of being *earthly* things, and space has the sense of being *earthly* space. This is true not only of

---

14. Such suspension would in effect undo—that is, suspend—another suspension explicitly outlined in Husserl's text, assuming that *aufheben* as Husserl uses it can be rendered by *suspend*. Referring to the earth as a noncorporeal basis, Husserl notes that at higher levels of constitution it comes to be constituted as a basis-body, as corporeal, and that this constitution suspends (*aufheben*) the earth's originary basis-form. *Suspension* could thus be made to cover both the cancellation of the originary earth as well as the recovery, hence the preservation, of it—that is, *suspension* could itself be suspended between the two significations, the two operations, indeed in a certain proximity (which would need to be marked precisely) to the determination that *aufheben* receives in German Idealism.

inanimate things (*Körper*) but also of living things, those with an animate body (*Leib*). Husserl writes: "The totality of the We, of human beings, of 'animate beings', is in this sense earthly [*irdisch*]—and in the beginning has no opposite in the nonearthly" (*GU* 318). One could say: in the beginning, in the domain of origin, the earth is so all-encompassing that everything, everyone, is earthly. Within this domain the very determination of sense is earthly, the very sense of sense is linked to the earth. Husserl declares even that this sense is rooted (*verwurzelt*), thus doubling metaphorically the reference back to the earth. He stresses, too, that it is to one and the same earth that "the totality of the We," that is, humanity as a whole, is referred back, that is, borne as by an ark. In his words: "The earth is, for all, the same earth" (*GU* 315).

But what about the possibility—still within the domain of origin—of another earth, of what Husserl himself calls "new 'earths' "? The second of the discourses, which is woven throughout much of Husserl's text, is addressed to this possibility. It is one of the things that occasions, in the course of the text, so many references to flight—to the flight of birds, of airplanes, indeed even of spaceships. And it is especially this preoccupation with flight, the phantastical narratives thus produced, that gives the entire discourse a tone most unusual for Husserl, one that could almost be called comic. When, in the midst of what one takes to be rigorously scientific considerations, Husserl suddenly interjects: "Suppose I were a bird and could fly" (*GU* 315), when, again, he abruptly metamorphizes into a bird flying away from the earth off to some celestial body such as the moon (see *GU* 324)—it is not only of the Kantian dove that one thinks. Or rather, what matters is perhaps not so much what one thinks of such phantastical flights but rather their proximity to a comic image that has seldom ceased haunting the philosopher, picturing him— as in the classical instance—precisely as suspended above the earth, communing with the air and learning of higher things. A proximity of which Husserl had, no doubt, not the slightest suspicion.

Husserl poses, first of all, the case in which from a very high-flying plane one can see that the earth is globe-shaped. The question is whether in such a case the plane cannot come to function as basis, replacing the earth-basis and allowing one to begin representing the earth as the globe-shaped body that Copernican science takes it to be. Husserl leaves this question unanswered, moving on to another case of flight, a case in which we would have the ability to fly—whether by boarding a plane or by virtue of some biological endowment is not clear—and in which there would be two earths between which we could fly. The question is whether by having one earth as basis we could represent the other simply as a body, reversing the order of basis and body with each flight between the two, determining the originary, determining *which* would be originary, merely by soaring—or flapping our way—across the space between them. Husserl answers with a qualified *yes*, though the qualification appears to carry considerably more weight than the slight affirmation. Here is what he says: "But what is meant by two earths? Two pieces of one earth with one humanity. Both together would become one basis and at the same time each would be for the other a body" (*GU* 218). Such—one could add—is the power of originary synthesis that, beneath the level at which the two would alternate reciprocally between basis and body, they would—despite a certain spatial separation—be unified into a single basis, a single earth, older, in a sense, than the others. What flight alone could not accomplish would be done by the power of synthesis.

From the case of two earths, Husserl turns to another, one in which there is a certain extension of the earth-basis. This case is like that of the high-flying plane, but now the vessels move on beyond the earth, travelling for extended periods in space. The phantastical narrative of flight thus comes to border on science fiction. Husserl writes of spaceships departing from and returning to the earth; on board, guiding the spaceships, are human beings, who, venturing off into space, leave behind the earth-basis on which they have properly their home. From the originary ark they embark in what Husserl calls flying arks, this designation indicating that such vessels can come to function as basis in a way that is not merely relative but more akin to the way of the earth-basis. But what enters decisively into the constitution of these new earths is one's *birth*. If one were born on such a vessel, travelling in space with one's family for a considerable time, then the spaceship could function as one's initial earth-basis until such time as one came to realize the link to the earth itself. However much mankind may be, as Husserl says, "earthbound" (*GU* 316), it is possible under such conditions for there to be another basis-place and so, as he says, a plurality of home-places (*Heimstätten*), at least in the interval between birth and the eventual—perhaps virtually inevitable—unification of them—as in the case of the two earths—into a single basis-place. The possibility of such an interval, of such a plurality of home-places, Husserl names with the word *historicity* (Historizität): each person, he says, has his historicity with respect to his way of being made at home (*beheimatet*).

Husserl turns to the case in which one is born on a ship, not in space but at sea. If one grew up on the ship, then one would not apprehend it in relation to, moving relative to, the earth, at least not until the conditions became such that a certain synthesis came into play. Up until that time, says Husserl, the ship "would itself be my 'earth', my originary home [*Urheimat*]" (*GU* 319).[15] Husserl adds that every I has an *Urheimat*, as does every originary people (*Urvolk*). Husserl moves very quickly to a most remarkable conclusion: Every people—every *Volk* and every *Übervolk*—"is ultimately made at home [*beheimatet*] naturally on the 'earth', and all developments, all relative histories, have to this extent a unique originary history [*Urhistorie*] of which they are episodes" (*GU* 319). Such a history, he adds, may name a togetherness of peoples living and developing in complete separation. A curious history, to say the least. A history constituted by humanity's being made at home on the earth, having the earth as originary home (*Urheimat*). If it is a history at all, it is a kind of history of the earth, though of an entirely different kind from the account given by Copernican astrophysics. This originary history, running its course within the domain of origin—even apart, it seems, from what might come to be constituted at higher levels—would be a history belonging to the earth as the ultimate, natural *Urheimat*, to the earth in its unique capacity for *Beheimaten*, for making human beings at home, for granting them a *Heimat*.

The third discourse poses, within the domain of origin, a kind of opposite to the originary earth: "If earth is constituted . . . , then sky too is necessary as the field of what is outermost yet still spatially experienceable for me and for all of us—from the earth-basis [*vom Erdboden aus*]" (*GU* 318). The sky is the outermost horizon or limit at which what can be experienced as a distant physical thing finally disappears as such; Husserl's text "The World of the Living Present" calls it the outermost or utmost remoteness (*äusserste Ferne*), noting that something quite similar occurs on the earth's surface in the form of a very distant, perceptually undifferentiated background seen at or near the horizon.[16]

---

15. Husserl leaves unconsidered whether, at least at an intermediate stage, the sea would not be apprehended as one's basis, one's "earth," and whether having the sea as basis would not be precisely a way of having the earth as basis. At the very least one would need to consider the consequences of the sea's being *of the earth* in a way that ships, things as such, are not. Is the sea (and here too the article functions peculiarly) any more a body, a thing, than is the earth?

16. Husserl, "Die Welt der Lebendigen Gegenwart und die Konstitution der Ausserleiblichen Umwelt," *Philosophy and Phenomenological Research*, 6:326.

It is as if at the horizon there were a transition from earth to sky, communication between the elements. This curious meeting—indeed the very phenomenon of the horizon in the ordinary sense of the word—serves to indicate that the opposition posed between earth and sky is a very different kind from, for instance, that between rest and motion. In Husserl's text—in all of Husserl's texts as far as I have been able to determine—one finds little more than the posing of the opposition as an opposition between originary basis and originary limit, both basis and limit understood in a very specific, though still undeveloped, experiential connection. This other kind of opposition—one might well call it an older opposition, elemental opposition—remains to be thought at or beyond the limit of Husserl's texts.

The fourth discourse outlines a decisive move, a turn or return, within the domain of origin. The intensity of its appeal increases toward the end of the text until, in response to the challenge issued by the voice of Copernican science, it becomes almost shrill. The move is one that turns toward the transcendental ego, referring everything constitutively to it, even within the domain of origin, thus including even—and most remarkably—the originary earth. Husserl writes: "But everything comes down to this: not to forget the pregivenness and constitution belonging to the apodictic ego, to me, to us, as the source [*Quelle*] of all actual and possible sense of being [*Seinssinn*]" (*GU* 323). Everything, he goes on to say, "relates back to this historicity of transcendental constitution," so that "all beings have sense [being-sense, *Seinssinn*] only from my constitutive genesis" (*GU* 324). This does not mean that the earth proves to be simply another constituted thing; on the contrary, the earth has a privileged role in the constitutive genesis, which, says Husserl, proceeds "in an earthly manner" (*irdisch*). Yet, however privileged as the originary ark of humanity, even the earth is submitted to the reference back to transcendental life, which in the final order of origins would precede the very ark by which it, at least in the form of existing human beings, would be borne.

The voice of Copernican science charges the phenomenologist with the most unbelievable philosophical hubris for rejecting the scientific worldview and for attaching original significance to the earth and to the humanity borne by it. For, from the scientific standpoint, one knows that, for example, it is possible that other celestial bodies may crash into the earth, destroying it along with humanity. Yet, even before such a charge and such possibilities, Husserl insists that one must not retreat. Rather, one must respond in such words—with such questions—as the following: "What sense could the collapsing masses in space have, in a space constructed a priori as absolutely homogeneous, if the constituting life were eliminated? Does not such an elimination itself have sense, if at all, only as an elimination of and in constituting subjectivity?" In the domain of origin, in the most radical return to the origin, one will affirm that "the ego lives and precedes all actual and possible beings" (*GU* 325).

Let me conclude with a general topological question, developing it, letting the questions multiply along three somewhat different lines.

The question is: Where does Husserl's text leave the earth?

First of all, one can say that it leaves the earth neither in motion nor at rest but rather prior to this opposition, as the originary ark that continues to bear those who live on. Yet, as such, Husserl's text leaves the earth as something *constituted*. Indeed the very opening of the text onto the analysis of the earth is a description—though still at an undifferentiated level—of the synthesis by which the earth comes to be represented. The question is whether in taking the earth to be constituted—even if at the most originary level—Husserl has not already left behind a still older earth. Is the earth, instead, pregiven in advance of such synthesis as Husserl describes? Or—to press further—is it not so much *given*— givenness remaining determined by concepts of presence and synthesis—as rather imposed, self-imposing in the sense of claiming (Husserl says we are *earthbound*) and especially in the sense of "making at home" (*Beheimaten*)? Would it, then, be appropriate to call this still older earth *origin*, granted an erosion here of those senses of origin gathered in the history of metaphysics, granting a certain slippage, a twisting, in a direction that might be called elemental: earth-origin as elemental grant of *Heimat*? Thus rewriting—and not just in reverse—the classical progression from στοιχεῖα to ἀρχή.

Where does Husserl's text leave the earth? It leaves the earth, in the second place, suspended from transcendental life, from constituting subjectivity. Everything, including the earth, depends on the return, the referral back, to this most originary origin. The character of the latter is expressed most precisely as the living present (*lebendige Gegenwart*) with its retentional and protentional horizons. In the manuscript "Die Welt der lebendigen Gegenwart" Husserl speaks of the living present as the originary present (*Urgegenwart*) and continues: "In this authentic present of perception there is constituted the perceptually present world, thus the first world of perception, and therein the constitution of rest."[17] The connection left implicit in this passage is more openly expressed in a section in *Experience and Judgment* where Husserl mentions the earth in connection with—in *its* connection with—time as the "form of all forms."[18] Derrida's discussion of the passage makes the connection explicit: "In this section, the unity of the Earth is grounded in the unity and oneness of temporality, the 'fundamental form' (*Grundform*), the 'form of all forms' " (*Int.* 79). The earth is, then, in effect, referred back to the living present; and in the long and remarkable note that the *Introduction to Husserl's Origin of Geometry* devotes to the Husserlian fragment on the earth, Derrida describes the living present as "the rest and absolute maintenance of the origin in which, by which, and for which all temporality and all motion appear." It is as if, in the grounding, in the constitutive reference, of the earth back to the living present, the latter not only would be confirmed as most originary of origins but also would come to assume, at this level, the proto-rest in reference to which motion and rest would appear, almost as if usurping the role otherwise ascribed to the earth, that of being a basis, the ark of humanity.

This outcome is closely allied with another tendency to which Derrida's long note calls special attention. Especially toward the end of the Husserlian fragment, the tendency is for the earth to assume what Derrida calls "a more formal sense," which he contrasts with the sense of the earth as "the originary *here* whose facticity would finally be irreducible." This tendency is most pronounced in a certain assimiliation of the sense of the earth to that of the world; hence, says Derrida, "it is to the World that the transcendental immutability attributed to the Earth returns, since the Earth then is only its factual index" (*Int.* 80). This tendency to conflate earth with world is most explicit in *Experience and Judgment*: the world "is, in the most comprehensive sense, as the *life-world* for a human community capable of mutual understanding, *our earth*."[19]

In any case, Derrida's reading of Husserl has shown—I refer primarily to *Voice and Phenomenon*, or rather, in this context simply assume its perspective, without taking time even to summarize its argument—that time itself fractures the living present, or, if you will, that the very pro-

---

17. Ibid., 334.
18. Husserl, *Erfahrung und Urteil* (Hamburg: Claassen Verlag, 1964), 191.
19. Ibid., 189.

duction of the present is irreducible to presence. To say nothing of inter-subjectivity, of the possibility of an intersubjective origin or of an original intersubjectivity, noting only that Husserl's text on the earth constantly invokes the other, not only in the form of humanity as such, but also at the very beginning, in the initial description of the synthesis by which the earth comes to be represented: this comes about, he says, in a way similar to the synthesis of the experiential fields of an individual—"except that I appropriate analogically the reports, descriptions, and findings of others" (*GU* 308). Derrida is already explicit in *The Problem of Genesis*: "Transcendental intersubjectivity, the originary presence of 'the alter ego' in the monodic 'ego', is, it seems, the impossibility of any absolutely simple originary."[20] More generally, one could say—here, it goes almost without saying, I reduce to a few words an immense problematic (such is the problem of time!)—that the living present, the would-be originary origin, is contaminated by time and the other. This is why Derrida can, as he says, specify the intention of *Voice and Phenomenon* by noting "that phenomenology seems to us tormented, if not contested from within, by its own descriptions of the movement of temporalization and of the constitution of intersubjectivity" (*V* 5). Time and the other come to complicate—have always already complicated—what would have been the simple origin. In *The Problem of Genesis* Derrida asks: "How can everything begin with a complication [*par une complication*]?"[21] And in the Foreword written for this text more than three decades later, Derrida reinforces the force of this question: "It is a question always of an originary complication of the origin, of an initial contamination of the simple."[22] The question is whether these complications of the origin can remain isolated or whether they will be carried over to that allegedly constituted earth suspended from transcendental life. The question—to be heard in various registers—is: Can the earth not have been contaminated? Is one, then, drawn back toward an earth withdrawn, toward an earth that will never have been constituted, an older earth? If one can say that Husserl's text leaves the earth in the hope of returning to a purer, more originary origin, thus again—as since the Greeks—taking up the upward way, one can hardly not suspect that

---

20. Derrida, *Le Problème de la Genèse dans la Philosophie de Husserl* (Paris: Presses Universitaires de France, 1990), 30.
21. Ibid. 12.
22. Ibid., vi–vii.

there will be also a draft drawing it back earthward, enjoining it to remain true to the earth. Such a draft would interrupt, in its classical form, the question of origin, diverting the question toward what could come to be another locus for the "question" of the question: the unquestionable, unsuspendable earth, on and by which one will always already have been *beheimatet* when one comes to question, to take up, for instance, the question of the earth.

Where does Husserl's text leave the earth? Where, finally, in time? At what time? In what time? In what kind of time?

Is the time of the earth the same as the time of the living present? Is it a time to be measured by presence? Is it even—as with the time that fractures the living present—to be measured, or at least determined, by the production of presence?

Or is it *un autre temps*? Another time? A time whose discourse would require a tense other than the present? Also other than—as we say—the present perfect?

Is it not—if one follows the most radical strain in Husserl's text—a time linked to *Beheimaten*, as in the case of that originary history to which this text refers.

Is it not at least a time more profoundly determined by absence and death than the time of the living present can ever be? In this regard one cannot but be astonished by Husserl's efforts near the end of the text and in response to the hypothetical destruction of the earth and of humanity—his efforts to think death, or, as he says, not to retreat even before the problem of death. Here is how he expresses the phenomenological conception of death: "In the present, I as something present [*als Gegenwärtiges*] am progressively dying. Others die for me when I do not find a present connection with them." It would seem that death is simply the falling away, the slipping away, of life, the loss of presence.

Is it in passing over—as it seems—the time of death and the time of the earth—is it especially then and there that Husserl's text leaves the earth, taking flight, taking up the upward way, a way on which—one cannot but suspect—the originary power of the earth will remain concealed?

4

The Truth That Is Not
of Knowledge

In Heidegger's 1925–26 lecture course *Logic* (*GA* 21) the bonds are still in place, those that bind truth to knowledge and knowledge to intuition and presence. Indeed, it is precisely in these lectures that these bonds are displayed, not only as governing the phenomenological defense of logic against the assault by psychologism, but also as bonds that have held throughout the history of philosophy, that serve even to mark, if not to define, the unity of that history. And yet, in the very display of these bonds there are signs that Heidegger has begun to loosen them, or rather, that the very movement of the things themselves has made them begin to fray.

Near the beginning of the lectures Heidegger orients philosophical logic to the question of truth. The central question of such a logic would be: What is truth? Yet, before such a logic can commence, before it can take up its question of truth in a positive way, it is necessary to dispel the specter of scepticism that has haunted logic since the ancients, the specter that has challenged the question of logic by attempting to interrupt it with another question, with the question "whether the very idea of truth is not a phantom" (*GA* 21: 19). Heidegger resumes the classical responses to the threat of scepticism: for example, that in order to be able to set about determining whether truth really exists or is only a phantom, one must already have some understanding of truth, must already know *what* it is; so that, even if it should eventually turn out that there is no such thing as truth, the very assertion that truth is only a phantom would presuppose some understanding of what truth is, of what it would be if there were truth. Yet, rather than regarding this and the other classical re-

57

sponses as sufficiently meeting and defeating the challenge of scepticism so as to banish its specter and clear the field for the commencement of philosophical logic, Heidegger proceeds to challenge these responses, exposing within them a series of fundamental, unexamined presuppositions. He considers, for example, the response that, calling attention to the sceptical assertion that there is no truth, observes that this very denial itself lays claim to being a true proposition and thus presupposes that there is truth, presupposes precisely what it denies, contradicts itself. But instead of merely confirming, reformulating, or even setting limits to the range of this response, Heidegger exposes within this perhaps most classical response a nest of fundamental presuppositions the force of which cannot but interrupt the response and leave it stammering no less than the scepticism whose challenge it was to have met: in the response it is presupposed that truth means propositional truth; and it is assumed that the issue raised by the sceptical assertion can be settled by appealing to the principle of contradiction, without any questions having been asked about what constitutes and gives force to a principle, without the slightest doubt having been raised about the ultimate status thus accorded the principle of contradiction (*GA* 21: 22f.). Because this classical response is integral to Husserl's critique of psychologism, Heidegger insists that the presuppositions he has exposed in that response continue to haunt Husserl's critique, even though the *Logical Investigations* is the one place "where vital questioning is today still to be found in logic" (*GA* 21: 24). More precisely, these presuppositions prevent Husserl's critique of psychologism from decisively expelling the specter of the sceptical question. Driving scepticism and psychologism from the field of pure logic is not a task that Husserl's Prolegomena to Pure Logic would already have completed but rather is carried on—and indeed first taken up in a decisive way—in the theoretical developments within the Investigations themselves.

The most germane of these developments is the theory of intentionality. For Heidegger makes it explicit that psychologism is to be rejected, not because it treads upon territory not its own, the domain of pure logic, but rather because it relies on a psychology that does not understand the very theme that would define the discipline. Not that it would be, then, simply a matter of replacing one psychology with another. Heidegger refers to the ambiguity in which the delimitation of psychology has been entangled from the beginning, the ambiguity involved in its being oriented both to βίος (hence belonging to ethics) and to ζωή (hence belonging to physics). Heidegger notes that this ambiguity still persists insofar as psychology is regarded "both as a natural science of living beings and as a science of human existence" (*GA* 21: 35); in the current phrase *human science*, one finds expressed much the same ambiguity. As a result of this ambiguity the delimitation of psychology, the very determination of what it is, remains fundamentally confused: "Thus, when in the sequel we speak of psychology, we must keep quite clearly in mind that fundamentally we do not know what it is" (*GA* 21: 36).

Nonetheless, the *Logical Investigations* makes a decisive breakthrough by uncovering intentionality as the fundamental character of the psychic; through this discovery a means is provided for understanding in a positive, descriptive way the distinction on which Husserl's entire critique of psychologism turns, the distinction between real and ideal. Though there are clear signs of Heidegger's reluctance to allow the distinction between real and ideal to govern his own analyses or even his appropriation of the Husserlian analyses (see *GA* 19: 98)—no doubt because of his keen awareness of how directly this distinction derives from the Platonic opposition between sensible (αἰσθητόν) and intelligible (νοητόν) (*GA* 21: 52)—he is no less insistent than was Husserl that only a psychology based on an understanding of the psychic as intentional could succeed in rigorously determining the basic concepts of logic and thus preparing the field of pure logic. The question is only whether such a psychology would be sufficiently continuous with what has been called psychology to warrant retaining this designation; even Husserl, who in the first edition of the *Logical Investigations* designated his work as descriptive psychology, soon came to regard the phrase as misleading and to elaborate the increasingly more complex distinction between phenomenology and psychology. Heidegger is still more hesitant about assimilating to psychology the phenomenological theory of intentionality opened up by the *Logical Investigations*, to say nothing of the more radical guise that the theory will assume in the analysis of Dasein carried out in *Being and Time*, already near completion at the time of the lecture course *Logic*.[1]

In order to take up the phenomenon of truth within the new domain of intentional analysis, Heidegger undertakes an analysis of knowing as

---

1. The text of the lecture course *Prolegomena zur Geschichte des Zeitbegriffs* (*GA* 20), presented in the semester just preceding that in which *Logik* was presented, is the penultimate draft of *Sein und Zeit*.

such; in effect, though without taking note of it, he thus affirms the bond between truth and knowledge, leaves it intact for the moment, tacitly assuming that the phenomenon of truth is to be found in the act of knowing. Heidegger's analysis retraces in more didactic form the intentional analysis of knowledge developed in the *Logical Investigations*. It is a matter of focusing on the intentional structure of knowing, and this requires, above all, marking the distinction between psychic content and the intentional object of an act. Whatever its specific character, an intentional act is always directed, not at contents within consciousness (such as sensations or images), but rather at the things themselves. In the perceptual act in which (to use Heidegger's example) one perceives a wall, one's act is directed to the wall itself and not to sensations or images within consciousness that would be supposed somehow to resemble the wall itself outside consciousness. The same holds if the act is one in which the thing itself is not actually perceived but only spoken of: if one speaks of the table that is behind one's back, one still intends that table itself and not some mental content that would only represent it; but now, instead of seeing the thing in its bodily presence, one merely intends it, means it in an intention empty of intuitive givenness, represents it (*vorstellen*). In both cases, representation and perception, what is meant is the thing itself; but only the latter type of act, in which the thing is had originarily, in the flesh, is an act of knowing. But, in turn, such having of the thing itself in the flesh is precisely what phenomenology designates as intuition (*Anschauung*). Thus is knowledge bound to intuition, the latter taken in the broadest sense: it includes not only vision but also hearing (as of a musical piece), as well as the intuitive "understanding" involved when one "sees," for example, that two plus two equals four. Hence, intuition is not limited to the sensible, to perception; rather, intuition is involved in every mode of comportment in which the thing meant is present in the flesh (*leibhaftig anwesend*). It is because intuition presents the thing itself, because it is demonstrative, that it is bound to knowledge.

Heidegger interrupts—briefly—the series of phenomenological analyses, as if to insert in parentheses a divergence from the primacy accorded to intuition and presence by those analyses, a divergence that *Being and Time* will release across the entire field, undoing the bonds that the lectures will have left largely intact. The question inserted is whether for the most part things are had in their bodily presence when one has to do with them within one's most proximate surroundings. Heidegger's example: while writing at a table, one feels the resistance of the table, which to that extent is given in the flesh; and yet, in the strict sense it is not the table that is there in the flesh (*leibhaftig da*), present to the writer, but rather the words that he is writing and the meaning of what is being written. Heidegger mentions that the concept of bodily presence, of *Leibhaftigkeit*, is oriented to theoretical knowledge, in distinction from the usual manner of dealing with things in one's most proximate surroundings, where for the most part they are not directly and expressly given in the flesh. Thus does Heidegger broach—in unmarked parentheses—the radical divergence from presence that *Being and Time* will produce through its orientation to the most proximate surrounding world (*die nächste Umwelt*) (*GA* 21: 103f.).

Closing the parentheses, Heidegger turns to an analysis of the demonstrative character distinctive of intuition. Intuition is demonstrative because it serves to fulfill those intentions in which something is merely meant; as when, merely speaking of something behind one's back, one then turns toward it and, by seeing it in the flesh, there before one's perceptual gaze, one demonstrates what one has said, demonstrates that it is true. The intuition thus fulfills the empty intention executed in speech, filling it with the intuitive content given in the flesh, also bearing out the expectations that lay in the empty representation; now one *sees* there upon the wall that very picture hanging askew that previously one only *said* was hanging there askew. In demonstration there is a coincidence of what is intuited with what was emptily represented; and yet, such demonstration does not, as it were, live only in the things but involves also a moment of unreflective self-understanding, which phenomenology calls *Evidenz*, the experience of truth.[2] Thus it is that the legitimacy (*Rechtmässigkeit*) of knowledge is not something to be established *nachträglich*, for instance, through some further act of knowledge that would legitimate the first and that, once invoked by a theory of knowledge, would expose that theory to "senseless consequences" such as that of an infinite regress of acts of knowledge, each required to legitimate the one preceding it.

In the intentional fulfillment in which the intuited comes to coincide with the meant, what gets demonstrated and is "known" to be therein demonstrated is the *truth* of what was meant. Thus Heidegger's defini-

---

2. "Evidenz ist vielmehr nichts anderes als das 'Erlebnis' der Wahrheit" (*LU* I: 190).

tion: "Truth is the sameness of the meant and the intuited" (*GA* 21: 109). Knowledge occurs when the intuited comes to coincide with the meant, and truth is the sameness of the meant and the intuited, the sameness that is demonstrated through the coincidence. Thus are they bound together: knowledge, truth, intuition. Through intuition they are bound also to presence, even though Heidegger has begun, parenthetically, to loosen the bond.

To truth as thus determined, intuitive truth (*Anschauungswahrheit*), Heidegger traces back the more derivative determination of truth as propositional (*Satzwahrheit*): a proposition can be true, can be a locus of truth, precisely insofar as it can belong to an act of identification in which something intuited comes to coincide with what is meant in the proposition. Focusing on the question of the primacy of intuitive truth, Heidegger proceeds finally to trace out quite succinctly the bonds with which the entire series of analyses has remained deeply involved. First, regarding the bond of truth to knowledge: truth is a determination of knowledge in such a primary way that one can call the expression *true knowledge* a tautology. Only if knowledge is true, is it knowledge; and something apprehended as false is precisely *not known*. In turn, knowledge is bound to intuition: Heidegger says even that knowledge has been—in the analyses—determined as intuition, though he adds that this does not mean that every instance of knowing is an intuiting, only that intuiting is proper knowing (*eigentliches Erkennen*), at which all other knowing aims, to which it is oriented as the ideal (*GA* 21: 113).

Then, suddenly, Heidegger opens the phenomenological analysis to the entire history of philosophy: "By radically comprehending the concept of intuition for the first time, Husserl thought the great tradition of Western philosophy through to its end" (*GA* 21: 114). There follows a series of brief discussions in which Heidegger indicates how the relevant bond has been affirmed throughout the history that Husserl is said to have brought to its end by finally thinking that bond radically. The bond that has been affirmed is that of knowledge to intuition, which, conjoined with the tautological bond of truth to knowledge, has sustained a determination of truth as essentially intuitive, that determination that Husserl has thought through to its end. The bond of knowledge to intuition is openly expressed in Husserl's so-called principle of all principles, which requires of all principles that they appeal ultimately to intuition; intuition is thus posited as the source from which all knowledge is to be legitimated (*Rechtsquelle der Erkenntnis*). For Kant, too, knowledge proper is intuition; even though thought is set over against intuition in the Kantian conceptuality, it is in the end only a means in service to intuition, a means of compensating for the finitude of human intuition, which Kant contrasts with the *intuitus originarius* of the divine intellect. Heidegger extends the bond, binding together the exemplary moments of the history of philosophy, from Leibniz through Descartes to Scholasticism, in particular to Thomas Aquinas, to Augustine, and eventually back to Aristotle; only at the end of these discussions does Heidegger turn back to enclose Hegel too within this history, referring to the Hegelian concept of knowledge as self-intuition, as νόησις νοήσεως[3]. He concludes: "But it is the task of philosophical logic as characterized to question whether in fact this undiscussed predetermination of truth is or is not something final, something grounded in itself, or whether in the end it is not a prejudice" (*GA* 21: 124). Having thus displayed the bonds that sustain this predetermination, especially the bond linking knowledge to intuition (knowledge, in turn, being bound tautologically to truth), having shown how these bonds and the predetermination they sustain have the effect of binding together the entire history of Western philosophy, the task is to loosen the bonds, at least sufficiently to examine them more closely even than did Husserl in thinking this history through to its end. The task is also to open the possibility of a "more radical question" of truth, "over against this predetermination of truth" that has held sway since the Greeks—in short, to stretch and twist the bonds, perhaps to break them, perhaps even to venture a truth that is not of knowledge as intuition.

---

3. Heidegger notes that Hegel's logic seems to break through this idea of knowing as intuition, but he insists that this is mere seeming, semblance. No doubt it is because the case of Hegel is less apparent that Heidegger turns to it only after the unity of the history has been established. The very brief remarks to which he limits himself hardly suffice to enclose Hegel decisively within that history. To suggest that there is a moment in Hegel's thought that breaks the bond to presence and to intuition taken as correlate of presence, it suffices to cite the following passage from Hegel's *Wissenschaft der Logik*: "One can easily perceive that in absolute clearness one sees just as much, and as little, as in absolute darkness, that the one seeing is as good as the other, that pure seeing is a seeing of nothing. Pure light and pure darkness are two voids which are the same. Something can be distinguished only in determinate light or darkness . . . " (*Gesammelte Werke* [Hamburg: Felix Meiner, 1985], 21:80). In the 1923 lectures *Hermeneutik der Faktizität*, Heidegger is even less receptive to a radical moment in Hegel's thought: "All dialectic really lives always on what it takes from the table of others. The illuminating example: Hegel's *Logic*. . . . The dialectic is bilaterally nonradical, i.e., basically unphilosophical. It has to live from hand to mouth . . . " (*GA* 63: 45f.).

In fact, at the time of the lecture course *Logic* such a venture had already in effect been launched: most thoroughly in the lecture course of the previous semester, *History of the Concept of Time*, but in a sense from the very moment that Heidegger began sketching the project that came to its (limited) fruition in *Being and Time*.[4] For that project vigorously displaces intuition and presence (at least in its determination as *Vorhandenheit*, though implicitly in all its traditional determinations, which depend on the correlation of presence with intuition). By displacing intuition, the project stretches and twists the bond that had, since the ancients, kept truth bound to intuition. When, finally, in *Being and Time* Heidegger turns to a radical redetermination of truth, the bond is broken.

In *History of the Concept of Time* Heidegger begins with phenomenology. He outlines its fundamental discoveries (intentionality, categorial intuition, the original sense of the a priori), traces the developments that these themes underwent in the decade following the *Logical Investigations*, and calls finally for an investigation of what these developments had left undetermined: an investigation of the Being of the intentional, hence, of the Being of that being that is intentional, the being that Husserl had distinguished as consciousness, but without questioning the ontological differentiation on which the distinction of consciousness from reality was dependent. To his initial discussion of phenomenology, Heidegger then adds an elaborate sketch of the investigation called for, an analysis of the being that is intentional, now designated no longer as consciousness but as Dasein, an analysis of Dasein oriented to the question of the meaning of Being. In this sketch almost the entirety of the First Division of *Being and Time* is included in a form only slightly less detailed and precise than in the published work.

The relevant displacement is produced through the analysis of the most proximate surroundings; this is the analysis to which Heidegger also alludes in the *Logic* but in such a way as to keep it distinct from the phenomenological analysis. In *History of the Concept of Time* Heidegger develops this analysis and allows the displacement that it produces, the displacement of intuition and presence, to come into play, even though (and this is one of the instances of less precision) a certain language of presence (in the form of the words *Präsenz* and *Anwesenheit*) remains temporarily intact. The differentiation is clearly marked: what

---

4. The project is sketched as a whole as early as July 1924, in the lecture that Heidegger gave to the Marburger Theologenschaft: *Der Begriff der Zeit* (Tübingen: Max Niemeyer, 1989).

is genuinely given most proximally are not perceived things present in the flesh, in their *Leiblichkeit*, but rather the familiar things of concerned preoccupation (*das im besorgenden Umgang Anwesende*), the things with which one deals concretely in one's proximate surroundings, things that are thus embedded in a referential totality, a world, from which they receive their particular sense, the things that Heidegger calls by the name *das Zuhandene*, displacing eventually even the very word *Ding* because of the predetermination linking it to *das Vorhandene* (*GA* 20: 264).[5] The mode of access to the latter, to things as present-at-hand, the mode of access in which one foregoes concernful dealings with things and merely perceives them, is a founded mode that comes to be constituted only through a certain interruption of what is in play in one's concernful dealings, an interruption especially of the operation of the referential totality, of the world in which each thing is linked up referentially with others and the totality oriented to certain tasks to be done, certain possibilities for Dasein (*GA* 20: 300). As the table on which one is writing has its place in the room along with the chair on which one sits while writing, along with the lamp that illuminates the top of the table, across from the door that is closed so that the writer will not be disturbed, all of these things displaying in their mutual references an orientation to certain tasks, certain kinds of dealings in which they serve their purpose, certain of Dasein's possibilities, for instance, of writing.

In *Being and Time* the same displacement is produced through an analysis that is even richer in its concrete descriptive elaboration and that calls attention specifically to the displacement produced. The displacement is linked to what the analysis demonstrates regarding Dasein's sight (*Sicht*): first, that the sight by which Dasein deals concernfully with things and solicitously with others is not a matter of just perceiving but rather of apprehending things and others in their involvements in the world; hence, that sight is grounded in understanding, the moment of comportment in which Dasein projects upon the referential structure of its world in such a way that things and others can show themselves (in their involvement in the world) to Dasein's sight. These determinations of Dasein's sight produce the displacement: "Through the demonstration of how all sight is grounded primarily in understanding . . . , pure intuition is deprived of its priority, which corresponds

---

5. Regarding *Ding*, see *SZ* 67f.

noetically to the priority of the present-at-hand [*des Vorhandenen*] in traditional ontology" (*SZ* 147).

What does this displacement of intuition and presence entail with regard to the bond between knowledge and intuition? Heidegger touches upon this question in the course of tracing in *Being and Time* the genesis of the theoretical attitude, specifically, in his discussion of the thematizing that objectifies things as present-at-hand and that thereby carries out the scientific projection of nature. In order to situate such objectifying within the temporal interpretation of Dasein, Heidegger identifies it as a distinctive presenting (*Gegenwärtigung*) and then adds in a note: "The thesis that all knowledge has 'intuition' as its goal has the temporal meaning: all knowing is presenting. Whether every science or even philosophical knowledge aims at presenting, need not be decided here" (*SZ* 363). The thesis that all knowledge has intuition as its goal is of course the one that in *Logic* Heidegger has traced throughout the history of philosophy. The question that Heidegger leaves open is whether all scientific and philosophical knowing exhibits such an orientation and, hence, in the terms of the temporal interpretation of Dasein, is a presenting. Yet, if Heidegger leaves this question open, he clearly does not leave open the question as to the founded character of such intuitive presenting, indeed of knowing as such in the sense sustained in the history of Western philosophy.[6] For when Dasein comes to present things so as to objectify and thematize them, it will have done so only by modifying the comportment that it will already have had to them in its circumspective concern, its dealings with them as *zuhanden*. Unless knowledge is to be redetermined in a way that transgresses the previous determinations, knowledge will also be displaced in the displacement of intuition and presence. The field will thus have been cleared for a radical redetermination of truth.

Such a redetermination is provided in section 44 of *Being and Time*, the only major analysis in the First Division that is not to be found virtually intact in *History of the Concept of Time*. And yet, it is remarkable how the analysis of truth evokes the discussions from the lecture courses, especially from *Logic*, situating those discussions within the context in which intuition and presence undergo displacement. Heidegger notes that "according to the general opinion, what is true is knowl-

---

6. See especially the discussion in which knowing the world is exhibited as a founded mode of Being-in-the-world (*SZ* §13).

edge" (*SZ* 216), his hint of irony beginning to stretch this bond that *Logic* still characterized as tautological, preparing the questioning that will clear the field for the analysis of truth. The statement of another general opinion furthers that questioning: it is said that knowledge is judging, and so it can be said, as has almost always been said in the history of philosophy, that truth has its locus in judgment. Heidegger follows for a moment the train of Husserl's reflections: in judgment one must distinguish between the real psychic process and the ideal content of judgment, the latter (in the case of a true judgment) standing in a relation of correspondence to the real thing judged about. But now Heidegger is more outspoken in his unwillingness to have recourse to what he now calls "the ontologically unclarified separation of the real and the ideal." Voicing his suspicion that this separation already perverts the question, he even takes—for a moment, in the guise of questioning—the side of psychologism: "Is not psychologism right in opposing this separation . . . ?" (*SZ* 217).

It is against this background that Heidegger then proposes his analysis, proposes it in the most rigorous phenomenological terms. Adhering still to the general opinion that truth belongs to knowledge, he asks: "When does truth become phenomenally explicit in knowledge itself?" His answer provides the primary direction for the analysis that is to follow: "It does so when knowing demonstrates itself *as true*" (*SZ* 217). What is required, then, is an analysis of demonstration, since it is precisely in demonstration that truth comes to show itself *as truth*. Yet, such an analysis has already been given in *Logic*, appropriated from Husserl's *Logical Investigations*, and so *Being and Time* has only to orient that analysis more rigorously to the methodological directive and, most significantly, to integrate it into the analysis of Dasein, exposing it to the displacement of intuition and presence that that analysis produces.

It is a matter, then, of an intentional analysis of the demonstration that occurs when, having asserted that "the picture on the wall is hanging askew" while standing with one's back to the wall, one then turns around and perceives the picture hanging askew on the wall. That is, it is a matter of repeating with this example the analysis of intentional fulfillment that Heidegger took over in *Logic* from Husserl's *Logical Investigations*, a matter of showing through that analysis that the truth of the assertion consists in its saying the thing itself just as that thing comes to show itself, in its uncovering that thing just as that thing proves demonstrably to be, in short, in its being-uncovering (*entdeckend-sein*).

Heidegger could have extended the analysis and integrated it more radically into the analysis of Dasein, had he gone on to introduce another example, one in which the self-showing of the thing spoken of would have taken the form, not of perception, but of circumspective concern. For at least to this extent truth would, then, have been detached from knowledge as intuition. That Heidegger does not pause to develop such an example is a measure of the decisiveness that he attaches to the move that he broaches almost immediately upon having established the character of truth as being-uncovering. The move is announced as a regress from truth to its ontological condition of possibility: "Being-true as being-uncovering is, in turn, ontologically possible only on the basis of Being-in-the-world" (*SZ* 219). The move is a doubling of *truth*, doubling truth as being-uncovering, doubling it with the originary phenomenon of truth, which is the ontological condition of possibility of truth as being-uncovering. Though Heidegger does not elaborate the move descriptively, it is clear how it could be shown concretely that both the assertion and the self-showing of what is spoken of, both the empty intention and its fulfillment, are possible only on the basis of Being-in-the-world, only on the basis of the disclosedness (*Erschlossenheit*) by which Dasein is its "there" ("*Da*"), by which it is there in the world from out of which things can then show themselves in such a way that what has been said of them comes to be demonstrated. Thus doubling *truth*, Heidegger encloses within the unity of the word both truth in the extended phenomenological sense of being-uncovering *and* the condition of the possibility of such truth. Indeed, he declares: "What makes this very uncovering possible must necessarily be called 'true' in a still more originary sense" (*SZ* 220)—declares it as if it were self-evident, doubly marking ("must necessarily") the necessity of this doubling of *truth*.

It is this doubling that decisively breaks the bond of truth to knowledge in its traditional determination as intuition. For disclosedness is a matter neither *of* intuition nor *for* intuition. The originary phenomenon of truth, truth as disclosedness, is a truth that is not of knowledge.

The consequences of this doubling move to truth as disclosedness are virtually unlimited, and one could take it even as the point of departure for a rigorous narrative on the way forged by Heidegger's thought after *Being and Time*. Along that way such a narrative would be compelled constantly to mark consequences of the doubling.

For instance: the way in which during the 1930s Heidegger's lectures on Nietzsche put into question that tautological bond between truth and knowledge, marking that bond as one that even Nietzsche has in common with Plato, hence as binding even Nietzsche to the unity of the history of Platonism[7]—proposing then over against this history a thinking of a truth, most notably in art, that would be explicitly not of knowledge.

And then: the way in which "The Origin of the Work of Art" determines the truth in art as a truth that happens, that takes place in being set into the work of art, a truth therefore that is not of knowledge, that could be linked to knowledge only if knowledge were to be radically redetermined outside, at least, its bond to intuition, a redetermination that Heidegger broaches in this very text in his discussion of the preservation (*Bewahrung*) of the work of art, which he characterizes as a knowing (*Wissen*) constituted by "the ecstatic engagement of existing man in the unconcealment of Being" (*GA* 5: 55).

Until finally: in "The End of Philosophy and the Task of Thinking" Heidegger comes to retract the doubling, or, more precisely, the doubling of *truth*, insisting that the double, which he has come to call unconcealment (*Unverborgenheit*), clearing (*Lichtung*), and ἀλήθεια, is not to be equated with truth, since it is what first grants the possibility of truth, insisting—more disruptively—that the question of unconcealment is not the question of truth, so that it was, says Heidegger, "inadequate [*nicht sachgemäss*] and misleading to call ἀλήθεια in the sense of clearing, truth."[8] Thus, even if he will no longer say that what makes truth possible "must necessarily be called 'true' in a still more originary sense," what remains decisive is the doubling. Even if the double ought not be called truth, ought not be called even the originary phenomenon of truth, still what remains decisive is the turn to that which grants truth; and it is, above all, in order to safeguard the difference, the twofold, that Heidegger retracts truth as a name for that granting, that opening, that can be neither an act nor an object of knowledge. Unless *knowledge* is itself doubled along the lines proposed by "The Origin of the Work of Art"—

---

7. *Nietzsche* (Pfullingen: Günther Neske, 1961), 1:176, 188; hereafter: *N*. It is imperative to note that Heidegger's enclosing of Nietzsche's thought within the very Platonism that Nietzsche sought to overcome is only one moment in Heidegger's interpretation, a moment along with which one ought to mark, with Heidegger and perhaps more extensively than Heidegger, the moment of Nietzsche's twisting free (*Herausdrehung*) of Platonism (see *N* 1: 242). I have proposed to mark this latter moment also in Nietzsche's early work (see *Crossings: Nietzsche and the Space of Tragedy* [Chicago: University of Chicago Press, 1991], esp. 1–8).

8. *Zur Sache des Denkens*, 76f.

with the same risk no doubt that calling the double *knowledge* will be just as inadequate and misleading as in the case of the double of truth—it will need to be said and to be *thought* how unconcealment, *die Sache des Denkens*, can be—nonetheless—decisively not of knowledge.

5

Interrupting Truth

"Das Wesen der Wahrheit ist
die Un-wahrheit."

Heidegger, *Beiträge
zur Philosophie*

The question of truth cannot be merely one among several questions to be taken up by a thinking secure in itself. It can never have been—however much it may have seemed to be—a question to be addressed by a thinking already established from the outset, already fully determined as philosophical thinking. On the contrary, the development of the question of truth belongs to the very determination of philosophy, to its most classical determination, for example, as ἐπιστήμη τῆς ἀληθείας.[1] It is not as though philosophy is first delimited as such and then brought to bear on the question of truth; rather, the way in which the question of truth is addressed, the way in which truth is determined as such, determines the very project of philosophy, even if, in turn, that project must already have been broached in the determination of truth. In the formulation developed in Heidegger's 1937–38 course, *Basic Questions of Philosophy*, the question of truth is that by which philosophy is first brought to itself, gathered to itself, concentrated in its proper simplicity (*GA* 45: 13).

The trajectory of Heidegger's thought cannot, then, but have been determined in large measure by the question of truth. Thus it is that Heidegger's thinking of the history of metaphysics thematizes this history as that of the determination of truth: from the Platonic determination of

---

1. Aristotle, *Metaphysics* 993b20.

71

truth as correctness (ὀρθότης) or correspondence (ὁμοίωσις) to the utter inversion that this determination undergoes in Nietzsche's definition of truth as *the kind of error* without which a certain kind of living being could not live."[2] What is called for by the end that such inversion marks is a thinking of truth that is more originary, a recovery of truth within a dimension of origin that remained concealed in the history of metaphysics, that concealment belonging even to the very condition of the possibility of metaphysics, a concealment that will (prove to) have made metaphysics possible precisely by holding in reserve a truth that otherwise could not but interrupt metaphysics, an interrupting truth. The task of thinking at the end of metaphysics is, then, to translate the truth of metaphysics back into the interruptive truth, the ἀλήθεια, that in this manner precedes metaphysics.

The question of truth remains, then, always in play in Heidegger's work, from the courses of the Marburg period such as *Logic: The Question Concerning Truth* (1926–27, *GA* 21) up through such very late texts as "The End of Philosophy and the Task of Thinking" (1964)[3] and the Zähringen Seminar (1973, in *GA* 15). Yet it is during the 1930s, more precisely, during the period 1927–1943, that the question of truth assumes the greatest urgency in Heidegger's thought and comes to determine most powerfully and most transparently the itinerary of that thought. Within the methodological structure of *Being and Time* (1927) the analysis of truth (§44) serves as a pivot, gathering up the entire series of preparatory analyses of Dasein (Division One), concentrating the results of those analyses in such a way as to prepare for the more originary project disclosive of temporality as the meaning (*Sinn*) of the Being of Dasein (Division Two). In the attempt—later identified as having been undertaken from 1930 on[4]—to deploy the question of *Being and Time* in a more originary way, to shape its *Fragestellung* more originarily, the question of truth becomes still more prominent, entitling in fact a number of the discourses that engage most directly in the move—or rather, the break—to the more originary. The lecture that was eventually to be published as "On the Essence of Truth" (1943, in *GA* 9) was first presented in 1930 under the title "Philosophizing and Believing: The

---

2. Nietzsche, *Der Wille zur Macht*, ed. Peter Gast and Elizabeth Förster-Nietzsche (Stuttgart: Alfred Kröner, 1959), §493.

3. In *Zur Sache des Denkens*.

4. Ibid., 61.

Essence of Truth"; it was repeated several times and revised quite extensively, and indeed one can discern in the difference between the 1930 lecture and the 1943 published text certain of the most decisive moves in the transformation that Heidegger's thought undergoes, in that more originary deployment to which it submits its questioning. There is, in addition, the 1937–38 course cited above, which belongs to the very years in which Heidegger composed *Contributions to Philosophy* (*Beiträge zur Philosophie*). The latter, which remained unpublished until 1989, contains an extended series of discourses (*GA* 65: §§204–237) grouped under the title "The Essence of Truth"; among these discourses one finds some of the most decisive moves inscribed with a radicality that borders on the abysmal. During the same period there is also the series of texts in which Heidegger reflects on the transformation that he takes the essence of truth to have undergone in Plato's thought: the course entitled *On the Essence of Truth* (1931–32, *GA* 34), in which Heidegger presents his reading of the *Republic*; the course *Parmenides* (1942–43, *GA* 54), in which he extends (and complicates somewhat) that reading; and, finally, the published work, *Plato's Doctrine of Truth* (written in 1940, first published in 1942, now in *GA* 9).

I shall not undertake here to follow this itinerary as a whole. Rather, I shall focus on a single decisive indication that the *Contributions* gives regarding the question of truth; then, circling back to the analysis of truth in *Being and Time* and drawing out a single strand of the development to which Heidegger's work in the 1930s submits that analysis, I shall attempt to broach some understanding of the interruption announced by the indication from the *Contributions*, even though that interruption could not but produce also a certain break in Heidegger's very delimitation of understanding.

The indication on which I want to focus is given in a section of the *Contributions* (§226) entitled: "The Clearing of Concealment and ἀλήθεια [*Die Lichtung der Verbergung und die* ἀλήθεια]." This section is divided into four untitled subsections. The first stresses the need for questioning to engage concealment itself and not merely to think it as something superseded (*aufgehoben*) by revealment (*Entbergung*) and clearing (*Lichtung*). Heidegger enforces this demand by writing: *Wahrheit als die Lichtung für die Verbergung.* He broaches even "the captious formulation: truth is untruth"; and though insisting that this formulation can too easily be misinterpreted, he grants that it serves "to indicate the strangeness [*das Befremdliche*] involved in the new projection of essence." The indication on which I want to focus draws what appears to be a consequence of this strangeness of the essence of truth. It is given in the second subsection:

> But the previous attempts in *Being and Time* and the subsequent writings to carry *this* essence of truth through, as the ground of Dasein itself, in opposition to the correctness of representation and assertion, had to remain insufficient, because it was still carried through by *opposition* [*aus der* Abwehr] and so was still oriented to what it opposed, thus making it impossible to know the essence of truth by way of its ground [*von Grund aus*], the ground as which it itself essentially unfolds [*west*]. For this to succeed it is necessary no longer to hold back the saying of the essence of Being and to put aside the opinion that, in spite of the insight into the necessity of the advancing project [*des vorspringenden Entwurfs*], it is in the end still possible to clear a way step by step from the previous [view] to the truth of Being. But this must always fail. (*GA* 65: 351–52)

The passage indicates the insufficiency of an attempted transition, the transition *from* truth as the correctness of representation and assertion *to* that essence of truth that would be the ground of Dasein itself and that can also be called the truth of Being. This is the transition that was ventured by the analysis of truth in *Being and Time*. Now Heidegger insists that it remained oriented to the metaphysical determination of truth, even if by opposition; and thus circulating still within the opposition, it could not advance to the essence of truth as unfolding ground. Or rather, its attempt to advance step by step from the metaphysical determination of truth to that essence of truth that would be the truth of Being cannot but be interrupted.

How does this interruption occur? What is it that comes to interrupt the move from truth to truth (if in this dimension one can still appeal to the classical question τί ἐστι . . . ?)? From what kind of advance must one have returned in order to identify what appeared to be a transition as indeed an interruption?

In *Being and Time* a certain orientation to the traditional concept of truth is quite evident from the outset. Heidegger identifies three theses constitutive of the traditional concept, and his discussion of these theses serves to introduce his own effort at undercutting them, his attempt to move to a more originary concept of truth, from which (it could subsequently be shown) the traditional concept would have arisen. Thus, the point of departure of the analysis of truth is one of opposition, though indeed an opposition that aims not at rejection but at a move to the more originary. What Heidegger's analysis opposes in the traditional concept of truth is its distance from the originary phenomenon of truth. His analysis would move across that distance and recover the more originary phenomenon from which the traditional concept would have arisen. Beneath that concept, nearer to the origin, his analysis would bring to light the originary phenomenon that the traditional concept of truth would prove hitherto to have concealed.

Heidegger begins with the three theses:

> Three theses characterize the traditional conception of truth and the view of how it was first defined: 1. The "locus" of truth is assertion (judgment). 2. The essence of truth lies in the "correspondence" of the judgment with its object. 3. Aristotle, the father of logic, both assigned truth to the judgment as its originary locus and also launched the definition of truth as "correspondence." (*SZ* 214)

From the outset the analysis is thus both phenomenological and de(con)-structive. By means of phenomenological analysis it is to undercut the first two theses, to show that truth has a more originary locus than assertion and that correspondence between judgment and its object is grounded in a more originary phenomenon. The effect of carrying this analysis through and of engaging in the movement that it makes possible will be to clear away what has blocked access to the originary sources from which the essence of truth was first determined by the Greeks. Thus, the analysis would loosen up the "hardened tradition" (*SZ* 22), breaking apart the ossified concept passed on by tradition, interrupting that truth in the interest of recovering a truth nearer the origin. In the end it is to be a matter of recovering the force of an elemental word: ἀλήθεια.

Neither the word nor the concept as such is the primary object of the analysis of truth. Rather, it is a *phenomenological* analysis in the sense, first of all, determined in the Introduction to *Being and Time* (see *SZ* §7). That determination prescribes that the analysis must be one that proceeds in reference to the *way truth shows itself*; that is, it must be an analysis that attends to the process within which truth comes to show itself *as truth* and that thematizes what, within such a process of self-showing, truth shows itself to be. This is why Heidegger begins by asking: "When does truth become phenomenally explicit in knowledge itself?" He answers: "It does so when knowing demonstrates itself [*sich . . . ausweist*] *as true*" (*SZ* 217). Truth shows itself as truth in the context of demonstration. Such is, then, the phenomenal context to which the analysis must attend: it is a matter of thematizing what truth shows itself to be when in the course of demonstration it comes to show itself as truth.

The analysis involves two phases, two distinct movements toward the more originary. The first begins at the level of the traditional theory of truth, though the effect of the analysis is to subvert that theory for the sake of a more originary determination of truth. For this phase of the analysis Heidegger requires less than two pages (*SZ* 217–18). The second phase carries out the movement from the more originary determination of what the traditional concept took to be truth *to* a more originary phenomenon that while making truth in its traditional sense possible would, on the other hand, have been largely passed over by the tradition. For this phase of the analysis Heidegger requires only a few sentences (*SZ* 220).

Let me review once more the remarkable analysis with which Heidegger begins and which constitutes the first phase of the analysis as a whole. It is remarkable for its simplicity, for the directness with which it brings the decisive breakthrough of Husserl's phenomenology into play precisely in analyzing the things themselves and with a certain independence of Husserl's specific formulations.[5]

Heidegger begins with the situation in which a person, with his back to the wall, makes the true assertion: "The picture on the wall is hanging askew." The demonstration occurs when the person turns around and perceives the picture hanging askew on the wall. Then it is that the assertion comes to be demonstrated, that it proves to be true; its truth becomes manifest as truth. It is a question, then, of what exactly occurs

---

5. In *History of the Concept of Time* Heidegger takes up the same problems within a more specifically Husserlian context. Here too he insists, as in *Being and Time*, on the complexity of what is required by the phenomenological injunction "to the matters themselves" ("*zu den Sachen selbst*"): "We must free ourselves from the prejudice that, because phenomenology calls upon us to apprehend the matters themselves, these matters must be apprehended all at once, without any preparation. Rather, the movement toward the matters themselves is a long and involved process which, before anything else, has to remove the prejudices that obscure them" (*GA* 20: 36–37). The simplicity of the analysis in *Being and Time* is not simply in opposition to the complexity that characterizes this long and involved process; rather, it is precisely through its peculiar simplicity that the analysis, breaking up the ossified concept, removing the obscuring prejudices, opens up the complexity of the question of truth.

in such demonstration. Just how does truth show itself in the demon-stration? One could say that it shows itself as a kind of agreement. One could say even that it shows itself as a kind of agreement between knowledge (i.e., the assertion) and the thing known (i.e., the thing about which the assertion is made). To this extent the traditional concept can be declared correct. And yet, the question remains: Just what kind of agreement is this? In what sense can knowledge be said to agree with things? How can there be agreement between terms as disparate as knowledge and things?

Heidegger asks: To what is the speaker related when he initially makes the assertion? Can one say that the asserting relates to a repre-sentation of the picture, to a mental image of the real picture, a picture of the picture? Heidegger says: to insert such a representation is "to fal-sify the phenomenal state of affairs" (*SZ* 218). With these words he brings into play that decisive breakthrough that Husserl carried out in the *Logical Investigations* under the title *intentionality*: the character of consciousness as consciousness *of* requires that all such mediating rep-resentations, all images that would stand between an act that means something and that which is meant be expelled. Hence, when it is as-serted that the picture on the wall is hanging askew, this asserting re-lates, not to a picture of the picture, but to the picture itself, to the thing itself. What one means in the assertion is the real picture itself and noth-ing else: "The asserting is a Being toward the thing itself" (*SZ* 218).

What happens, then, when the person turns around and actually per-ceives the picture? What comes to be demonstrated? Heidegger an-swers: "Nothing else than *that* it *is* the very being that was meant in the assertion" (*SZ* 218). Hence, the correspondence that comes to be demon-strated is not an agreement of a representation (something psychic) with the thing itself (something physical) but rather an agreement between what is meant and the thing itself; more precisely, it is an agreement be-tween the thing itself *as* meant and the thing itself as perceived, as it shows itself concretely. In Heidegger's words, what occurs is that "that about which the assertion is made, namely the being itself, shows itself *as that very same being. Confirmation* signifies the self-showing of the being in its sameness" (*SZ* 218). In Husserl's terms, it is a matter of iden-tification through intentional fulfillment.

What, then, does the demonstration serve to demonstrate about the as-sertion? Heidegger answers: "What comes up for confirmation is that the assertive Being toward that of which something is asserted is a pointing-out [*Aufzeigen*] of the being, that such Being-toward uncovers [*entdeckt*] the being toward which it is. What gets demonstrated is the Being-uncovering [*Entdeckend-sein*] of the assertion" (*SZ* 218). In other words, what is demonstrated is that the assertion points out that about which it is made, that it uncovers that being; what is demonstrated is that the asserting is an uncovering, a pointing-out, of the thing itself.

How, then, is truth manifest? In such demonstration of the truth of assertion, how does truth show itself as such? What character does it show itself to have? Heidegger answers:

> To say that an assertion is true signifies that it uncovers the being in itself. It asserts, it points out, it lets the being be seen (ἀπόφανσις) in its uncoveredness. The Being-true (truth) of the assertion must be understood as Being-uncovering [*entdeckend-sein*]. (*SZ* 218)

The truth of the assertion lies in its character as uncovering, and in demonstration it comes to show itself as such, as being-uncovering.

Thus, Heidegger's analysis—or rather, the first of its two phases—proceeds in a way exemplary of phenomenology: the preconceptions that obscure the phenomena are set aside, and the analysis attends simply to the self-showing in which truth comes to show itself as such. The result is essentially a reinscription of the classical Husserlian analysis within the project of fundamental ontology.

The second phase of the analysis is different. For it does not simply undertake to clear away the traditional misconceptions so as to let the phenomenon be thematized in its self-showing, thus bringing to a self-showing the same phenomenon that was inadequately thematized in the traditional concept of truth; rather, in its second phase the analysis ventures a transition to another level, one that was not in play in the traditional concept of truth; it ventures a *move from* the phenomenon of truth as correspondence or being-uncovering *to another phenomenon* that can also be called *truth*. The second phase of the analysis is thus a regress to what Heidegger calls the originary (*ursprünglich*) phenomenon of truth, or even the *most originary* phenomenon of truth. Not that the analysis simply ceases in this phase to be phenomenological: it begins to gather up the entire complex of phenomenological analyses that the First Division of *Being and Time* has carried out and to bring the resources of those analyses into play in relation to the question of truth. And yet, however thoroughly inscribed within its phenomenological context, this move has a character that cannot but appear quite traditional, at least as long as it is carried out this side of the redeterminations that would have been produced by the never-published Third Division: it is a move from truth as being-uncovering to the ground of the possibility of such truth.

Heidegger does not actually carry out the move but only, identifying the ground to which the analysis moves, refers to previous analyses (specifically, that of the worldhood of the world) as having in effect already carried it out. Recalling those analyses, one could say—to give the very briefest indication—that in order for Dasein to comport itself to things in a way that uncovers them (as in assertion), world must already be disclosed. For at least two reasons: because world is that within which things can be intended, meant, as in assertion; and because world is that from out of which things can show themselves in such a way that a demonstration of an assertion becomes possible. Hence: "That beings within the world come to be uncovered *is grounded* in the disclosedness of world [*die Entdecktheit des innerweltlichen Seienden* gründet *in der Erschlossenheit der Welt*]" (*SZ* 220). Truth—that is, being-uncovering as a mode of intentional comportment in which, as in assertion, beings can be uncovered—is possible only on the basis of *disclosedness.*

Near the beginning of the short passage that announces this move, Heidegger proposes a peculiar extension of the word *truth,* a doubling in the direction of ground: "Being-true as Being-uncovering is a way of Being of Dasein. What makes this very uncovering possible must necessarily be called 'true' in a still more originary sense" (*SZ* 220). Thus it is that Heidegger calls disclosedness *truth,* not only *more* originary but indeed *most* originary: disclosedness is "the most originary phenomenon of truth" (*SZ* 220–21).

But what about this doubling of truth? What is the necessity—redoubled in Heidegger's formulation: ". . . must necessarily be called 'true' . . ."—that compels Heidegger to extend the word *truth* to that which makes truth possible? Or does the redoubling formulation betray some uncertainty regarding the move, as if Heidegger were attempting in the formulation to reinforce a move whose force, whose necessity, might otherwise seem insufficient? For is it indeed necessary that the ground be called by the same name as that which it would make possible? In other instances is it even the case that the ground is called by the same name as that which it grounds? Or is the difference between ground and grounded not usually marked linguistically in a more emphatic way than merely by employment of the comparative and superlative degrees? Is the difference between ground and grounded only a matter of degree? Or does its presentation as a matter of degree perhaps serve to mask the difference, to make ground and grounded seem more homogeneous than they may be? Does the doubling and the appeal to its necessity have the effect of concealing the complexity—or even the impossibility—of the transition from the traditional or phenomenological concept of truth to the other phenomenon, which *Being and Time* calls disclosedness, which in the 1930s will be called the truth of Being, but which finally will not be called truth at all but only ἀλήθεια? Is this effect, this facilitating of the transition, not carried even further when Heidegger goes on in *Being and Time* to round out the analysis of truth by showing how the traditional concept must have arisen from the originary phenomenon of truth? For then it turns out that—once one gathers up the results of the preparatory analysis of Dasein—one not only can move directly from the traditional concept of truth to that most originary phenomenon that is its ground and that is also called truth; but also one can proceed back from originary truth to the traditional concept, proceeding step by step, completing the circle. Even if Dasein is not only in the truth but also in the untruth. Even if it is essential to Dasein not only to uncover but also to conceal, to cover up and close off. Fundamental ontology will have broken through all that kept even the originary phenomenon of truth itself covered up in the history of metaphysics.

The simple doubling to which the name *truth* is submitted and its enforcement of a certain homogeneity between the traditional concept of truth and the originary phenomenon have the effect of constraining the analysis within an opposition; it is thus that the attempt in *Being and Time* to address the question of truth remained, as the *Contributions* charges, "still oriented to what it opposed." Thus too was it "impossible to know the essence of truth by way of its ground, the ground as which it itself essentially unfolds," for the phenomenon constitutive of the ground or essence of truth continued to be thematized too exclusively by its opposition—that is, *within* its opposition—to the traditional concept of truth as redetermined in the phenomenological analysis.

Yet, how is it that the simple opposition comes to be broken apart, broken off, and the originary phenomenon so twisted free of it that every attempt to clear a way leading step by step from the traditional concept of truth back to the originary phenomenon must, as the *Contributions* insists, "always fail." What comes to interrupt that move that seemed so assured—though no less decisive—in *Being and Time*?

What releases the interruption is a certain transformation—or, more precisely, a decentering, a dislocation—to which the phenomenon of truth is submitted in those texts of the 1930s that take up the question of the essence of truth. The transformation is reflected in the methodological character of these texts in contrast to that of *Being and Time*. Both the 1930 lecture and the 1943 published text that evolved from it begin by considering what one ordinarily understands by truth and by discussing what is commonly meant by the word *truth*. It is from this point that the essence of truth is then unfolded through its series of ever more originary determinations: correspondence, openness of comportment, freedom, letting-be. What is striking, especially in the point of departure, is that the phenomenological injunction is not sounded: Heidegger does not proceed by analyzing a situation in which truth comes to show itself as truth but rather begins with what is commonly meant by the word *truth* and proceeds by way of a series of analyses that, though too complex to analyze here,[6] are manifestly not phenomenological in the direct way exemplified in *Being and Time*. Even if one insists that these texts remain phenomenological in a sense such as that which Heidegger later adumbrates retrospectively,[7] it is clear that a decisive methodological shift has reoriented the discourses on truth broached after *Being and Time*: they are no longer simply oriented to self-showing.

Even before Heidegger begins to consider what is commonly meant by the word *truth*, the discourse of "On the Essence of Truth" is interrupted by the demands and attacks of common sense, its demand for the actual truth and its attack on all such questions as that of the essence of truth. The discourse on the question of truth has hardly begun when common sense—Heidegger will call it also sophistry—interrupts with its suspicion that the question of the essence of truth is "the most inessential and superfluous that could be asked" (*GA* 9: 177). Nonetheless, a certain unfolding of the essence of truth does ensue, and it produces a double series of redeterminations, redetermining both *essence* and *truth*. This discourse is haunted by a subdiscourse on un-

---

6. See below, chap. 6, "Deformatives: Essentially Other than Truth," for a detailed discussion of these analyses.

7. See *Zur Sache des Denkens*, 81–90.

truth, which keeps returning throughout the series of redeterminations: at first it is only a reminder that truth has an opposite, untruth, and that the discourse on truth will eventually have to be rounded out by a discourse on this opposite. One is reminded of the way that untruth is brought in at the end of the analysis of truth in *Being and Time* (Dasein is both in the truth and—as *verfallen*—also in the untruth); or rather, one would be so reminded were it not for the almost compulsive repetition of the subdiscourse and, most decisively, the dislocation that takes place at what would be the center of "On the Essence of Truth." For it turns out that the discourse on untruth is anything but a mere rounding out of the prior discourse on truth. Its effect is, rather, to interrupt that discourse by inscribing untruth within truth, by—as the 1930 lecture expresses it—letting the nonessence into the essence. In the 1943 published text the interruption is still more decisive: not only does untruth, concealment, belong to the essence of truth, but within that essence untruth is *older* than what would have been called truth (see *GA 9*: 193–94). In the word *older* Heidegger would say—but in a way that could also unsay—an ordering that would exceed all the words by which it has been named in the history of metaphysics. It is this excess, this reserve of concealment, that withholds the essence of truth from the demand for self-showing and that limits the possibility of a phenomenological discourse on the essence of truth. It limits also—and finally interrupts—every progression by which one would attempt to move step by step—that is, by reiterated appeal to evidence, to self-showing—from the traditional concept of truth to that essence of truth to which the still older untruth would—essentially, one would have said—belong. Indeed, as the concluding Note in the later editions of "On the Essence of Truth" indicates,[8] this very movement is what is enacted by that text, the movement now thought as that from the essence of truth to the truth of essence, the movement enacted in the text before finally being said in the nonproposition enunciated in the Note: "The essence of truth is the truth of essence." It is little wonder, then, that this text proves to be anything but a step-by-step progression; indeed its interruption is even such that in a note that Heidegger later wrote in his copy of the text he identifies the move from section 5 ("The Essence of Truth") to section 6 ("Untruth as Concealment") as a *leap*, as "*der Sprung in die (im Ereignis wesende) Kehre.*"

---

8. Beginning with the second edition (1949).

Contributions to Philosophy says the same when it declares, even if with caution: "The essence of truth is un-truth." Not only does this saying "bring nearer the strangeness of the strange essence of truth" (*GA* 65: 356) but also in saying this strangeness it bespeaks the very interrupting of truth.

6

Deformatives:
Essentially Other
Than Truth

What if truth were monstrous? What if it were even monstrosity itself, the very condition, the very form, of everything monstrous, everything deformed? But, first of all, itself essentially deformed, monstrous in its very essence? What if there were within the very essence of truth something essentially other than truth, a divergence from nature within nature, true monstrosity?

How could one then declare the truth—if it were monstrous? How could one even begin—as I have—to ask about a monstrous essence of truth? Would not the language of such declarations and questions have to become monstrous in addressing—and in order to address—such truth? Would not the deformation of truth, the operation of its deformatives, engender a deforming of language? Would it not require a commencement of deformative discourse?

There is perhaps no discourse more inextricably entangled in what it would address than discourse on the essence of truth. There is perhaps no questioning less capable of detachment from what it would interrogate. For to ask the philosophical question "τί ἐστι . . . ?", the question "What is it?", is to ask about the essence; and thus in the question "What is the essence of truth?" one merely repeats what is asked about, merely doubles the question. To say almost nothing of the way in which questioning is always already engaged with truth prior to any question: in coming to question one is already oriented to truth, that engagement from a distance constituting the very condition of the question.

Heidegger has much to say about such engagement—for example, the following, which I excerpt from that part of *Contributions to Philosophy* (*Beiträge zur Philosophie*) entitled "The Essence of Truth": "The essence of truth grounds the necessity of the *why* and therewith of questioning" (*GA* 65: 353). There will always already have been a response to the essence of truth—a believing (*Glauben*), as it is called in the *Contributions to Philosophy*—whenever questioning commences. Questioning will never have been simply outside the truth, other than the essence of truth, essentially other than truth.

Can there be, then, a question of an other? Under what conditions can the question of an essentially other than truth be raised? According to *Contributions to Philosophy* this question, the question of the relation of truth to an other, is inhibited, even prohibited (*verwehrt*), as long as ἀλήθεια is conceived in an originary way, *anfänglich begriffen als Grundcharakter der* φύσις, says Heidegger. One can ask about such a relation, he continues, only after the originary essence of ἀλήθεια has been given up and truth has become correctness (*GA* 65: 329–30). Thus the question of an other, of that which would be essentially other than truth, would not be an originary question. It would arise only in decline, in a falling away, in a certain return from engagement with the originary essence of truth.

It is a strange question, this question of the other of truth. For what could be more obvious than that truth has an other, an opposite, namely, untruth or error? Yet, what is the sense of other that is taken for granted when error is declared the other of truth? Can the sense of other be so rigorously stabilized that error can be declared simply *the* other of truth? Can the sense of otherness be restricted to opposition? Can the sense of opposition be itself rigorously controlled, its polysemy utterly reduced?

It will prove especially difficult to control the pairing of essence and other. One may say of course that error is essentially other than truth in that it falls simply outside truth itself, outside what truth itself is, outside the essence of truth. Indeed, in his most sustained discourse on the essence of truth Heidegger reaffirms this externality affirmed by both common sense and metaphysics. And yet, his reaffirmation is limited, not to say ironic, first of all because there is no simple outside: as the mere negation, the symmetrical opposite of truth, error is not essentially other but is dependent on the determination of truth. It is not essentially other than truth but only the other side of the determination of truth, the mere opposite.

Thus it is that when Nietzsche comes to think that final possibility with which the possibilities of metaphysics would finally be exhausted, he thinks truth as *"the kind of error* without which a certain kind of living being could not live."[1] This inversion, Nietzsche's reversal of Platonism, the end of metaphysics, proclaims that truth is error, that truth is untruth. In *Contributions to Philosophy* Heidegger repeats this proclamation, even though he encloses it within a double warning, marking it as captious and as too easily misunderstood. Nonetheless, it bears repeating, he grants, in order "to indicate the strangeness" of what is to be undertaken in this connection, the strangeness of what Heidegger calls a new projection of essence (*Wesensentwurf*) (*GA* 65: 351). The project is to reopen the essence of truth, redistributing the opposites. It is a matter of bringing a second moment into play along with the Nietzschean moment of inversion, of releasing a moment of displacement by which the very *Ordnungsschema* governing the opposition between truth and error would be transformed (cf. *GA* 43: 260). Now truth and untruth would be thought together differently; and through this deforming of the essence of truth, thinking would come to twist free of the metaphysical opposition.

Such thinking of the essence of truth is carried out most rigorously in the text "On the Essence of Truth." What I propose is a rereading of this text—or rather, here, an indication of the schema of such a rereading—one that would focus on the moment in which the text twists free, that would trace the displacement in which the mere opposite would become a proper untruth and would come to deform truth itself.

One should not underestimate the strangeness of this text, first presented as a public lecture in 1930 and repeatedly revised before finally being published in 1943.[2] If one compares the published text of 1943 with the still unpublished lecture of 1930, the impression of strangeness is only enhanced. The double text, enclosing a period of thirteen years, becomes even stranger if one unfolds within it another discourse on truth belonging within this period, the one contained in *Contributions to Phi-*

---

1. *Der Wille zur Macht*, §493.
2. In a note in *Wegmarken* Heidegger explains that the work first published in 1943 "contains the repeatedly revised text of a public lecture, which was thought out in 1930 and presented several times under the same title (in the fall and winter of 1930 in Bremen, Marburg a.d.L., Freiburg i.Br. and in summer of 1932 in Dresden)" (*GA* 9: 483). According to the text that I have examined of the Marburg version, the lecture was presented there to the Faculty of Protestant Theology. Also, despite Heidegger's remark in the note in *Wegmarken*, "The Essence of Truth" was only the subtitle in this version of the lecture. I shall return below to this question of titles.

losophy (1936–38) under the title "The Essence of Truth" (*GA* 65: 327–70). In the latter, for example, one finds a curious sequence of indications assembled under the title: *Worum es sich bei der Wahrheitsfrage handelt* (one might translate loosely, since it cannot strictly be translated: What the question of truth is all about) (*GA* 65: 338). The first indication in the sequence reads: "not a matter of a mere modification of the concept." The second reads, surprisingly, strangely: "not a matter of a more originary insight into the essence." The third continues: "but rather a matter of *den Einsprung in die Wesung der Wahrheit*"—a matter, one may say in lieu of the impossible translation, of stepping into the essential unfolding of truth. The indications become still stranger, the fourth reading: "and consequently a matter of a transformation of the Being of man in the sense of a *derangement* [*Ver-rückung*] of his position among beings." What is the question of truth all about? Human derangement, madness!

The strangeness of the text "On the Essence of Truth"—I refer to the published text of 1943—is less apparent, at least at the beginning. The objections by which common sense opposes any question of the essence of truth are sounded; and it is declared that common sense has its own necessity, that it can never be refuted by philosophy. Yet, almost from the outset a displacement of the common commences, giving way finally to the uncommon declaration of the proposition "The essence of truth is the truth of essence." What is perhaps strangest is the pairing of this declaration with a certain retraction. Heidegger says of the proposition: "It is no proposition [*Satz*] at all in the sense of a statement [*Aussage*]" (*GA* 9: 201). But if the proposition "The essence of truth is the truth of essence" is also not a proposition, then what is to be said of it, through it? A most uncommon saying: "the saying of a turning within the history of Being."

In its formal structure the text "On the Essence of Truth" displays a certain symmetry. It is divided into nine sections. The first four develop the question of the essence of truth. This development is gathered up in the fifth, the central section, which is entitled "The Essence of Truth." Then come finally four sections that appear to extend or round out what has been established, addressing the question of the relation of philosophy to the essence of truth and especially the question of untruth.

In the movement of the text, however, there is a certain eccentricity that finally transforms—or rather, deforms—this formal structure. Thus, most notably, the question of untruth is not simply reserved for the final sections of the text but is in play from the beginning, in play at least in Heidegger's ironic declarations of the legitimacy of deferring, if not excluding, its consideration. This operation of the question of un-truth throughout the text cannot but produce, in turn, a certain doubling of the center, hence finally a decentering of the entire discourse, even a monstrous decentering.

A certain uncommon movement is broached from the outset of the text. Heidegger begins: Vom *Wesen* der Wahrheit ist die Rede. The dis-course concerns the *essence* of truth. Heidegger italicizes *Wesen* (*essence*) and so in this opening calls attention to it. In a sense the entire opening section of the text is addressed solely to this word essence and to what is said in it. Heidegger observes that in asking about the essence of truth, one is not concerned with any specific kind of truth but rather disregards, abstracts from, the differences between, for example, scientific truth and artistic truth, attending rather to the one thing that dis-tinguishes every truth as truth. That one thing that all truths have in com-mon would constitute the *essence* of truth. Thus, essence means: the common—in Greek: κοινόν.

In this connection Heidegger refers also to common sense (*der gemeine Menschenverstand*). He not only refers to it but also speaks (almost) with its voice, and one realizes from the outset that various voices—a polyphony—are to be heard in this text. Heidegger voices—as a question—the objections that common sense makes to the question of essence: "Is not the question of essence the most inessential and su-perfluous that could be asked?" (*GA* 9: 177). It is as if common sense—opposing the question of the common—were in opposition to itself. Yet, the opposition that Heidegger stresses is that between common sense and philosophy, an opposition in a sense irresolvable: "Philosophy can never refute common sense" (*GA* 9: 178). Near the end of "On the Essence of Truth" Heidegger will again speak of common sense, and it will be necessary to consider what bearing the questioning ventured in Heidegger's text has on common sense, whether this questioning bears on it in any other than a purely extrinsic, negative way.

What first broaches an uncommon movement is a marginal comment written by Heidegger in his own copy of the third edition (1954) of "On the Essence of Truth" and now, along with other marginal comments, in-cluded with the text in the *Gesamtausgabe*. These marginal comments are not simple additions to the text, and their function cannot be limited to mere clarification. Not only do they introduce in the margin of the text later developments in Heidegger's thought that presuppose the way laid out in the text; but also within the text itself many of the marginal comments produce a disordering, announcing at the outset of a development in the text a result that is to be reached only by way of that development. For instance, at the beginning of section 1 Heidegger sets out to consider what one ordinarily understands by the "worn and almost dulled word 'truth' " (*GA* 9: 178–79). Yet, before he can even begin to declare what this most ordinary understanding is, the text is interrupted by a marginal comment keyed to the word *truth*: the comment refers *truth* to *clearing* and, hence, leaps over the entire development that is just commencing and that will be required in order to translate the discourse on truth into a discourse on clearing. The marginal comment carries out the translation instantaneously; its discourse, disordering the text, is heterogeneous with the discourse of the text—or rather, renders the text a scene of double writing.

A similar disordering, a drastic foreshortening, is produced by the marginal comment keyed to the word *essence* in the opening sentence of "On the Essence of Truth." The comment reads: "Essence: 1. quidditas—the what—κοινόν; 2. making-possible [*Ermöglichung*]—condition of possibility; 3. ground of the making-possible" (*GA* 9: 177). Thus, prior to the determination of essence as the common, as κοινόν, the comment indicates that this initial determination is not the only one that will come into play, that there are at least the two other senses of essence mentioned in the comment. Thus, the text is to put into question not only the essence of truth but also the very sense of essence. It could not be otherwise, granted that Heideggerian reading of Plato that links the determination of truth as ὁμοίωσις to the determination of Being as εἶδος, hence to the determination of *essentia*, essence. Thus is the text "On the Essence of Truth" oriented from the beginning to that non-proposition to which it will finally lead: the essence of truth is the truth of essence.

What one finds, then, in the text "On the Essence of Truth" is a *double series* of redeterminations, beginning with the ordinary concept of truth and the common sense of essence and then proceeding to the more originary determinations mentioned in the marginal comment.

Heidegger begins by circumscribing the ordinary, i.e., the common, concept of truth. What one ordinarily understands by *truth* is that which makes a true thing true, more specifically, that by virtue of which a thing or a proposition is true. As such, truth has, then, the character of accordance or correspondence (*Übereinstimmung*). In the case of a thing it is a matter of accordance with a certain preunderstanding; for example, true gold, genuine gold, is gold that accords with what one understands in advance by *gold*. In the case of a proposition, it is a matter of accordance with that about which the proposition is asserted, of correspondence with the thing spoken of. Heidegger traces this concept of truth back to its origin in the medieval definition: *veritas est adaequatio rei et intellectus*. Here there is a double accordance, rooted in the medieval conception of the relation between God, nature, and man. A thing is true only if it accords with the divine idea, the archetypal idea in the divine intellect; thus, in this case truth consists in accordance of the thing to the divine intellect (*adaequatio rei ad intellectum*). But in the case of the human intellect, that is, of human knowledge as expressed in propositions, the structure is more complex: on the one hand, a human idea is true by according with the divine idea, just as anything creaturely is true by according with the divine archetype; on the other hand, a human idea is true by according with the thing known, and it is in this connection that truth consists in *adaequatio intellectus ad rem*. The connection is this: a human idea can correspond to the known thing only on the basis of a double correspondence (of the human idea *and* of the thing) to the divine idea. As Heidegger writes: "If all beings are 'created', the possibility of the truth of human knowledge is grounded in the following: that thing [*Sache*] and proposition measure up to the idea in the same way and therefore are fitted to each other on the basis of the unity of the divine plan of creation" (*GA* 9: 180–81). A marginal comment puts it still more succinctly: "Because of correspondence with the creator, therefore [correspondence] *among themselves* (as created . . .)" (*GA* 9: 181). By thus tracing the common concept of truth back to its medieval origin, Heidegger carries out a kind of desedimenting of it, referring it to this, its "most recent," origin in such a way as to broach its *Destruktion*. In order to disrupt the obviousness that common sense takes it to have, he shows that this concept of truth is rooted in medieval ontology, in a certain interpretation of Being, that, consequently, the concept of truth as accordance (correspondence) is anything but obvious when, as in modern thought, it comes to be detached from that interpretation of Being. By linking the allegedly ordinary concept of truth to its medieval origin, by demonstrating its historicity, Heidegger indicates that outside medieval ontology it is not at all obvious what is meant by accordance of an idea with a thing, of a statement with that about which it is said. By desedimenting this concept of truth, he releases its questionableness: "What is it about statements that still remains worthy of question [*Fragwürdiges*]—granted that we know what is meant by accordance of a statement with the thing? Do we know that?" (*GA* 9: 182).

The irony is more veiled in what Heidegger says at this first stage about untruth. But only slightly so: Heidegger links what is said about untruth to the very obviousness that the entire discussion has aimed at subverting: it is considered obvious that truth has an opposite, namely, untruth, which would, then, consist in non-accordance. Heidegger concludes that untruth, so conceived, "falls outside the essence of truth." He continues: "Therefore, when it is a matter of comprehending the pure essence of truth, untruth, as such an opposite of truth, can be put aside" (*GA* 9: 182). As mere opposite, untruth belongs outside; its consideration can be left aside or at least deferred until the essence of truth has been secured.

What drives Heidegger's text on to its second stage is the question: What is meant by *accordance* (*Übereinstimmung*) in the definition of truth as accordance of a statement with the thing about which it is made? How can there be an accordance between a statement and a thing, considering how utterly different they are? Heidegger's answer reaches back to Husserl's *Logical Investigations*: such accord is possible only because the statement is not just another, though utterly different thing but rather is a moment belonging to a comportment to the thing about which the statement is made. Heidegger's formulation is most concise in the 1930 lecture text: "It is only because the statement is also a comporting [*Verhalten*] that it can in its way accord with something." What kind of comporting occurs in the assertion of a true statement? A comportment, says Heidegger, that presents the thing as it is. Or rather, since he writes the word with a hyphen, *vor-stellen*, distinguishing it from *vorstellen* in the modern epistemological or psychological sense, let it be said that such comportment sets the thing there before us as it is. But what is thus required? What must be involved in a comportment that— in the appropriate sense—presents the thing as it is? Heidegger answers—I cite the 1943 published text:

> This can occur only if beings present themselves along with the presentative statement so that the latter subordinates itself to the directive that it speak of beings *such-as* they are. In following such

a directive the statement conforms to beings. Speech that directs itself accordingly is correct (true). (*GA* 9: 184)

What is required, then, is "a binding directedness [*eine bindende Richte*]" to things, a subordinating of speech to them in such a way that one speaks of things in just *such* a way *as* they are.

At this juncture let me double the text, bringing into play alongside the published text of 1943 the original lecture text of 1930. For in the earlier double of the text one finds a different formulation of the same matter. Heidegger refers to two characteristics of such comportment as occurs in the assertion of a true statement: on the one hand, revealing or making manifest (*Offenbaren*), on the other hand, letting-be-binding (*Verbindlich-sein-lassen*). Thus, such comportment reveals things, shows them as they are, *and yet* is bound precisely by those things. Heidegger raises the question of the relation between these two characteristics, the question as to which is prior. In a sense it is less simply a question than a paradox, which one might formulate as follows: one's comportment would have to be bound by the things, governed by them, in order to reveal them *as* they are; and yet, that comportment could be bound by them only if one had already revealed them so as to take one's bearings from them as they are. This paradoxical formulation indicates the necessity of Heidegger's conclusion: "The two characteristics of comportment, revealing and letting-be-binding, . . . are not two at all but rather one and the same." They must, then, be thought together, thought as one and the same.

In the 1943 text Heidegger gathers up the requirements that must be met in order that comportment be such that true statements can arise in it; he gathers them in the phrase: openness of comportment (*Offenständigkeit des Verhaltens*). He concludes: "But if the correctness (truth) of statements becomes possible only through this openness of comportment, then what first makes correctness possible must with more originary right be taken as the essence of truth" (*GA* 9: 185). Such is, then, the second pair of determinations in that double series: more originary than the common essence is essence as *making-possible*; and more originary than truth as accordance (correctness) is the essence of truth as openness of comportment.

Heidegger's move to the third stage seems quite classical: it is a regress from the openness of comportment to the *ground* of that openness. In the 1943 text the move is carried out very quickly, requiring only a few sentences. Let me attempt to reinscribe those sentences—still more economically—by extending the doubling of the text, again bringing into play the description of open comportment provided by the 1930 text. The first of the two characteristics, revealing beings, involves presenting them, setting them there before—and so, over against—us; that is, it involves setting them within what the 1943 text calls "an open field of opposedness [*ein offenes Entgegen*]," "an open region [*das Offene*]" (*GA* 9: 184). The other characteristic of such comportment, letting beings be binding, involves maintaining a binding or pregiven directedness toward those beings so as to present them *as they are*. Thus, the openness of comportment requires a certain *engagement* in the open region and a certain *openness* to what is opened up there, namely, to the beings to which speech would submit. Such engaged openness is to be called: *freedom*. Thus, the ground of the making-possible of truth as accordance is freedom. Heidegger concludes that the essence of truth is freedom.

Such is, then, the third pair of determinations in the double series: essence as *ground* and the essence of truth as *freedom*.

The essence of truth is freedom: Heidegger observes that this proposition cannot but seem strange. Strange—not merely because it offends common sense by appearing to submit truth to human caprice, but because, far beyond the reach of common sense, it broaches in the word *freedom* an opposition that borders on the unthinkable, an engaged openness, an engagement that "withdraws in the face of beings in order that they might reveal themselves" (*GA* 9: 188–89). Will these ever have been thought as one and the same? Can freedom be thought as such?

It would appear that freedom comes to be thought in the move onward toward the center of the text "On the Essence of Truth." The very title of the fourth section, "The Essence of Freedom," would appear to indicate the course of the further regress that such thinking would follow: from freedom to the essence of freedom. Indeed Heidegger asks explicitly: "How is this essence of freedom to be thought?" (GA 9: 187–88). Yet also, at the beginning of this section he hints that this regress will be a *double move*:

Consideration of the essential connection between truth and freedom leads us to pursue the question of the essence of man in a regard which assures us an experience of a concealed essential ground of man (of Dasein), and in such a manner that the experience transposes us in advance into the originarily essential domain of truth. (*GA* 9: 187)

Thus, it is to be: (1) a move to the (concealed) essential ground of man, this ground constituting presumably the essence of freedom; and thereby (2) a transposition to a domain of truth that Heidegger ventures to call "originarily essential."

Heidegger begins by identifying freedom as *letting-be*: freedom lets beings be the beings they are and so has the character of letting-beings-be (*das Seinlassen von Seiendem*). Letting-be is not of course a matter of neglect or indifference. In the words of a marginal comment, it is "not negative"; it is rather, in the formulation given in another marginal comment, "to allow what is present its presence, to bring nothing else . . . in between" (*GA* 9: 188). Also, however, it is no mere dealing with beings, no tending, managing, or even preserving; rather, it requires that one "engage oneself with the open region and its openness [*das Offene und dessen Offenheit*] into which every being comes to stand" (*GA* 9: 188). Heidegger adds that in the beginning of Western thought this open region was conceived as τὰ ἀληθέα (he translates: *das Unverborgene*, the unconcealed) and its openness as ἀλήθεια (*Unverborgenheit*, unconcealment). One cannot but note also the connection with the phenomena of world and disclosedness (*Erschlossenheit*) developed in *Being and Time*.

By introducing letting-be, Heidegger reorients somewhat those two opposed moments that were found to drive the concept of freedom almost to the point of contradiction. In place of an engagement in revealing, in presenting beings, that would be coupled with a withdrawal, a holding back, so as to be bound by beings, engagement is now thought preeminently as engagement *in the open region*, whereas it is a matter of withdrawal *in the face of the beings* that come to presence in that open region. It is still a matter of thinking these together, even if also in their difference:

> To engage oneself with the disclosedness [*Entborgenheit*] of beings is not to lose oneself in them; rather, such engagement withdraws in the face of beings in order that they might reveal themselves with respect to what and how they are and in order that presentative correspondence might take its standard from them. (*GA* 9: 188–89)

Such engagement, which sustains letting-be, has the character of exposure (*Aussetzung*) to beings as such in the open; it is a matter of being set out into the open region in which beings come to presence. It is a matter of being *ek-sistent*, of standing outside oneself, out into the open in which beings come to presence.[3] Heidegger insists that, when conceived as ex-posure, as ek-sistence, freedom can no longer be regarded as a property of man but rather must be considered that which first lets man be *as* man: "Man does not 'possess' freedom as a property. At best, the converse holds: freedom, ek-sistent, disclosing Dasein possesses man . . ." (*GA* 9: 190).

Hence one movement of the double move: to the concealed essential ground of man, namely, freedom as ek-sistence—that is, the essence of freedom determined as ek-sistence.

But in this determination of the essence of freedom how is the sense of essence determined?—if I may continue for the moment to mark with the word *sense* a question belonging to a region in which this word cannot but become ever more questionable. Most remarkably and in utter contrast to the previous three stages, Heidegger now says nothing whatsoever about the sense of essence, not even in the marginal comments. Yet, something can be said—even if with all the withholding that the matter here exacts, even if such reticent saying also borders on the unthinkable, reproducing the opposition that would be said in the word *freedom*, reproducing it as freedom of speech. Something can be said if one sets side by side two almost identical propositions bearing on the determination of freedom. The first reads: "the essence of freedom manifests itself as exposure to the disclosedness of beings." The other: "Freedom is . . . engagement in the disclosure of beings" (*GA* 9: 189). Both freedom and the essence of freedom are the same—namely, exposure to or engagement in the disclosedness or unconcealment of beings. Thus, the essence of freedom is freedom—that is, freedom itself, freedom proper. In the word *essence* one is now to hear: the "itself," the proper.

And yet, what is most remarkable is that this would-be delimitation of freedom itself, of freedom proper, has the effect precisely of disrupting the "itself," the "proper." For to be ek-sistent, to be engaged in, exposed to, the unconcealment of beings is to be referred beyond oneself, referred *essentially*, one might venture—not without also withholding

---

3. This analysis parallels that found in "On the Essence of Ground" (1929), though the language of the latter remains closer to *Being and Time*. In the 1929 text the concept of freedom is introduced following the development of the concept of world: "The passage beyond to the world [*Der Überstieg zur Welt*] is freedom itself. . . . Freedom alone can let a world hold sway for Dasein . . ." (*GA* 9: 163–64). This passage beyond beings to the world Heidegger also calls transcendence.

it—to say. It is to be outside oneself, ecstatic, in a manner that cannot leave the "oneself," the proper, the essence, intact.

Thus it is that Heidegger writes: freedom "receives its own essence from the more originary essence of uniquely essential truth" (*GA* 9: 187). Let it be said: freedom is submitted to unconcealment, to ἀλήθεια. This submission constitutes the second moment of the double move: a transposition to the originarily essential domain of truth. Hence, the double move as a whole consists in the regress to the essence of man (freedom, ek-sistence) *and then*, precisely because it is ek-sistent, ecstatic, the referral of this essence beyond itself, what one would like to call its *essential* reference beyond itself (were the reference not deformative both of essence and of its doubling). One could say that there is a deeper sense in which freedom is not a property of man (were the deformation of essence, now broached, not also a deformation of sense, of the sense of sense, to say nothing of the implied order of depth): freedom, as ek-sistence, is the very *dispropriation* of the essence of man.

Thus it is, too, that at the center of "On the Essence of Truth," in that section in which the entire movement would be gathered under the title "The Essence of Truth," so little is said. What one finds there is a discourse that bespeaks unmistakably the submission to ἀλήθεια, a discourse on attunement (*Stimmung*), the very way of being submitted to the open, to ἀλήθεια. It is *almost* as if at its center the text "On the Essence of Truth" had come essentially to its end. Almost as if it would require still only perhaps some final rounding out.

Almost—but not quite.

For at the center there is also another discourse, a discourse on untruth, one that resumes a subdiscourse that has haunted the text all along its way toward the center. Even after the regress to freedom as the essence of truth, the question of untruth is addressed in nearly the same form as at the outset: untruth is declared both the opposite of truth and the non-essence of truth and, with an irony that anticipates what is to come, it is said to be excludable "from the sphere of the question concerning the pure essence of truth" (*GA* 9: 187). Then, following the disruption of freedom proper that is announced under the title "The Essence of Truth," Heidegger introduces an untruth that would consist, not in mere non-accordance, but in covering up or distorting (in a certain opposition to letting-be). Then, most decisively, he withdraws untruth from the domain of the merely human. Untruth, too, must be referred beyond all proper freedom, beyond man himself: "The non-essence of truth cannot first arise subsequently from mere human incapacity and negligence. Rather, un-truth must derive from the essence of truth" (*GA* 9: 191). To think the essence of truth will thus require thinking also the non-essence (un-truth). Thus begins—at the very threshold of the center—the decentering that drives the text onward: not only the decentering already under way, the decentering of man, the decentering by which he is displaced, dispos-sessed, in the direction of originarily essential truth; but also now—still more disruptively—a decentering of truth itself, a displacement by which it ceases to be simply (properly) set over against its opposite (untruth). It is a decentering of opposition as such that now drives the text onward.

Onward to the would-be center—which, contrary to what its title and the apparent symmetry of the entire text would suggest, culmi-nates, not in a declaration of the essence of truth, of truth proper, but rather in a discourse on untruth. This discourse proclaims a still more intimate adherence of untruth to truth: "Letting-be is intrinsically at the same time a concealing [*Das Seinlassen ist in sich zugleich ein Verber-gen*]. In the ek-sistent freedom of Dasein . . . there is concealment [*Verborgenheit*]" (*GA* 9: 193). Thus is broached a monstrous decenter-ing of the essence of truth, an opening of it to an other that would no longer be merely a symmetrical opposite but that would be intrinsic to it, that would belong to it. Thus, at its center the text broaches a mon-strous decentering, which cannot but deform the text itself. From this point on it will become ever more monstrous—beginning with the pas-sage from the would-be center to the remaining sections of the text, a monstrous transition that is thus not a passage or transition at all but rather a leap. A marginal comment marks it as such—as "the leap into the turning (that essentially unfolds in *Ereignis*) [*der Sprung in die (im Ereignis wesende) Kehre*]" (*GA* 9: 193).

Hence the monstrous phrase that follows this leap—the phrase with which Heidegger refers to concealment as: the un-truth that is *most proper* to the essence of truth. Now untruth belongs most properly to the essence of truth, belongs to what would have been the proper of truth, had that very proper not been disrupted by the submission of freedom to ἀλήθεια. It is time to read the discourse onto which the phrase opens:

Here non-essence does not yet have the sense of inferiority to essence in the sense of the general [*das Allgemeine*—what is com-mon to all] (κοινόν, γένος), its *possibilitas* (making-possible) and the ground of its possibility. Non-essence is here what in such a sense would be a pre-essential essence. But "non-essence" means at first and for the most part the deformation [*die Verunstaltung*] of that already inferior essence. Indeed, in each of these significations the non-essence remains always in its own way essential to the essence and never becomes unessential in the sense of something indifferent. (*GA* 9: 194)

Truth becomes monstrous: a deformation of what is natural (i.e., of the essential); a divergence from nature, something unnatural, within nature (non-essence within essence). Here the sense of essence is disrupted so decisively that it erases its very designation as a disruption of *sense*, namely, by disrupting the very operation of the concept of sense as well as the sense of concept. Concealment as non-essence is a deformative so decisive as to require that one begin to write differently, that a deformative writing commence.[4] One would say that now the structure of essence is such that the non-essence belongs to it rather than falling outside it, that essence is such as to include non-essence within it. But one would also have to pair with such saying an unsaying that would grant the deformative effect upon such words as *such*, *within*, and *itself*. Little wonder that, when Heidegger comes finally to propose the answer to the question of the essence of truth, he must pair that proposal with a denial that it is a proposition.

Let me extend the discourse in that direction by mentioning—all too briefly—three moments in the discourse on untruth that has now commenced.

The first is the extension that the deformative move undergoes through the introduction of *errancy*. Thus would Heidegger name—alongside the concealment already introduced into the essence of truth as its proper non-essence (*eigentliche Un-wahrheit*), what he now calls *the mystery* (*das Geheimnis*)—another form—or rather, deform—of untruth belonging to the essence of truth, belonging to it as its essential counter-essence (*das wesentliche Gegenwesen*). Hence, there is a doubling of untruth, into non-essence and counter-essence. But, in turn, errancy is determined as a double movement. On the one hand, it is a

---

4. Also a double writing, a rewriting or rereading of Heidegger's text that would release into it what certain rhetorical strategies (primarily irony) hold in reserve up to the center. For though untruth comes into play as proper to the essence of truth only at the center of the text, it cannot but have been in play (even if as repressed) in all the determinations retraced from the beginning of the text.

concealing of concealment, that is, a covering up of the mystery that holds sway throughout Dasein's engagement in the open. On the other hand, it is a turning toward readily available beings, away from the (concealed) mystery: "Man clings to what is readily available and controllable even where ultimate matters are concerned" (*GA* 9: 195). Thus is man left "to his own resources," in a kind of abandonment or destitution (*Seinsverlassenheit*).

Hence, there is not only a doubling of untruth but even a redoubling inasmuch as errancy is thus determined as a double movement. Such proliferation of deformatives cannot but deform ever more the essence of truth, inasmuch as essence in all its senses hitherto—thus, one would like to say: essence in its essence—has been determined primarily in relation to unity, not duplicity. But now, as truth becomes essentially duplicitous, it becomes also ever more monstrous.

The second extension gives an indication of the force of the disruption. Heidegger writes:

> But to speak of non-essence and untruth in this manner goes very much against the grain of ordinary opinion and looks like a dragging up of forcibly contrived *paradoxa*. Because it is difficult to eliminate this impression, such a way of speaking, paradoxical only for ordinary *doxa* (opinion), is to be renounced. (*GA* 9: 194)

Such a way of speaking, this double talk about an essential non-essence, *speaks against* ordinary opinion, literally contradicts common sense. For common sense insists on the mutual exclusion of opposites, insists that one cannot have, in the same connection, both truth and untruth, certainly not as constituting the very essence of truth. This mutual exclusion is precisely what is enforced by the so-called law of non-contradiction. Little wonder that Heidegger proposes a certain indirection or renunciation: he is speaking against the law of non-contradiction. Could there be a discourse more monstrous than one that dares contradict the law of non-contradiction?

The third extension indeed attests to something still more monstrous. Now it becomes a matter not only, as the 1930 text expresses it, of letting the non-essence into the essence, but of putting into question the priority of the essence proper over the non-essence. The 1930 text denies such a priority, granting instead that concealment is "as old as the very letting-be of beings." The 1943 text goes still further and reverses the priority:

The concealment of beings as a whole, untruth proper, is older than every openedness of this or that being. It is also older than letting-be itself which in unconcealing already holds concealed and comports itself toward concealing. (*GA* 9: 193–94)

Thus it is said—and will soon have also to be unsaid—that within the essence of truth non-essence is older than what was previously called essence, untruth older than truth—the word *older* here replacing all the words with which a thinking short of such deformity would still attempt to say such orderings. *Contributions to Philosophy* says the same differently: "The essence of truth is un-truth"—a saying that, even if risky, serves nonetheless, as the *Contributions* continues, "to bring nearer the strangeness of the strange essence of truth" (*GA* 65: 356).

In the final section of "On the Essence of Truth" Heidegger proposes an answer to the question of the essence of truth. The proposal takes the form of a translation. The proposition—it will also be declared not a proposition—to be translated is introduced as follows: "The question of the essence of truth finds its answer in the proposition: *the essence of truth is the truth of essence*" (*GA* 9: 201). In preparation for translating this proposition, Heidegger establishes four points: (1) The subject of the proposition, though written at the end, is: *the truth of essence*. In the translation the proposition will be rewritten accordingly, inverted. (2) In *the truth of essence*, essence is to be understood verbally: as *wesen*. Here there is already a problem of translation, of translating *wesen* into English, or rather, an impossibility, in face of which one can only resort to some such locution as: to unfold essentially. (3) In *the truth of essence*, *truth* says: sheltering that clears (*lichtendes Bergen*). In turn, *sheltering that clears* simply says the essence of truth as it has finally been determined in Heidegger's text: unconcealment (clearing) as including double concealment (mystery and errancy), which might be written as ἀ–λήθεια. Such sheltering-that-clears Heidegger identifies as the *Grundzug* of the Being of beings: its basic character, to be sure, but, more literally, the basic draught, drawing, movement, by which beings can come forth in their Being, come to presence. Putting (2) and (3) together, one may translate *truth of essence* as saying: *sheltering-that-clears* (i.e., the drawing of ἀ-λήθεια) essentially unfolds. . . . (4) In *the essence of truth*, as this occurs in the proposition to be translated, essence means whatness and truth is understood as a characteristic of knowledge, i.e., as accordance.

These preparations let one see that the proposition *the essence of truth is the truth of essence* encompasses the full course through which "On the Essence of Truth" has moved. Heidegger's translation makes this explicit: "Sheltering-that-clears is—i.e., lets essentially unfold [*lässt wesen*]—accordance between knowledge and beings" (*GA* 9: 201). But then, having translated the proposition, Heidegger abruptly denies that it is a proposition: "It is no proposition [*Satz*] at all in the sense of a statement [*Aussage*]" (*GA* 9: 201). Presumably, one is to understand: it is not a proposition, a statement, because it is a saying of that which first makes possible all propositions in the sense of statements with their claims to be in accordance with things.

At the outset and indeed throughout "On the Essence of Truth" Heidegger refers to the opposition between philosophy and common sense (*der gemeine Verstand, der gesunde Menschenverstand*). By voicing—as an ironically endorsed question—the opinion of common sense that the question of essence is "the most inessential and superfluous that could be asked" (*GA* 9: 177), he alludes to a very traditional interpretation of this opposition: that philosophy is *eine verkehrte Welt*, standing common sense on its head. The opposition is one that philosophy cannot simply dissolve; common sense has, to be sure, its own weapons, most notably, the appeal to obviousness. Philosophy cannot refute it, says Heidegger, for it is blind to the essence of philosophy (in the language of the 1930 text), or (according to the published text) "deaf to the language of philosophy" and "blind to what philosophy sets before its [own] essential vision" (*GA* 9: 178). Furthermore, common sense constantly threatens to ensnare philosophy:

> Moreover, we ourselves remain within the sensibleness of common sense to the extent that we suppose ourselves to be secure in those multiform "truths" of practical experience and action, of research, and belief. We ourselves intensify that resistance which the "obvious" has to every demand made by what is questionable. (*GA* 9: 178)

Or in the more direct language of the 1930 version:

> The common understanding, who is that? We ourselves, even and precisely philosophy, we ourselves who now conjecture about the question of the essence of truth as about just any other question, which we tend to pose just like the question of the weather or any such thing.

One could say, then, that common sense is not just an opposite set deci-sively and securely outside philosophy; rather, the opposition between philosophy and common sense is such as also to open up *within philos-ophy itself*. Thus would the non-essence of philosophy (common sense) belong to its essence, the deformation of essence thus coming to deter-mine philosophy itself, or rather, in strictest terms, to deprive it of itself, submit it to dispropriation.

A traditional name for this non-essence that invades the essence of philosophy is *sophistry*. Heidegger alludes to the relevant configuration:

> However, in the same period in which the beginning of philosophy takes place, the *marked* domination of common sense (sophistry) also begins. Sophistry appeals to the unquestionable character of the beings that are opened up and interprets all thoughtful ques-tioning as an attack on, an unfortunate irritation of, common sense. (*GA* 9: 199)

Heidegger leaves it unsaid whether he takes the opposition between phi-losophy and common sense (sophistry—though certainly it is not *sim-ply* common sense) to represent a decline from another thinking that would be free of such opposition or whether such opposition is to be re-garded as necessarily belonging to any thinking, however displaced it may be from the beginning of philosophy.

There is something about the 1930 version of Heidegger's text that I have left unsaid until now: the title "The Essence of Truth" is given only as the *second* of two titles and even as such is placed in parentheses, as a subtitle subordinated to the first of the titles, the main title: "Philoso-phizing and Believing" ("*Philosophieren und Glauben*"). Furthermore, Heidegger announces in the opening paragraph that—

> the task of the lecture is stated by the main title. The main title says what is to be dealt with, philosophizing and believing, thus not philosophy and theology. The subtitle states how we are to set about the task . . . , [viz.,] by questioning concerning the essence of truth.

Heidegger asks: "But is believing not then already excluded?" He an-swers: "Certainly, and yet we deal also with believing in passing over it in silence." Indeed, there is only silence: after the opening paragraph, believing is not mentioned again. And in the 1943 version of the text there is only the most passing of references to believing.

In order to elucidate this strange situation, one must turn to *Contributions to Philosophy*, specifically to the section entitled "Belief and Truth" (*GA* 65: 368–70,§237). Let me deal—very schematically—with a series of points. (1) Heidegger refers, first of all, to the task of the section: to conceive the essence of believing on the basis of the essence of truth. The affinity with the stated task of the 1930 lecture is evident. (2) Focusing on believing and noting its opposition to knowing (*Wissen*), he offers the following characterization: believing is a *Für-wahr-halten* of something that withdraws from knowledge; to believe is to hold as true (to hold to be true) something that withdraws from insight. Heidegger mentions the example of believing a report whose truth cannot be directly confirmed. (3) But then he asks: What is authentic knowing (*das eigentliche Wissen*)? His answer: it is that knowing "which knows the essence of truth and thus only determines itself in the turn from out of this essence." It is *das Sichhalten im Wesen der Wahrheit*; or, in the terms of "On the Essence of Truth," ek-sistence. (4) Heidegger calls this knowing "essential knowing [*das wesentliche Wissen*]" and gives it priority over all believing: it is more originary than every believing, for the latter is always related to something true (*ein Wahres*) and hence presupposes knowing the essence of truth. He adds that such knowing is no mere representing of something encountered (*vorstellen*—written now without the hyphen). (5) And yet, he continues: "If one takes 'knowing' in the prevailing sense of representing [*vorstellen*] and possession of representations, then essential knowing is indeed not a 'knowing' but a 'believing'." One could say: essential knowing is a believing because it is linked, not just to *something* that withdraws, that is concealed, from insight, but to the very concealment in the draught of which things can come to be concealed, to withdraw from insight, the concealment that Heidegger has identified as the (double) non-essence belonging "properly" to the essence of truth. (6) Heidegger concludes: "This originary believing is not at all a matter of accepting that which offers immediate support and makes courage superfluous. This believing is rather a persisting in the uttermost decision [*Ausharren in der äussersten Entscheidung*]."

No doubt, then, the main title of the 1930 lecture was not simply a rhetorical means for linking the lecture to the particular audience to which it was delivered (to the Faculty of Protestant Theology in Marburg). And yet, one cannot but wonder that the theme expressed in that title remains so undeveloped and in the version published in 1943 disappears entirely. Was it perhaps a believing that proved so monstrous that it had to come to be called otherwise? For example, by a word that already, inconspicuously appears in the 1930 text: *Gelassenheit.*

Then Heidegger would have said *from* the strange essence of truth, beginning from the truth of essence, that dispropriation for which even eksistence and ecstasis (to say nothing of believing) seem still too centered: no longer letting-be, but being-let, or rather, having (always already) been let (into the open in which beings can come to presence). Yet, the strangeness that sounds in *Gelassenheit* when it is heard with the ears of technological man resounds, in the end, from the strange essence of truth, from "the strangeness of the strange essence of truth."

In the wake of this strangeness—a wake that has perhaps only just begun, a wake in which we are to mourn nothing less than the passing of truth itself—what is to become of the essentially other than truth? No longer is it the mere opposite that could be kept securely outside the essence of truth. Nor is it an other that truth could appropriate in such a way that the otherness would be retained within a new unity attesting the priority of truth. Nothing is kept more explicitly at a distance from Heidegger's text(s) on the essence of truth than dialectic. The untruth that is essentially other than truth remains essentially other even within the essence of truth; in the word used in *Contributions to Philosophy* it remains as something oppositional (*als Widerstandiges*) within the essence of truth (*GA* 65: 356). It is even—as Heidegger would say in that perhaps most monstrous saying—something within the essence of truth that is older than truth itself.

Thus, what is essentially other than truth belongs to the essence of truth, even though within that essence its otherness is preserved, not just dialectically but as oppositional, even as older than truth. Presumably this is why—to return to that passage in *Contributions to Philosophy* to which I referred earlier—the question of the relation of truth to an other is prohibited as long as ἀλήθεια is thought in an originary way.

This prohibition is what allows Heidegger to broach a discourse on the possibility of experiencing errancy itself (*die Irre selbst*) in such a way as to escape being drawn into (along by) it (*GA* 9: 197). To experience it thus would be to overcome its essential otherness. Yet, how could one experience errancy itself? Is there errancy *itself*, errancy proper? What of the prohibition that would have the effect of holding it within reach of such an experience?

Is it perhaps just this prohibition that we shall have to ponder in that still immeasurable wake that marks the passing of truth itself? Not to question, perhaps not even to think, but to ponder, to weigh, to test the weight of the prohibition against saying an other so essentially other that it would not belong to the essence of truth, an other that would be outside the essence of truth without becoming again a mere opposite unable to withstand the logic of appropriation. An other that would engender, not πόλεμος, but outrage. An other so essentially other than truth that it would be absolved from truth, as absolutely as madness can be. Let us, then, ponder whether what the question of truth is all about is, in the end, akin to madness.

7

Spacing Imagination

Spacing imagination.

Hence, already, between the two there is a space, spacing them. It could not be otherwise.

A spacing that keeps them apart in the very draft by which one is drawn to the other, imagination to spacing.

Thus, also, it will be a matter, in the transitive sense, of spacing imagination, of withdrawing it from the submission to presence that could not but have been in force in the history of metaphysics, thus releasing it also from the horizon of reason and perception to which its flight could not but have been constrained. It will be a matter of drawing imagination out toward the intervals that interrupt presence, of drawing it to the limit of presence and on beyond being as presence, of letting it hover ἐπέκεινα τῆς οὐσίας.

It goes almost without saying that the escape and flight will not have been managed without enlisting the aid of imagination, turning it upon itself, even if always eccentrically.

Thus, too, it will be a question of a spacing that sets imagination apart from itself, separating it from itself along the line drawn grammatically by the differentiation between subjective and objective genitive. A question, then, of spacing imagination so as to install in it the space of a turning on itself—spacing of imagination. The turning would be not only eccentric but also rigorous—that is to say, executed phenomenologically.

It will be a matter, then, of focusing on Husserl's phenomenological analysis of imagination, rethinking this analysis in such a way as to prepare for spacing imagination, even if, in the end, the escape and flight of imagination cannot but threaten the most profound securities and the strongest solidarities of phenomenology, calling thus for a redetermination of rigor that could not remain simply phenomenological. The threat will appear most obtrusively in the guise of a certain incoherence in the very spacing of imagination that the phenomenology of imagination puts into play.

(a)

Husserl's phenomenological analysis of imagination is centered in the distinction between phantasy and image-consciousness (*Phantasie und Bildbewusstsein*).[1] Or, more precisely, it is around this distinction, toward one side or the other, that the most decisive moves of that analysis occur. It is also at the site of this distinction, in the turning of the analysis around it, that some of the most unsettling displacements are broached, displacements that threaten to disturb the very limits, the solidarities, by which a phenomenology of imagination would be defined.

Husserl brings the distinction to bear upon certain experiences (*Erlebnisse*) or acts (*Betätigungen*), in contrast to powers or faculties (*Vermögen*), which would not belong to the phenomenological sphere of the truly given.[2] As first announced in the *Logical Investigations*, the two forms of imagination marked by the distinction correspond to the two ways in which the object of an act of imagination can appear, either straightforwardly and directly or as representing another object that resembles it (*LU* II/1: 424). The first form is that of phantasy, the second that of image-consciousness. Husserl calls for a rigorous analysis of the intentional structure of these two types of acts; such an analysis will serve to differentiate them precisely from one another and from other types of intentional acts such as memory and perception.

---

1. The terminology is not entirely stable. *Phantasie* is also called, for example, *freie Phantasie* and sometimes *freie Imagination* or *schlichte Imagination*. *Bildbewusstsein* is also *Bildobjektbewusstsein* and *Bildlichkeitsbewusstsein*. See the discussion in Maria Manuela Saraiva, *L'Imagination selon Husserl* (The Hague: Martinus Nijhoff, 1970), 58. As will be seen with respect to the terms *schlichte Phantasie* and *eikonische Phantasie*, the variations in terminology are not always as extrinsic as they might seem but sometimes directly reflect developments in Husserl's analyses.

2. Edmund Husserl, *Phantasie, Bildbewusstsein, Erinnerung: Zur Phänomenologie der Anschaulichen Vergegenwärtigungen*, Husserliana 23, ed. Eduard Marbach (The Hague: Martinus Nijhoff, 1980), 3. Subsequent references to this volume will be indicated in the text by *Hus.* 23, along with the page numbers.

One result will be to submit to the rigor of phenomenological analysis a connection that has been in play throughout much of the history of metaphysics, often reductively, almost always elusively—for example, as the connection between φαντασία and εἰκασία.[3] It is this connection that would constitute the very unity of the concept of imagination, that would determine whether there is *a* concept of imagination.

Another result will be to subordinate imagination to perception, to declare it secondary, inferior to perception.[4] The critique that the Fifth Logical Investigation brings to bear upon the so-called image-theory of perception is emphatic regarding the proper order of founding: one cannot explain perception on the basis of image-consciousness, that is, as consciousness of an image within that would resemble the object without, because consciousness of something as an image requires that it first be given in perception. In short, imagination in the form of image-consciousness is founded on perception.[5]

The differentiation is extended in the Sixth Logical Investigation through the analysis of meaning fulfillment. Here perception and imagination (again in the form of image-consciousness) are treated as two different kinds of acts by which a meaning intention can be fulfilled. Husserl contrasts the respective fulfillments thus: in perception "the object 'itself' appears and does not merely appear 'in an image ' " (*LU* II/2: 56). Thus the superiority of perception lies in the fact that it presents the object itself, presents it directly. In perception the object is actually present, and it is only in perception that that final fulfillment can be achieved in which the object comes to be present just as it was intended. In *Ideas* I the differentiation is extended to phantasy: whereas phantasy renders

---

3. See Saraiva, *L'Imagination selon Husserl*, 22. Also my *Delimitations: Phenomenology and the End of Metaphysics* (Bloomington: Indiana University Press, 1986), chap. 1.

4. See Saraiva, *L'Imagination selon Husserl*, 41.

5. "Since the apprehension [*Auffassung*] of anything as an image presupposes an object intentionally given to consciousness, we should plainly have an infinite regress were we again to let this latter object be itself constituted through an image or to speak seriously of a 'perceptual image' immanent in a simple perception, by way of which it would refer to the thing itself" (*LU* II/1: 423). The relative instability of the distinction between phantasy and image-consciousness in the *Logical Investigations* produces a certain vacillation or even conflation that renders Husserl's argument against the image-theory less than compelling. Whereas the image that Husserl shows to be founded on perception, hence to presuppose it, is that of image-consciousness—he gives the example of a painting—the image on which the image-theory would found perception would—if there were such—have a character like that of a phantasy image. Hence, from the beginning the differentiation and subordination of imagination to perception will have proved much less easily accomplished than Husserl supposed.

somehow present something that is not present (here Husserl repeats the Kantian determination), perception presents the object itself in its bodily presence (*leibhaftiger Gegenwart*).[6] The differentiation is between two ways of making the object present, of coming to have it present to oneself; it is a differentiation between *Vergegenwärtigung* and *Gegenwärtigung*, between the inferior, somehow incomplete presence of a phantasy object and the full bodily presence of the perceptual object. Husserl calls it "the fundamental distinction," "an ultimate and felt distinction [*ein letzter und fühlbarer Unterschied*]" (*Hus*. 23: 106).

Let me underline one point, namely, that the differentiation and the subordination of imagination to perception turn entirely upon a differentiation within presence, upon a differentiation between, on the one hand, full bodily presence, which functions as a telos, and, on the other hand, certain inferior modes of presence linked to images. Husserl has virtually reconstituted one of the oldest oppositions, that between image and original, reconstituted it precisely in its traditional role of serving for the differentiation of presence.[7] Little wonder that he breaks off the questioning by calling the distinction fundamental, by designating it as an ultimate distinction. And yet, one cannot but wonder how it could also be a felt distinction (one capable of being felt—*fühlbar*) and how, even if it were, that would serve to confirm that it is fundamental. What does the opposition between image and original have to do with feeling? Is it something felt? Or is the appeal to feeling only the disguise of a solidarity with the history of metaphysics with which phenomenology will never have broken?

Thus submitted to phenomenological analysis, imagination proves to be secondary, inferior. And yet, a double sense is operative in the genitive (phenomenology *of* imagination), which is to say that it is not only a matter of submitting imagination to analysis. Indeed, in Husserl's work imagination proves to be not only an object or theme of phenomenological analyses but also, according to the methodological reflection accompanying the analysis, an indispensable component of the agency by which such analysis would be carried out. The analysis is performed both *upon* imagination (as theme) and *by* imagination (as agency), even if always in conjunction with other types of acts. This distinction is no

---

6. *Ideen zu einer reinen Phänomenologie und phänomenologischen Philosophie*, erstes Buch, Husserliana 3, ed. Walter Biemel (The Hague: Martinus Nijhoff, 1950), §43. Hereafter: *Hus*. 3.

7. "Perceptual appearance and phantasy appearance are so closely akin, so similar, that they immediately suggest the idea of the relation between original and image" (*Hus*. 23: 10).

less central to Husserl's phenomenology of imagination than is the distinction between phantasy and image-consciousness; and the two distinctions, thoroughly interpenetrating, constitute the primary grid of Husserl's analysis.

Yet, how is it that there is an operation of imagination in phenomenology and, *a fortiori*, in phenomenology of imagination? Any such operation would seem to be ruled out by the demand for rigor under which phenomenological analysis stands: whereas phenomenology would attend to the things themselves as they themselves show themselves, imagination would seem quite oblivious to things themselves, engaging rather, as we say, in flights of phantasy, flying away toward pure fiction. Husserl does not minimize the paradox but rather, marking his very phrase as paradoxical, declares "that *'fiction' constitutes the vital element of phenomenology* . . . , that fiction is the source from which the knowledge of 'eternal truths' draws its sustenance" (*Hus.* 3: §70).

Not only are the phenomenological operations of imagination, that is, of phantasy and of image-consciousness, quite complex, but also they can be described, in their bearing on phenomenological epoche and on essential insight, only on the basis of the general analysis of phantasy and of image-consciousness. On the other hand, it remains to be seen whether that analysis suffices for determining the power that is in effect ascribed to these forms of imagination by virtue of the role given them in the execution of phenomenological epoche and of essential insight. At this point let me merely underline a more specific form of that paradox to which Husserl calls attention. Whereas phenomenological analysis establishes the primacy of perception over imagination, a primacy determined by orientation to the telos of full presence, there is with regard to the agency of phenomenology a reversal of this primacy: "There are reasons why, in phenomenology . . . , *free phantasies* acquire *a privileged position over against perception* and do so *even in the phenomenology of perception*" (*Hus.* 3: §70). How is it, then, that imagination can assume the very opening of phenomenology, both the epoche and essential intuition being inseparable from it, while within phenomenology, submitted to analysis, it can be declared secondary, inferior?

I shall not attempt to resolve this tension. Nor is it certain that it can be resolved without violating the constitutive parameters of Husserl's analyses. But before engaging it as such, let me focus on the analyses that Husserl brings to bear upon imagination, leaving out of account for the moment—as does Husserl himself—the turning of imagination itself upon those analyses, its empowering of them. Within these analyses, leaving their restriction intact, other tensions will appear, tensions within their development, tensions that—one cannot but suspect—effect a certain twisting of the phenomenology of imagination, twisting it perhaps into a shape less readily assimilable to the circle of metaphysics.

(b)

Husserl's analyses of imagination stem largely from the Göttingen period; most of them postdate the publication of the *Logical Investigations* (1900–1901) and predate the appearance of *Ideas* I (1913). Most notable is a course that Husserl gave during the winter semester 1904–1905 entitled "Hauptstücke aus der Phänomenologie und Theorie der Erkenntnis." This course, which in 1906 Husserl described as preparatory for a phenomenology of reason and eventually for a critique of reason, consisted of four parts devoted to the phenomenology of perception, of phantasy, of time, and of the thing, respectively. The part that is said, retrospectively, to be devoted to phantasy is in fact devoted almost equally to image-consciousness, moving constantly between these two primary forms of imagination. The context in which the analysis of imagination is here first taken up will remain decisive for Husserl: to the end, even in the few relevant texts stemming from the later, Freiburg period, the problem of the relation to perception and to the perceptual world retains a certain dominance, which, in turn, is enforced by the orientation to the problem of reason. I shall want to suggest that in taking the measure of imagination from reason, Husserl not only situates the analysis within the most classical framework but also releases certain forces that begin to twist that framework, that perhaps even prepare imagination to be twisted free from it.

That part of the course of 1904–1905 devoted to imagination has been edited by Eduard Marbach at the Husserl Archive in Leuven, along with numerous research manuscripts on imagination dating from as early as 1898 and as late as 1924. Published as Volume XXIII of the Husserliana under the title *Phantasie, Bildbewusstsein, Erinnerung,* the entire volume runs to more than 700 pages. Here I can refer only to a few of these texts.

Let me focus first—and indeed primarily—on the text from the 1904–1905 course. Husserl begins with some critical remarks directed at previous analyses such as those by Brentano; specifically, he criticizes those analyses that attempt to differentiate between perception and phantasy solely in terms of content, as though phantasies were only faded, less enduring, less lawful perceptions. The difficulty with all such approaches derives from their lack of what Husserl calls the concept of objectivating apprehension (*objektivierende Auffassung*) and of the essential distinctions generated by this concept (*Hus.* 23: 7–10). Husserl's reference is of course to the theory of intentionality as formulated in the *Logical Investigations.* An objectivating apprehension is an intentional act that apprehends an immanent, experienced (*erlebt*) content in such a way as to objectivate it, in such a way that an object is intended. Thus, it is essential to distinguish properly between the three principal moments of intentionality: the act of apprehension, the experienced sensible content, and the intentional object. One needs especially to note—and Husserl returns to this difference again and again—that the intentional object is not, like the experienced content, something immanent, that it is not a real component of the experience. Conversely, the sensible content is not what is perceived, is not the object of a perceptual act: one does not see color-sensations but colored things, one does not hear tone-sensations but the singer's song (*LU* II/1: 374). In the analysis of phantasy, then, it is imperative that one not confuse the sensible content that is experienced in phantasy—the phantasm, as Husserl will term it—with the object of the phantasy, the object intended by the act of phantasy.

Thus, phantasy is to be submitted to the framework of the theory of intentionality. Thereby it is also submitted, in advance, to a classical distinction between act and content, a distinction that Husserl draws primarily from the analysis of perception. Not that Husserl then simply poses the distinction beyond the reach of all analysis: again and again in the research manuscripts he will return to the distinction, especially to the parallelism that it sets up between sensation and phantasm. And yet, the appropriateness of the distinction to phantasy is never seriously challenged. Must one not, finally, ask whether phantasy includes a component that would correspond to the sensible content that allegedly belongs to perception? Are there, in the end, any phantasms in phantasy? In the end—that is, once Husserl's analysis is carried through and all the tensions that it releases are allowed to come into play.

The analysis proper begins with image-consciousness. It begins by distinguishing the three objects that together constitute the full intentional object of image-consciousness. The first is the *physical image*, for example, the painted canvas as a thing that can be torn or bent or hung on the wall. The second Husserl calls the *image-object* (*Bildob-*

jekt); this is the image as image, the image in its imaginal or representational capacity, the canvas not just as a thing but as depicting something. The third, the *image-subject* (*Bildsubjekt*) is that which is depicted, that which is imaged by the image-object, the landscape represented by the painting. Phantasy is, then, distinguished from image-consciousness by its lack of the first of these three moments; that is, in phantasy an image-object occurs without any connection to a physical thing, without being borne by a physical image. Quite remarkably, Husserl does not hesitate to call such an image-object a mental image (*ein geistiges Bild*) and even, reversing the order of determination, to characterize the image-object of image-consciousness as a mental image that is awakened by a physical object. Not that Husserl fails in these connections to take precautions. He is careful to set aside the naive interpretation that would erroneously consider such a mental image to be something really immanent in consciousness. Also he is careful to stress that a mental image is not an image-thing, that it has no existence either physically or psychically. And yet, one cannot but wonder at the appropriateness of calling a painting, precisely *in its capacity as imaging*, a *mental* image—however imperative it may be to distinguish between that capacity and the character of the painting as a thing. For it is *in the thing*, on the surface of the painting, that the imaging occurs; it is in the thing, even if as image-object, that the image-subject appears. Neither can one help wondering whether the identification of the phantasy image as a mental image does not also dislocate the imaging and remain thereby in a certain complicity with the very subjectivism that Husserl's precautions are supposed to exclude. I shall have to return to these questions.

In contrast to the more complex, threefold structure of image-consciousness, the structure of phantasy always includes, according to Husserl's initial analyses, the duality of image-object and image-subject (*Hus*. 23: 21). Husserl's example is meant to fix this duality:

If the Berlin castle hovers before us in a phantasy image [*uns im Phantasiebild vorschwebt*], then it is the castle in Berlin that is meant, that is the represented thing. But from it we distinguish the image hovering before us, which of course is not an actual thing and is not in Berlin. (*Hus*. 23: 18)

Correspondingly, it is necessary to distinguish in phantasy two apprehensions (*Auffassungen*), two intentional acts, and to regard the act correlative to the image-subject as founded on the act by which the image-object is intended.

Phantasy is thus more complex than perception, in which there is a single apprehended object. In phantasy—at least according to Husserl's initial analyses—there are always two interrelated apprehensions by which are intended two objects: the phantasy image, which appears, and the image-subject, which is imaged in that appearance and which is intended in an apprehension built upon that of the phantasy image. In phantasy there is always mediation (*Mittelbarkeit*) (*Hus*. 23: 24). In contrast to perception, one rarely takes the appearance to be the self-appearance of the object. Rather—at least according to Husserl's initial analyses—one lives entirely in the new apprehension founded on the appearance: "In the image one intuits the thing [*im Bilde schaut man die Sache an*]" (*Hus*. 23: 26). Both in phantasy and in image-consciousness the image-subject is apprehended without there being an appearance simply corresponding to it; it does not itself appear independently but only in and through the appearance of the image-object. Husserl will say even that in phantasy "we have only one appearance, that of the image-object" (*Hus*. 23: 30). In this appearance the image-subject is represented in a manner that Husserl contrasts with representation by an analogical symbol or an arbitrary sign. The representation is a matter of imaging, or, in the terms that Husserl introduces: *Verbildlichen, Veranschaulichen, Vergegenwärtigen* (*Hus*. 23: 30).

It has not taken long for Husserl's analysis to arrive at the security of that fundamental distinction that at the end of the text from the 1904–1905 course Husserl will be willing to declare an ultimate and felt distinction. In imagination it is always a matter of *Vergegenwärtigung*, in distinction from the *Gegenwärtigung*, the presentation of the thing itself, that is achieved in perception.

And yet, even if the distinction is finally to be declared ultimate, Husserl does not yet shield it from the analysis that it would to an extent have secured. I want, then, to underline precisely the turns in the analysis where it is brought to bear on that very distinction that would seem eventually to be declared beyond analysis. There are three such turns, each broaching a determination of imagination that essentially distinguishes it, as *Vergegenwärtigung*, from perception.

First of all, Husserl refers again to the fact that one rarely takes an imaginal appearance to be an appearance of the thing itself. Rather, in the portrait it is *as if* the person himself appeared. Husserl proposes, therefore, that in imagination "the appearance has a character that prevents it from being taken as self-appearance in the most proper sense" (*Hus*. 23: 33). Presumably, this character, marking an appearance as imaginal, must be somehow manifest in the very appearing of the image-object.

Husserl refers, secondly, to the difference between the respective fields, between the unity of the perceptual field with its enduring connections between objects and the senseless confusion with which phantasies run through one another so as to evoke a consciousness of mere imaginality (*Bildlichkeit*) (*Hus*. 23: 33). One could say: in the two cases the spacings are different, and the peculiar spacing that belongs to imagination is such as to make manifest the imaginality of the appearance. Such manifest imaginality is presumably that character that marks the appearance as imaginal.

The third reference is to the duality of image and original, the difference between image-subject and image-object. Husserl declares that even in the case of utter similarity, even in the case of sheer coincidence of the corresponding intentions, this duality, this difference, would not collapse into the simple schema of perception; for in such a case, he explains, one would need only to refer to the external moment, to distinguish the portrait from the person (*Hus*. 23: 32)—that is, to recall the difference that makes similarity and coincidence possible. One cannot but wonder about the condition of such recall. If one has only the appearance of the image-object, must it not itself somehow betray that it is only image and thus evoke the reference beyond? In other words, must not its imaginal character, its manifest imaginality, involve a reference to the duality? Does not the portrait itself attest that it is a portrait, independently of all merely external reference?

In any case the duality is—at least according to Husserl's initial analyses—essential to imagination. Without this structure, that is, if the imaginal function were to be cancelled, imagination would be transformed into perception. The puppets that one would have apprehended *as if* they were men might come then to be seen simply *as* men, without any difference, that is, mistaken for men. And phantasy, bereft of its imaginal function, would become the vision of the visionary whose world of phantasy has become his actual world (*Hus*. 23: 40–42).

(c)

There are two additional analyses that I would like to outline, the first a closer analysis of the image-object in image-consciousness, the other a closer analysis of phantasy that leads Husserl eventually to a certain reversal of the results of his initial analysis.

The first analysis focuses on certain conflictual moments in the appearance of the image-object. Husserl begins with the question of the relation to the physical image: Is the appearance of the image-object founded on the appearance of the physical image? It would seem to be, as Husserl's analysis up to this point has tacitly assumed. And yet, Husserl continues, "it becomes dubious as soon as the question is raised concerning the contents of apprehension [*Auffassungsinhalte*] of these two appearances. The image-object and the physical image do not, after all, have separate and different contents but identically the same" (*Hus.* 23: 44). Whether one apprehends a picture merely as points and lines on paper or as a form depicting something, exactly the same sense-content is involved, and what differentiates the two cases are the different apprehensions. The same content gets apprehended, now as points and lines on paper, now as a form depicting something. The conflict (*Widerstreit*) is, then, between these two different apprehensions of the same content. Insofar as the image-object comes to appearance, the corresponding apprehension comes to dominate and fuses with the content. Nonetheless, the other apprehension does not simply disappear. Furthermore, its object, the picture as points and lines on paper, links up with the appearances of the surroundings; as something actual it has those normal, stable connections with the actual surroundings that are not had by the image-object, with which it remains therefore in conflict. Husserl concludes: "The surroundings are *actual*; also the paper is something actually present [*wirkliche Gegenwart*]. The image appears, but it conflicts with what is actually present, thus it is mere 'image'; however much it may appear, it is a nothing [*ein Nichts*]" (*Hus.* 23: 46).[8] Thus the conflict, almost resolved in favor of the image-object, also expels the victor from the field, drives the image-object out beyond what is actually present. Or, more precisely, the spacing of the perceptual field, with which the physical image links up, is such as to exclude the image-object from that field. And yet, the image-object is not utterly excluded but still appears

---

8. Husserl continues to stress this exclusion of the phantasy object from the well-ordered perceptual field. For example: "while all perceptions with regard to the objects intended in them join together in a unity and have reference to the unity of a single world, the objects of phantasy fall outside this unity; they do not join together in the same way with the objects of perception in the unity of a world intended as such" (*Erfahrung und Urteil*, ed. Ludwig Landgrebe [Hamburg: Claassen Verlag, 1948], 195).

as mere image, as nothing; indeed it appears as such on that very scene from which it is excluded. It is a question, then, of another spacing: What must be the spacing of the image-object, of its appearing, in order that it appear on the scene of actual presence and yet not be present? How is it that its spacing withdraws it from presence precisely in letting it appear on the scene?

The scene is, of course, also temporal and not just spatial in the narrow sense; spacing will always have opened and distributed both, as in the spacing of the profiles of a perceptual object. Thus one may also characterize the appearance of the image as, in Husserl's phrase, "the appearance of the not-now *in the now.*" The appearance is, Husserl continues, "*in* the now insofar as the image-object appears in the midst of perceptual actuality . . . , but, on the other hand, it is a 'not-now' insofar as the conflict makes the image-object a nothing, which indeed appears but is nothing and which can only serve to represent a being [*ein Seiendes darzustellen*]" (*Hus.* 23: 47–48).[9] The image-object appears *on* the scene without being *of* the scene either spatially or temporally. Its spacing withdraws it from the scene in letting it appear there.

The other analysis that I would like to outline focuses on phantasy. It begins by returning to the comparison of phantasy with image-consciousness. Whereas the initial analysis regarded the two forms as identical except for the lack, in phantasy, of the third moment, i.e., the physical image, Husserl now observes that this lack essentially alters the corresponding image-object. Since it lacks the conflictual identity of content with a physical image, the image-object of phantasy does not appear in the midst of actuality; it does not appear on the scene of actual presence. As a result, its appearance is different; and now Husserl produces a series of analyses delineating various specific differences: for example, that the phantasy object typically appears like an empty schema, with unsaturated colors and vague contours; that it is fleeting and changes, as Husserl says, in protean fashion; and that in the series of appearances in phantasy there is discontinuity to a degree that exceeds any found in perception. In view of the immense difference thus exposed between the image-object of phantasy and that of image-consciousness, Husserl poses the question that threatens to revoke the basic parallel on which the entire analysis thus far has turned:

---

9. "What is phantasied is always something temporal . . . ; but its time is a quasi-time" (ibid.).

"In phantasy is there really constituted an image-object through which an image-subject is intuited?" Husserl confesses that he has serious doubts (*Hus*. 23: 55).

A supplementary text dated 1905 formulates the question and the doubt still more pointedly. The question is whether the phantasy image is of such a character as to refer beyond itself, whether it is in this sense an image. Husserl asks whether the image/original structure characteristic of image-consciousness has not been externally imposed upon phantasy, attributed to it perhaps on the basis of our knowledge of the difference between appearance and actuality. Husserl declares: "When I live in the phantasy, I notice no representational consciousness at all; I do not see an appearance before me and grasp it as representative of something else; rather I see the thing, the events, etc." (*Hus*. 23: 150).

In the final sections of the text from the 1904–1905 course, Husserl tends more and more to free phantasy from the structure of image-consciousness. Since there is neither a physical image nor, now, an image-subject to be apprehended, phantasy is no longer to be regarded as containing a manifold intention, at least not essentially, not in itself. As such it relates to its object just as unifoldly (*einfältig*) as does perception. Such phantasy in itself, phantasy as such, Husserl now calls *simple phantasy*, proceeding analytically from imaginal phantasy, that which includes the dual structure of image-object and image-subject, *to* simple phantasy as the founding moment within imaginal phantasy. In simple phantasy the phantasy object has no representational character whatsoever, though it may of course come to have also an imaginal reference beyond itself, simple phantasy thus being transformed into imaginal phantasy (*Hus*. 23: 84–87).

This fundamental reorientation is consolidated in the manuscripts immediately postdating the 1904–1905 course. For instance, a text from 1909 refers to the progress made since the course and declares that apprehension in phantasy is to be essentially distinguished from genuine apprehension of an image (*Hus*. 23: 276). Finally, in a manuscript from 1912 Husserl carries the development one step further, at least terminologically: the form previously called image-consciousness is now termed *eikonic phantasy*, in distinction from so-called immediate phantasy (*Hus*. 23: 383–85, 450). The reversal is explicit: whereas initially phantasy was determined in reference to the structure of image-consciousness (as inner image-consciousness, to recall the least cautious expression), now the determination is reversed and image-consciousness is regarded as a form of phantasy to which an imaginal function and an icon have been added.

Granted this reversal, the analysis of phantasy becomes more decisive and more imperative than ever. How, then, is phantasy to be analyzed once it has been detached from all imaginal structure?

In the final sections of the course and in the manuscripts from the immediately following years, Husserl pursues the analysis of phantasy in two ways, which, corresponding to the distinction between experienced content and apprehension, ought to be complementary. First, then, he takes up the distinction between the respective contents of perception and of phantasy, between (in his terms) sensations and phantasms. It is a matter of an originary phenomenological distinction (as it is called) between, on the one side, sensation, which is such as to resist being taken as a mere image of something, which is itself the very hallmark of reality, which is primary actual presence (*primäre, aktuelle Gegenwart*); and, on the other side, phantasm, the sensible content of phantasy, which is given as nonpresent (*gibt sich als nichtgegenwärtig*), which is such as to resist being taken as present, which bears the character of irreality (*Hus.* 23: 80–81).

One can hardly avoid having the impression that Husserl is only reiterating the difference rather than developing an analysis of it. The question is, after all, *how* in phantasy something can be *given as nonpresent*, that is, how something nonpresent can somehow come to presence as nonpresent. One can hardly avoid suspecting that to shift the problem to the interiority of a subject, in which content would, in turn, somehow itself be present, is not only to compound the problem but also to risk simply falling back into that content-based approach that was to have been excluded by the theory of intentionality. Would it not be more in keeping with the rigor required of phenomenological analysis if one were to orient the analysis to the respective sites of appearance rather than attempting to recover some even relatively preintentional content?[10]

Husserl's other way of pursuing the problem, by focusing on the respective acts of apprehension in perception and in phantasy, is less bound by the old schema. For he is led beyond the mere distinction between two kinds of apprehension corresponding to two kinds of content (sensation

---

10. As early as 1909 Husserl came to have serious reservations about the schema of apprehension/content. His reservations stemmed largely from the difficulty that he found in the supposition of a given content that would be simply preintentional. Most notable in this regard is the manuscript of 1909 entitled "Phantasie als 'durch und durch Modifikation.' Zur Revision des

and phantasm), replacing this schema with the theory of intentional modifications. A later manuscript not included in the volume *Phantasie, Bildbewusstsein, Erinnerung* expresses the matter quite succinctly:

> It was false to regard phantasy as a peculiar apprehending whose apprehension-contents would be "phantasms." Phantasy is a modification of the corresponding perception, phantasy-contents are modifications of the corresponding sense-data. . . .[11]

As another manuscript puts it: in phantasy everything remains as in the corresponding perception except that "everything is modified into the *quasi*, the imaginary [*imaginativ*]" (*Hus.* 23: 214).

Still another manuscript, repeating that everything is carried over with modification from perception to phantasy, offers an example to show how the reality of the perceptual world, its character as real, is carried over as a quasi-reality to the phantasy world. The example is quite simple: one is to imagine that a rock strikes a window and passes through it without breaking it. Husserl insists that such a phantasy involves conflict, the event imagined conflicting with the quasi-reality of the phantasy world, carried over from the perceptual world in which such an event could not really occur (*Hus.* 23: 281).

And yet, one cannot but wonder about the constraint thus brought to bear upon phantasy, about the reduction—in the example—of difference to conflict. In the imagined scene something happens that is different from what could happen in the real world of perception and that appears as different—that is, the difference is manifest. If the perceptual world is taken as the measure of the phantasy world, then the difference will be taken as deviation from this measure, as conflict. But is such a constraining of phantasy to the horizon of perception—the constraint that the theory of modifications would enforce—called for?

Inhalts-Auffassungs-Schemas," in which Husserl writes as follows: "But in the case of perception we do not first have, as the concrete experience [*Erlebnis*] in it, a color as apprehension-content and then the character of apprehension which produces the appearance. And likewise in the case of phantasy we do not have a color as apprehension-content and then an altered apprehension, that which produces the phantasy-appearance. *Rather: 'Consciousness' consists through and through of consciousness, and sensation as well as phantasm is already 'consciousness'* [Vielmehr: 'Bewusstsein' besteht durch und durch aus Bewusstsein, und schon Empfindung so wie Phantasma ist 'Bewusstsein']" (*Hus.* 23: 265).

11. "Es war falsch, die Phantasie als ein eigentümliches Auffassen anzusehen, dessen Auffassungsinhalte die 'Phantasmen' seien. Phantasie ist eine Modifikation der entsprechenden Wahrnehmung, die Phantasieinhalte sind Modifikate entsprechender Empfindungsdaten . . ." (Manuscript L I 19 9b).

Or is it not reductive, reducing to a mere conflict a difference that also marks a transgression in which phantasy would exceed perception? Would a world in which a rock could strike a window and pass through it without breaking it merely conflict with the real world in which such an event would never be possible? Or would it not be a world in which new possibilities might be envisaged, opened up? One may recall, then, the words of Rousseau: "It is imagination that extends for us the measure of the possible. . . . "[12] But one will also need to observe that Husserl himself ascribes to imagination a power not unlike that of opening possibilities. This ascription comes, however, not in Husserl's analyses of imagination, but rather only when he turns to consider what imagination empowers in phenomenology: then he accords to imagination a power without which there could hardly occur any insight into essences. Yet essential being would delineate the realm of the possible, and thus imagination, empowering essential insight, would open up and extend our measure of the possible.

(d)

But before following that turn and putting in play its spacing of imagination, let me outline the reorientation within the analysis of imagination that I have repeatedly attempted to broach. The reorientation is prompted by several of Husserl's analyses despite the solidarity of phenomenology, even in its very concept of rigor, with the determination of being as presence and despite the massive constraints that Husserl thus employs to restrict imagination to the horizon of perception.

It is preeminently a matter of reorienting the analysis to the site of appearing. In the case of image-consciousness, with its threefold structure, that site, a site of imaging, is the image-object. In thus orienting the analysis to the image-object, it would be necessary to resist a certain tendency that Husserl shows, more in the *Logical Investigations* than in the concrete analyses of the 1904–1905 course and the related manuscripts, a tendency to place the very constitution of imaginality utterly under the power of the intentional apprehension.[13] For to be an image is

---

12. J.-J. Rousseau, *Émile*, in *Oeuvres Complètes* (Paris: Gallimard, Pléiade, 1959), 4: 304.

13. "Resemblance between two objects, however precise, does not make the one be an image of the other. Only a presenting ego's power to use a similar as an image-representative of a simi-

not simply to be used by consciousness as an image, nor is it simply a matter of consciousness positing an original behind it. Rather, it belongs to the character of an image to be intuitive (*anschaulich*),[14] and for it to be intuitive means that it appears as such before our very eyes, detaching itself from the physical image and opening onto the image-subject—that is, inviting one to follow its lead and be shown something.

It is, then, at this site, in the appearing of the image-object, that the hold of presence is broken and imagination is drawn to spacing. In detaching itself from the physical image, the image-object withdraws from the actually present surroundings; it is excluded by the spacing of the perceptual field. And yet, it still appears, even if, in Husserl's words, as a mere image, as a nothing. Its spacing withdraws it from presence precisely in letting it nonetheless appear. And yet, it not only itself—as nothing—appears but also in that very appearing shows itself as an image, that is, images an original, an image-subject. The spacing of the image, withdrawing it from presence in letting it nonetheless appear there, is equally the opening up of a distance, a depth, behind the image; it is the opening of a space for a showing of an original.

Such an imaging would also belong to the spacing of phantasy insofar as an imaginal structure, the duality, is retained. But in phantasy it would be a matter of opening a space distinct from the perceptual field without its being opened by differentiation from that field. It would be a matter of opening a space in which—to take another of Husserl's examples—a flute-playing centaur could phantastically appear, could come to presence as nonpresent, without ever belonging at all to one's perceptual field.[15]

Such a reorientation of the analysis of imagination could not but move at the limit of metaphysics, a limit whose complexity one could hardly exaggerate, a movement that could not but constantly risk falling back into the security of presence. For in the history of metaphysics imagina-

---

lar—the first similar given intuitively, while the second similar is nonetheless *meant* in its place—makes the image *be* an image. This can only mean that the image as such is constituted in a peculiar intentional consciousness" (*LU* II/1: 422).

14. The subtitle of Husserliana 23 is "Zur Phänomenologie der anschaulichen Vergegenwärtigungen."

15. "The phantasy image does not appear in the objective context of present reality, the reality that is constituted in actual perception, in the actual field of vision. The centaur that now hovers before me in phantasy does not seemingly cover a part of my visual field. . . . The phantasy field is completely separated from the perceptual field" (*Hus.* 23: 49). See *Hus.* 3: §23.

tion could not have been understood otherwise than in reference to presence, as intuition of a secondary, partial, or somehow degraded presence. Not that one could now think imagination without reference to presence; this would be literally nonsense, that is, no thinking at all. But one could undertake to think it in reference to an appearing, an imaging, a showing, that would never be a matter simply of presence or of degrees or modifications of presence but rather also of spacings that would fracture presence, letting an image show itself on the scene of presence precisely in being withdrawn from that scene—letting it hover there.

(e)

One could engage the turn to the spacing of imagination, to the imaginal empowerment of phenomenology, by retracing with Husserl the affinity between the phenomenological epoche and the primary forms of imaginal consciousness. Then, it would be a matter of focusing on the operation of phenomenological epoche as the neutrality-modification by which the general thesis of the natural standpoint, the belief effective in the positing of things as actually existing, would be suspended. It would be a matter of marking the affinity between the epoche, so determined, and phantasy, that mere phantasy (*blosse Phantasie*) that, says Husserl, "posits nothing," that "free phantasy" that "contains as such no mode of positing at all" (*Hus.* 23: 254):[16] both the epoche and phantasy would involve a neutrality-modification of the natural, straightforward orientation to things. And yet, one would need also to mark the limits of the affinity: for while phantasy is indeed *a* neutrality-modification, it does not effect the universal neutrality-modification as such that is envisioned in the methodological demand for the epoche, and, consequently, "it is of fundamental importance not to confuse *this* modification"—namely, phantasy, regarded as a neutrality-modification of remembering (*Erinnerung*) in the broadest sense—"with that neutrality-modification that we set over against every 'positing' experience" (*Hus.* 3: §111). While thus acknowledging the restricted scope of phantasy, one would need still to take up the question of its privilege: Would phantasy serve to announce from within the natural attitude the transition to the properly

---

16. "In phantasy in the narrower sense a belief-character is lacking" (*Hus.* 23: 178).

phenomenological, the transcendental attitude, providing thus a certain prephenomenological opening onto phenomenology, a natural way, as it were, to the suspension of the natural?

If one were to engage the turn in this direction, in reference to the phenomenological epoche, one would need, perhaps even more, to mark the affinity that links the epoche to image-consciousness, not to image-consciousness as a whole but to that moment within it that corresponds to the image-object. Husserl's example traces the lines of the affinity: the act in which one intends Dürer's *The Knight, Death, and the Devil*, the act in which, specifically, one's intention aims neither at the engraving as a perceived thing nor at what is depicted in it but rather at the image *as image*, foregoing, interrupting, the usual, aesthetic passage beyond the depiction to the depicted—this act, says Husserl, is "an example of the neutrality-modification of perception." For: "This *depicting image-object* stands before us *neither as being nor as not-being*, nor in any *other positional modality*; or rather, we are conscious of it as being, but as quasi-being in the neutrality-modification of being [*als gleichsam-seiend in der Neutralitätsmodifikation des Seins*]" (*Hus.* 3: §111).

But it is not primarily along these lines that I want to engage the turn to the spacing of imagination. For beyond Husserl's invocation of the neutrality of phantasy, beyond his depiction of a moment of neutrality in the face of Dürer's engraving, there is another occasion that promises even richer fruitfulness. I have referred to it already and cited, in essence, the declaration belonging to it. It is an occasion on which Husserl puts down his guard and strews seeds far beyond the boundaries that nearly always he keeps in force through the rigor of phenomenology, by the power of its principle of all principles. This occasion, this dissemination, is not without its specific textual indications: the declaration that Husserl ventures is embedded in a set of marks that serve to announce the relaxing of limits that on this rare occasion he is willing to allow. He marks, first of all, the paradoxicality of the declaration: it is something that one can actually say "if one loves paradoxical speech" (*Hus.* 3: §70). He marks also its ambiguity: it is something that one can say in strict truth "if one well understands the ambiguous sense." At the end of the declaration he marks its vulnerability, adding a footnote describing it as "a sentence that should be especially appropriate as a quotation for bringing under naturalistic ridicule the eidetic way of knowledge." Even within the declaration itself such supplementary marks are put into play:

when he declares that fiction constitutes the vital element of phenomenology as of all eidetic science, he takes the precaution of enclosing *fiction* in quotation marks, though he then removes them as he goes on to declare that fiction is the source from which the knowledge of eternal truths draws its sustenance—the marks, as if transferred from fiction, coming finally to enclose *eternal truths*, providing at least a modicum of protection for this all too vulnerable phrase, which naturalism would indeed like to equate with fiction.

Here, then, is the full declaration: "So, if one loves paradoxical speech, then one can actually say, and say in strict truth if one well understands the ambiguous sense, that *'fiction' constitutes the vital element of phenomenology as of all eidetic science*, that fiction is the source from which the knowledge of 'eternal truths' draws its sustenance" (*Hus.* 3: §70).

In order to underline just how paradoxical, ambiguous, and vulnerable this declaration is, it suffices to recall—once again—the bond of phenomenology to the things themselves, the bond that constitutes its very rigor. Its principle of principles is precisely the demand for evidence, the demand that whatever be put forth as truth be drawn from the things themselves, the demand that, as Husserl says at the beginning of the *Logical Investigations*, one "leave the last word to the things themselves" (*LU* I: x). How, then, can fiction constitute the vital element of phenomenology? Is it not precisely in fiction that the things themselves as they show themselves in their actual bodily presence count least of all? Is it not precisely in fiction, in the flight of imagination, that one soars beyond the things themselves, inventing stories that are uncontrolled by the demand for evidence and that in the end can only distort and conceal the truth of things? Is there any other way in which fiction might bear upon things? Is there any way in which—like a δεύτερος πλοῦς—the flight beyond the things themselves might serve to bring one back more effectively before the things themselves?

The declaration that draws phenomenology into the element of fiction, imagination, phantasy occurs in the culmination of a very remarkable section (§70) in the Third Part of *Ideas* I. It will be imperative to follow with utmost care the sequence of moves by which Husserl here prepares for the declaration, interrupting the operation of the limits that would otherwise prohibit the dissemination and prevent the seeds of phenomenology from being cast into what seems such a foreign element. But, if the effect of this dissemination is to be gauged, it is equally imperative to observe that it comes into play long before the elaboration found in this section; indeed it comes into play in the opening move of Husserl's text, in the wake, as it were, of the very first move carried out in this text. The boundaries thus exceeded will have been exceeded from the beginning. From the very opening of its discourse, phenomenology will have cast its seeds into a seemingly foreign element.

The first move could not be more classical, even though Husserl proceeds without the slightest reference to any ancient texts, the transliterated word *eidos* providing the least covert indication that much more may be at stake than can be gathered—at least in an opening move— from the manifest things themselves. Husserl's first move reopens—as if from the things themselves—the difference that has been both open and continuously at stake since Plato, the difference that Husserl expresses as that between fact and essence, between individual and eidos.

How does Husserl construe this classical differentiation? Focusing on essence (*Wesen*), on the word "essence," marked as word by the quotation marks that enclose it and separate it from essence as such, Husserl enacts a move from the word to its meaning, from the word "essence" to the meaning or essence—namely, essence as such—that the word would designate. This move to the essence that the word "essence" designates, to the essence of essence, Husserl carries out by delimiting essence as such within the individual—not the individual determined in opposition to essence, but rather the individual as what one first of all encounters, prior to any such explicit differentiation. Here is what the word "essence" would designate at first (*zunächts*), prior to explicit differentiation: it is "that which is found in an individual's own being as its *what*" (*Hus.* 3: §3). On the one hand, then, the move beyond the word *essence* to its meaning, to essence as such, ends up merely circling back to the word, substituting for the word "essence" the word "what." But the word "what" functions here as a kind of shorthand for the question "What is . . . ?" (τί ἐστι . . . ?)—or rather, for that which would be put forth in answer to this most classical of questions. Thus, on the other hand, the move breaks with the mere circling within language; it appeals to that which is found, is to be found, can be found (*das Vorfindliche*), when one poses the question "τί ἐστι . . . ?" and seeks in the individual that which presents itself as answering the question, that is, as fulfilling intuitively that which is emptily intended in the question.

Husserl's language remains utterly classical as he marks a certain separation that is always possible, a detachment from the individual of the *what* found in the individual, or, more precisely, a doubling of the *what*. Husserl writes: "But every *what* can be 'posited in an idea' [*'in Idee gesetzt' werden*]" (*Hus*. 3: §3). It is in this doubling that the difference between fact and essence, between individual and eidos, is first opened up and that the very determination of individual being as such in distinction from essential being is first established. At the same time, since the *what* names a certain content shown forth from the individual being, that is, in the intuition of something individual, the question arises as to the possibility of a corresponding intuition of that content once it has been detached and posited in an idea, posited as essence. Yet Husserl does not so much raise the question whether such intuition is possible but, rather, affirms unqualifiedly the possibility: "*Experiential or individual intuition* can be transformed into *essential insight* (*ideation*)—a possibility that is itself to be understood not as empirical but as an essential possibility" (*Hus*. 3: §3). That which one would see in such essential insight Husserl designates, not just as *essence*, but—italicizing the adjective—as *pure* essence. He also calls it—transliterating the Greek—*eidos*. In essential intuition what one intuits is no longer just the *what* that one finds in the individual but the *pure* essence, detached— essentially detachable—from the individual. Husserl says: "*The essence (eidos) is a new kind of object*" (*Hus*. 3: §3).

On the other hand, Husserl stresses that between individual intuition and essential insight there is, not merely an external analogy, but a radical commonality (*radikale Gemeinsamkeit*). What is common to both is their intuitive character. No less than experiential intuition, essential insight is a consciousness of something that is self-given to that sight. Essential insight is intuition, an intuition in which something is originarily given. It is an intuition in which one grasps the essence—as Husserl says—"in its 'bodily selfhood' [*in seiner 'leibhaftigen Selbstheit'*]" (*Hus*. 3: §3). Almost as if having risked extending the commonality too far with this curious phrase, almost as if concerned that the mere quotation marks might not suffice to protect the proper sense (if there be one) in which an essence has bodily selfhood—as if to compensate, Husserl proceeds immediately to underline that, despite all commonality, essential intuition is an intuition of a peculiar and new kind.

But it is, nonetheless, the commonality, the continuity, that he stresses. Not only can essential insight arise from individual intuition, but in a sense it must arise from such a source, can arise only through transformation of individual intuition. Yet the sense of this link to origin is subtle, and everything—especially the dissemination being prepared—

depends on understanding it properly. Here is the passage in which Husserl begins to delimit this sense:

> Certainly the peculiar character [*Eigenart*] of essential intuition is such that it has as its ground a principal part of individual intuition, namely, an appearing of the individual, a being-visible [*ein Erscheinen, ein Sichtigsein von Individuellen*], though not indeed any grasping of the individual nor any sort of positing as an actuality. Consequently it is certain that no essential intuition is possible without the free possibility of turning one's sight to a "corresponding" individual and of forming an exemplary consciousness. (*Hus.* 3: §3)

Thus, essential intuition is grounded in individual intuition; or, more precisely, it has as its ground a principal part of individual intuition, a certain moment of the experientially intuited. Husserl identifies this moment as the *appearing* of the individual, its being-visible—or, one may say perhaps equally, its visible being, its visible presence. Here an initial question needs to be posed: What is the connection between this appearing of the individual, its being-visible, and the *what* that Husserl initially marked as to be found in the individual object, as fulfilling intuitively what is intended when one brings the question "τί ἐστι . . . ?" to bear upon the object? Are they the same, or is there already a transition involved between the sheer appearing and the intuitive *what*?

Husserl marks another moment, marks it precisely as *not* bearing on essential intuition: the grasping and positing of the individual as an actuality, its character as an actually existing individual, plays no role in the origination of essential intuition. From this exclusion a decisive consequence follows: in order for an essential insight to originate from a particular individual intuition, the latter must include the moment of being-visible, but it need not include the other moment, the character of being posited as actually existing. In other words, the intuitive exemplification required for the origination of essential intuition need not be furnished by an individual intuition to which belongs a positing of the intuited individual as actually existing. In short, the individual intuition need not be perception. The effect of Husserl's analysis is thus to disengage essential intuition from perception, to disengage it from necessary dependence on perception. The intuitive exemplification required for the origination of essential insight can be provided by any individual intuition that contains the moment of sheer appearing, of being-visible, that is, by any intuition capable of letting the individual object appear, of letting it be visibly present—hence, not only by perception but also by memory and by phantasy or imagination. Husserl stresses that, with a view to essential insight, one need not set out from perception but can set out *just as well* (*ebensowohl*) from non-experiential, imaginal intuitions. Hence: "In this connection it does not matter whether anything of the kind has ever been given in actual experience or not" (*Hus.* 3: §4).

Most remarkable is what he says of free fiction (*freie Fiktion*), the possibility—a kind of virtually impossible possibility—that he grants to it. If, through some psychological marvel, free fiction could produce an imagining of something that never occurred in any experience, nor ever will, this would make no difference as regards essential insight; such an imagined object, one never to be perceived, could serve just as readily for the origination of essential intuition as could the most ordinary and mundane perception. Pure fiction—Husserl is granting—could provide the origin of insight into essences and thus into the essential truths pertaining to the essential, the eidetic, those that have been called "eternal truths."

In section 70 Husserl resumes his analysis of essential insight, marking by means of a footnote reference a continuity with the opening move. But now, in this very remarkable section, he carries the analysis through in a way that, on the one hand, is more thorough and rigorous than ever and yet, on the other hand, has the effect of relaxing certain limits and extending more excessively the dissemination already broached by the opening move. The continuity is also marked by the statement of intent given in the first paragraph: it is to be a matter of accentuating certain especially important lines pertaining to the method of apprehending essences. These lines are drawn, as it were, between the two poles named in the title given to the section: "The Role of Perception in the Method of Essential Clarification. The Privileged Position of Free Phantasy." In a sense this title already says it all: it will be a matter of showing that phantasy, fiction, imagination not only provide, alongside perception, a possible origin for essential intuition, but constitute even a privileged origin for the production of eidetic insight.

Husserl begins by referring to the earlier result: essential intuition can be carried out on the basis of a non-perceptual, non-originary presentation of the exemplary individual, on the basis of *Vergegenwärtigung*, in distinction from the *Gegenwärtigung* characteristic of perception. Even phantasy (the form of *Vergegenwärtigung* that Husserl mentions) suffices to supply the visible presence of the exemplary individual, its sheer appearing, its being-visible. For essential intuition this is the only ground needed: that the phantasy-object merely hovers in its unreality before one's inner vision does not in any way impair its capacity to serve as the ground from which essential intuition can arise.

Husserl turns abruptly to perception. His focus throughout the remainder of the second paragraph is on the advantages had by perception, the advantages that it has *in general* over all forms of *Vergegenwärtigung*. The advantages are most pronounced in the case of external perception. Such perception has its complete clarity; it offers clear and stable details; and, as an act to be brought under reflection, it has the advantage of not dissipating under reflection in the way that, for instance, anger may dissipate when reflected upon.

The third paragraph is the hinge on which the entirety of section 70 turns. Here the text turns from one pole to the other, from perception with all those advantages that Husserl has just detailed *to* non-originary presentation, *Vergegenwärtigung*, and specifically to phantasy. Husserl begins by posing hypothetically a kind of order, a principle by which various kinds of experience could be ordered: it would be a matter of ordering them according to their degree of approximation to the originarity possessed by sensible perception. Such an ordering, Husserl observes, would indeed be called for if the advantages of originarity were methodologically very important. And yet, having posed this ordering, Husserl immediately sets it out of play: "But all this we can disregard" (*Hus.* 3: §70). For it can be shown that the advantages had by perception are, in the end, *not* methodologically so very important, that they do not serve to give perception a privileged role in essential intuition, however much they may justify its being privileged in other regards. In grounding essential intuition it is not perception but phantasy that has the privileged role: "There are reasons why, in phenomenology as in all eidetic sciences, *Vergegenwärtigungen* and, more precisely, *free phantasies* acquire *a privileged position over against perception*, and do so *even in the phenomenology of perception*" (*Hus.* 3: §70). The remainder of section 70 is devoted to elaborating these reasons.

Husserl elaborates them initially—in the fourth paragraph—with respect to geometry. The geometer, he observes, operates incomparably more in phantasy than in perception of figures or models. In phantasy there may no doubt be less clarity than needed, and the geometer will often resort therefore to figures or models in order to stabilize and give clarity to his intuitions. But to rely primarily on the perception of figures or models would be to restrict himself severely in contrast to phantasy in which he has, says Husserl, "incomparable freedom," the freedom to recast the figures continuously through an entire series of possible shapes, thus producing in phantasy an immense number (*Unzahl*) of figures. Husserl writes even more pointedly of this freedom, saying that it is what first of all opens up for the geometer access to the expanse of essential possibilities with their infinite horizons of essential knowledge. It is precisely in this freedom that the power of phantasy lies, and it is because free phantasy can bring before the geometer a greater range of examples that this power has a privileged position in enabling the geometer's essential intuition.

The fifth paragraph applies this result with utter directness to phenomenology. Just as in geometry, so, in the essential, phenomenological investigation of experiences and their objective correlates, the freedom of phantasy provides access to a range of possible forms that goes far beyond what is originarily given. Husserl concludes: "Here too at all events the freedom of essential research demands that one operate in phantasy" (*Hus.* 3: §70).

In the penultimate paragraph Husserl reiterates the dissemination: it is a matter of making rich use of phantasy, transforming the phantasized freely and virtually without limit, casting the seeds of phenomenology into the soil of imagination in order that fruitful growth might arise. And yet, if the harvest is to be most fruitful, a prior need must be satisfied, one preceding even the dissemination itself. Husserl turns abruptly to it, to what needs to have happened previously (*vordem*): one's phantasy needs to have been fructified (*befruchten*), made fruitful so as to be fully capable of producing fruitful growth from the seeds sown in it. It is not only a matter of opening phenomenology to the natural endowment of phantasy, but also of fructifying, cultivating, that soil. But how? By opening phenomenology even more widely. Not only will one need to fructify one's phantasy through the richness of one's perceptual experiences, but also, says Husserl, "Extraordinary use can be made of what is offered by history, and in still richer measure by art and especially poetry, which are, to be sure, imaginary but which, in the originality of their invention of forms, the abundance of their single features, and the unbrokenness of their motivation, tower high above the achievements of our own phantasy" (§70). Opened to phantasy, phenomenology is also to be opened to history, art, poetry—that is, to disciplines that it will not in advance have founded and recast within the founding order of transcendental phenomenology, regional ontologies, etc. In being opened to phantasy, in having its seeds cast into the soil of imagination, phenomenology will also be opened to other fields that it will not be able simply to govern; it will have its seeds cast even farther afield, disseminated beyond all hope of self-recovery and self-enclosure.

Thus would phenomenology be phantastical, the phantasy that it would put in play for the sake of essential intuition being, in turn, fructified by the products of art and poetry above all, by the fruits of artistic, poetic phantasy—phenomenological fiction fructified by artistic, poetic fiction. It is almost as if art and poetry empowered philosophy, made it possible in its genuine fulfillment.

Let me conclude with two sets of questions bearing on this occasion of dissemination in which phenomenology becomes phantastical and is opened to art and poetry.

The first concerns the specific role played by phantasy (fiction, imagination) in essential intuition. Husserl's descriptions of that role refer repeatedly to the freedom of phantasy, the freedom that allows virtually unlimited transformation of the phantasy object, so that in phantasy it becomes possible to run through and survey an immense number (*Unzahl*) of individuals exemplifying the essence to be intuited. But what about this unlimited accumulation of examples? Is it necessary for essential insight that one carry out such a survey, that one run through an immense number of examples? Is it not—at least often—the case that a few examples suffice to allow one to grasp the concept, the essence, at issue? Are there not cases even where a single example is sufficient? Is it ever a matter simply of accumulating and running through an immense number of examples? Or is it not rather a matter of a different way of apprehending the examples? Must not a different way of grasping them come into play if one is to move beyond individual intuition to essential insight? Can the sheer appearing of the individual, its being-visible, ever suffice to allow one to delimit *what* something is? To say nothing of detaching that *what* from the individual, positing it as a *pure* essence, even intuiting it as such.

In this regard it would be appropriate—though I cannot do it here—to reread, with the same care with which I have tried to read Husserl's text, those eleven pages of the *Critique of Pure Reason* that Heidegger once called "the core [*das Kernstück*] of the entire comprehensive work."[17] I refer of course to Kant's discussion of schematism—that is, of the way in which concepts become sensible, of the schema in which the transition is constituted between the essential and the intuitable individual. But rather than attempting, without sufficient precautions, to enter onto the tortuous way of the schematism, let me simply cite a single passage from a much later section of Kant's work, a section of the Transcendental Doctrine of Method in which, like Husserl, Kant addresses the method used by the geometer. He has just written of how one constructs by imagination—with or without the use of figures—a triangle that corresponds to the concept of triangle. He continues:

> The single figure that we draw is empirical, and yet it serves to express the concept, without impairing its universality. For in this empirical intuition we consider only the act whereby we construct the concept and abstract from the many determinations (for instance, the magnitude of the sides and of the angles), which are quite indifferent, as not altering the concept "triangle."[18]

It would be a matter, then, not of accumulating examples, adding through phantasy that immense number that one could hardly represent perceptually; rather what would be decisive in the transition from example to concept, from individual to essence, would be the power of imagination to use an example as a schema of the concept, considering, as Kant says, "only the act whereby we construct the concept." Is it not, then, precisely this intuitive constructing of the concept, this provision of the schema (Kant says: "The schema is in itself always a product of imagination")[19]—is it not in supplying the schema by which the essence becomes intuitable that the imagination plays its decisive role in essential insight? But then, would it be the essence *as such* that would come to be intuited? Would essential insight consist in an ultimately simple act of grasping the essence itself, the essence as such, in its bodily selfhood, assuming that this phrase could still retain a coherent sense? Would essential insight be simply essential intuition, a beholding of the essence, a beholding from which everything individual, however indispensable, would

---

17. Martin Heidegger, *Kant und das Problem der Metaphysik*, 4th ed. (Frankfurt a.M.: Vittorio Klostermann, 1973), 86.

18. Kant, *Kritik der reinen Vernunft*, A 713f./B 741f.

19. Ibid., A 140/B 179.

nonetheless finally disappear for the sake of its very own pure appearance—its pure *re*-appearance in and as the essence? Or would not the schematizing operation of imagination, its way of using the individual as an image of the concept—would this not have the effect of complicating the structure of essential insight, rendering unthinkable a simple intuitive beholding of the essence in a bodily selfhood, a proper presence, in which everything individual would have been, at best, *aufgehoben*.

To say almost nothing of how such a schematizing operation would complicate spacing imagination, how it would compound the spacing of imagination by way of a form parallel to image-consciousness, one that would let the essence appear in a manner structurally analogous to that in which an image-subject can come to appear through an image-object without ever *itself* appearing, without appearing *as itself, from itself.*

To say even less of a spacing already in play in the opening of imagination.

The other questions concern language. In the most direct form it is a question of whether essential insight is ever as independent of language as Husserl's analysis tends to imply, or whether it is not precisely the unity of the word that, in the simplest cases, orients one's vision to the essence. Is the *what* already in this sense linked to the operation of language, the discernment and detachment of it already a response to the classical question "τί ἐστι . . . ?"—that is, to a question borne by a certain history? And what about the fructifying of phantasy on which Husserl himself places such importance? Can phantasy be fructified by being opened to history, to art, and especially to poetry without becoming entangled in the web of language, contaminated, as it were, to the point that it could never free itself and become again a power of running through an immense number of examples along lines that would not ever have been drawn by words but only by the articulations of a sphere of pure essences?

8

Intentionality
and Imagination

In the *Logical Investigations* imagination is decisively submitted to intentionality. Indeed, the subordination thus established comes to function as if it were the very axiomatics of the relevant analyses, thus itself sheltered from all disruption, even from rigorous reexamination, through those analyses. Neither in the *Logical Investigations* nor in the extensive further analyses that Husserl undertook in the following decade does he ever bring fundamentally into question the subordination of imagination to intentionality. On the contrary, this subordination serves to provide the very order within which all questions of imagination are articulated and all analyses pursuant to those questions are carried out.

In this subordination there are two moments. The first lies in the construal of imagination as a mode of intentional experience. To investigate imagination phenomenologically thus requires submitting it to an intentional analysis, bringing into play the basic schema of intentionality and the general elements distinguished and related by this schema. Thus, in analyzing phantasy, for example, one will begin with the basic distinction between the phantasy act and the phantasied object intended by that act. In other words, the analysis will proceed on the basis of this distinction; prescribing the very course of the analysis, this distinction will itself be sheltered from analysis.

And yet, one cannot simply charge that the basic schema of intentionality is presupposed without analysis. For one finds in the *Logical Investigations* a more general level of analysis aimed precisely at legitimating the concept of intentionality, at establishing that consciousness is essentially intentional experience. Yet, despite the generality of the analysis, it is decidedly oriented to a mode of consciousness that Husserl will constantly privilege, namely, perception, in which things are presented as themselves there in their bodily presence. It is precisely this character that Husserl takes as warranting his privileging of perception, in contrast, for example, to imagination, which presents things, not in their originary presence, but only in and through an image. Thus the second moment in the subordination: imagination is subordinate to the primary mode of intentionality, namely, perception, and thus relegated to a secondariness that can never measure up to the presentation of things accomplished by perception. This distinction between originary and secondary presentation Husserl formalizes and generalizes in the distinction between *Gegenwärtigung* and *Vergegenwärtigung*.

In order to secure the subordination it is imperative that perception and imagination be rigorously differentiated and that the possibility of any encroachment of imagination upon perception be demonstrably excluded. If perception is to be decisively characterized as originary presentation, then presentation through an image can play no role whatsoever in it. Whatever images traditional theories may have alleged to play a presentative role in perceptual consciousness must now be expelled from such consciousness. And yet, such theoretical expulsion of images serves not only to legitimate the originary character of perception but also to establish the very sense of intentionality: the intentional character of consciousness consists precisely in its being directed to its object, in its aiming directly at the object rather than at an image within consciousness that would serve to represent the object outside. Indeed, this character is retained even in modes of consciousness in which what is intended is itself an image—or, more precisely, an image-object, as Husserl calls it in order to mark its distinction from the kind of image that traditional theories took to represent within consciousness something outside consciousness. Husserl would have us distinguish—at the most general level, prior to all further differentiation— between a genuine and a spurious form of imagination. In its genuine form, imaginal consciousness would intend an image *as its object*, in contrast to the spuriously conceived consciousness of an image within that would be taken to represent an object outside. For Husserl the fundamental error of traditional theories such as those stemming from Locke lies in their mistaking perception for such a spuriously conceived consciousness of images, conflating the two, or, at least, taking such consciousness of images to be operative at the very heart of perception.

I shall want to examine closely the analysis by which Husserl dissociates perception from such consciousness of images. But, before turning to his critique of the so-called image-theory, let me stress, at a more general level, the decisiveness of the breakthrough that Husserl accomplished in the *Logical Investigations* and especially through the concrete descriptive development of the concept of intentionality. I would venture even to call this development an irreversible advance. In any case there can be no question but that it thoroughly governs, without of course simply determining, the transcendental course that Husserl's thought takes up in *Ideas* and in the later texts and manuscripts. It is hardly less decisive for Heidegger: in the texts from his Marburg period Heidegger introduces his own analysis of Dasein as an extension and deepening of Husserl's concept of consciousness as intentional experience. And even if Heidegger puts into play a series of displacements no less decisive than the introduction of the concept of intentionality, he never ceases calling attention to the latter: even in the Zähringen seminar (1973) he speaks of the importance of the impetus that he received from the Husserlian concept of intentionality and describes his own work as an investigating of what is originarily contained in intentionality, that is, as a thinking that traces intentionality back to its ground in the ek-stasis of Dasein.[1]

Precisely because Husserl's concept of intentionality has been so decisive, there is need to return across the analyses it has governed, to turn back to the axiomatics of those analyses, the axiomatics in which, in particular, the submission of imagination to intentionality is codified. But what I shall attempt to trace will not be, as with Heidegger, simply a move back to the ground. It will not be simply a matter of regressing to the ground of intentionality, gaining access thereby to a more originary domain for analysis, while, on the other hand, leaving intentionality and its axiomatics intact at a certain non-originary level. Rather, I shall try to broach a move that is both less direct and less regressive, a move that, more integral to Husserl's general analyses, attempts to mark certain limits of those analyses, certain points of indecisiveness. Specifically, I shall address—all too briefly of course—four such limit-points, occurring, first, in Husserl's critique of the image-theory, second, in his analyses of phantasy, third, in his descriptions of sense-content, and, fourth, in his characterization of the intentional act. By marking these points at which Husserl's analyses remain indecisive, a certain slippage of the

---

1. Martin Heidegger, *Vier Seminare* (Frankfurt a.M.: Vittorio Klostermann, 1977), 122.

very concept of intentionality can be released. I shall want to show especially how this slippage interrupts the submission of imagination to intentionality.

(a)

Let me turn, then, first of all, to Husserl's critique of the image-theory. This critique forms part of an Appendix to that chapter of the Fifth Logical Investigation in which Husserl first develops the concept of intentionality systematically, namely, chapter 2, entitled "Consciousness as Intentional Experience." The critique, designated specifically as an Appendix to the section (§11) in which Husserl first distinguishes and assembles the elements of the schema of intentionality, is clearly meant to supplement the general analysis of intentionality by disposing of the traditional theory that is to be replaced by the theory of consciousness as intentional experience.

What is the image-theory? It is the theory that proposes a certain form of imaginal representation as an explanation of perception, or, more generally, of presentation (*Vorstellung*). The explanation offered by the image-theory is formulated by Husserl in these words: " 'Outside' there is the thing itself, at least under certain conditions; in consciousness there is an image as its representative [*Stellvertreter*]" (*LU* II/1: 421). So, according to this theory, perception of the thing outside would be accomplished through a consciousness of its representative image in consciousness.

This theory, says Husserl, "completely overlooks the most important point: that in imaginal representation [*im bildlichen Vorstellen*] we *mean* the imaged object (the *'image-subject'*) *on the basis* of the appearing *'image-object'* " (*LU* II/1: 422). The remainder of the critique is devoted to showing how this most important point, this characterization of imaginal representation, disqualifies the explanation of perception that the image-theory attempts in terms of imaginal representation.

It is a question of possibility. Of the possibility of transcendence, of what makes possible the transition from an image within consciousness to an object transcendent to consciousness. Of the possibility of representation, of how an image in consciousness can be representative of an object outside consciousness. The question is, in Husserl's precise words: "What therefore enables us to go beyond the 'image', which alone is given in consciousness, and to refer it as an image to a certain object foreign to consciousness?" (*LU* II/1: 422).

Even before posing this question explicitly, Husserl expresses an assurance that serves to render the question more pointed, more urgent. What is taken to be assured is that the image does not immediately reveal its character as an image so as to involve in itself a reference beyond itself toward something imaged. Yet, the single sentence in which Husserl formulates this assurance involves a curious divergence and sets off a certain vacillation that will prove to run throughout the critique of the image-theory. The sentence reads: "But the imaginality [*Bildlichkeit*] of the object that functions as image is manifestly not an intrinsic characteristic (not a 'real predicate'); as if an object were imaginal [*bildlich*] just as, for example, it is red and spherical" (*LU* II/1: 422). The point is that the imaginality of the image, its very character of being an image, is not something that—like the color and shape of an object—one would apprehend immediately in the image in such a way as to be referred beyond the image toward something imaged. But what is curious is the specificity of Husserl's formulation: he makes his point, not with respect to images in general, but specifically with respect to objects that function as images, that is, images which, as objects, possess such real predicates as color and shape. Yet, such images occur in only one type of imaginal representation. In the analyses elaborated in the decade following the publication of the *Logical Investigations*, Husserl designates this type as image-consciousness (*Bildbewusstsein*) and characterizes it as involving three moments corresponding to, first, the *physical image* (for example, the painted canvas that can be cut, stretched, and hung in a gallery), second, the *image-object* (the painting as depicting something), and, third, the *image-subject* (that which is depicted by the painting). These same analyses differentiate image-consciousness from phantasy (*Phantasie*), which—at least in the initial analyses—is said to have the same structure as image-consciousness except that it lacks the first moment; that is, the phantasy image does not occur in an object, is not first of all a physical image (*Hus.* 23: 18–23).

But what, then, about Husserl's assurance that the image does not reveal its character as an image so as, in and of itself, to refer beyond itself toward something imaged? Clearly the assurance that Husserl offers covers only the case of image-consciousness, in which there is an object involved, a so-called physical image. Clearly it does not—as formulated—apply to the case of phantasy, in which there is no such object involved. Can one say with any assurance that a phantasy image does not reveal its character as an image, its imaginality? In fact, Husserl's analyses in the decade following the *Logical Investigations* demonstrate precisely the opposite, marking the difference between the unity of the perceptual field with its enduring connections and the confusion with which phantasies run through one another so as to evoke a consciousness of mere imaginality, an awareness that they are images (*Hus.* 23: 33).

But if the assurance that Husserl offers fails to include the case of phantasy, it extends even less to that imaginal representation that the image-theory would install at the heart of perception. Is there any assurance that such images—if there are indeed such images—do not reveal their character as images so as to refer, in and of themselves, beyond themselves? What Husserl says, applying only to a type of image specific to image-consciousness, offers in effect no assurance whatsoever regarding the type of images to which the critique is purportedly directed. Diverting the discourse entirely toward image-consciousness, Husserl leaves the very point at issue *undecided.*

If one were assured that no image referred, in and of itself, beyond itself, then one could also be assured, as Husserl says, that "resemblance between two objects, be it ever so great, does not make one be an image of the other" (*LU* II/1: 422)—least of all when, as the image-theory would have it, one has access to only one of the two resemblant objects. One could be assured equally that the transition from image to imaged, the very opening of an image toward what it would then image, its very constitution as an image, could be produced only by an act that would enact that transition. Such is the assurance that Husserl expresses, repeating in effect that most important point with which the critique began: "Only through a presenting ego's capacity to use a similar as an image-representative of a similar, to have the one intuitively present and yet to mean the other in its place, makes the image become an image" (*LU* II/1: 422). Thus does Husserl submit imagination to intentionality: only where there is intentionality, only where through an image something else similar to it is meant, only in such a case is there imaginal representation. Husserl is explicit: "This can only mean that the image is constituted as such in a properly intentional consciousness" (*LU* II/1: 422). Apart from the intentional act there can be neither images nor imaginal representation. Nothing would be, in and of itself, an image.

In all these formulations there is a certain divergence toward that type of imaginal representation that Husserl calls image-consciousness. For instance, when, formulating that most important point overlooked by the image-theory, Husserl characterizes the image through which something else is meant, he calls it an *appearing* image-object. And when this point is repeated in the course of the critique, the image is described as intuitively present (*anschaulich gegenwärtig*). The example that Husserl then offers is still more explicit: "A painting is an image only for an image-constituting consciousness, whose imaginal apperception (here founded on a perception) first gives to its primary, perceptually appearing object the 'status' and 'meaning' of an image" (*LU* II/1: 423). It is in the wake of this example that Husserl finally formulates his basic critique of the image-theory. Here is the refutation in which the entire discussion culminates: "Since apprehension of something as an image presupposes an object intentionally given to consciousness, it would obviously lead to an infinite regress to allow the latter again to be itself constituted through an image, thus to speak seriously of a 'perceptual image' immanent in a simple perception, *by means of which* it would refer to the 'thing itself' " (*LU* II/1: 423). The point is: one cannot explain perception on the basis of imaginal representation, because the latter presupposes perception, involves a perceptual moment, the moment in which the image is perceptually given as the basis on which one means something else. And yet, the limit, the indecisiveness, of this critique is all too evident. For it is only in one type of imaginal representation that a perceptually given image is involved, only in what Husserl calls image-consciousness, where the image is inherent in a physical object. In the case of phantasy there is no such underlying perception. Even less does the imaginal representation pertinent to the image-theory involve anything like an underlying perception. Husserl's refutation would be decisive only if the image-theory proposed an explanation of perception in terms of image-consciousness. But this is not the case, and Husserl's point remains indecisive with regard to the image-theory.

Husserl's critique leaves phantasy untouched, and there would be nothing in principle to prevent one's proposing that a phantasy-like image functions within perception. Installing such an image would not rescind the operation of intentionality (indeed, its double operation): the phantasy-like image would itself be the intentional correlate of a phantasy-like act, and upon this act the further, properly perceptual act would be built, the act in which something else would be meant beyond the image.

Husserl's critique also leaves untouched that type of imaginal representation that the image-theory would install in perception. In this case—in contrast to image-consciousness and phantasy—the image would not be an intentional object, would not be correlative to an intentional act. Husserl insists that such a non-intentional immanent image could never as such refer to a transcendent object: "One must realize that an object is not represented for consciousness merely because a content somehow similar to the transcendent thing simply *is* in consciousness" (*LU* II/1: 423). Yet, even if this were realized, even if it proved to be the case, there would be nothing to prevent one's regarding such an image as the content for an intentional act that would then mean the thing. It would be a matter, not of eliminating the non-intentional image, but of supplementing it with an intentional act; the result would be, then, an analysis of perception virtually indistinguishable from that offered by Husserl himself in the Fifth Investigation.

The question is whether that supplement is necessary. Or whether such an image, in and of itself, refers beyond itself, keeping intact its character as an image without the necessary intervention of an intentional act. The question remains undecided, at least within the limits of Husserl's critique of the image-theory.

(b)

Nothing in the critique of the image-theory dictates against retaining the image within perception. The question is, rather, whether the image thus retained is to be regarded as an intentional correlate (like a phantasy image) or as non-intentional. This question is, in turn, linked to that of the act, to the question whether and at what point an intentional act intervenes in the constitution of perception. More generally, it is a question of what, if anything, comes to supplement the image in such a way that perception is accomplished. In short, then, a question of the image and of its supplement.

In order to develop these questions, it will be helpful now to turn briefly to Husserl's analysis of phantasy. The most extensive such analyses are those to which I have already referred from the decade following the publication of the *Logical Investigations*. Particularly notable is the text of Husserl's lectures on imagination in a course from 1904–1905, which provides the starting-point for a significant development in the analysis of phantasy, a certain transformation that commences in the lectures and that is carried further in a series of research manuscripts composed in the years following the lectures. These texts, left unpublished by Husserl, are now available in Volume 23 of the Husserliana entitled *Phantasie, Bildbewusstsein, Erinnerung.*

Near the beginning of the 1904–1905 lectures, Husserl formulates the distinction between phantasy and that other form of imagination that he terms image-consciousness. The distinction is based on the analysis—to which I have referred—that begins by differentiating the three moments involved in the intentional correlate of image-consciousness: the physical object, the image-object, and the image-subject. Image-consciousness as such would involve, then, three intentional acts corresponding to the three objective moments, these acts themselves linked by founding relations: the foundation would be provided by the first act, that of a perceptual consciousness intentive of the physical image, that is, the image not yet as an image but only as a physical object, the painted canvas that can be cut, stretched, and hung in a gallery. Upon this act would be founded the act in which the image comes to be intended as an image, thus the painting as depicting something. Upon this act, in turn, would be founded the act in which through the image one intends that which is imaged, that is, in Husserl's terminology, through the image-object one intends the image-subject, through the painting as depicting something, one intends that which is depicted, the landscape that, in this connection, does not appear independently but only in and through the picture, through the image, in an intuitive and yet imaginal representation.

Phantasy is initially characterized as a privative form of image-consciousness, a form in which the first moment is lacking. In phantasy an image-object is intended without that intention being founded on perception of a physical object. Marking its difference from an image borne by a physical object, Husserl sometimes calls the image-object of phantasy a mental image (*ein geistiges Bild*). In phantasy the image-object hovers there before one's inner vision, before (as we say) the mind's eye; it is neither embodied in a physical thing nor, as Husserl's analyses show, situated in the space of the perceptual world. But the image hovering there is an image *of* something, opening thus onto that which it images. According to Husserl's initial analyses, phantasy always includes the duality of image-object and image-subject. Husserl's example focuses sharply upon this duality: "If the Berlin castle hovers before us in a phantasy image [*uns im Phantasiebild vor-schwebt*], then it is the castle in Berlin that is meant, that is the represented thing. But from it we distinguish the image hovering before us, which of course is not an actual thing and is not in Berlin" (*Hus.* 23: 18). Correlatively, two intentional acts are to be distinguished in phantasy corresponding to the double object: one intends, first, the image-object, the phantasy image of the castle, and then, on that basis, one intends the image-subject, the castle itself in Berlin.

In the 1904–1905 lectures and in the related manuscripts of the following years, Husserl returns again and again to the analysis of phantasy. But rather than simply confirming and elaborating the initial analysis, Husserl comes more and more to call that analysis into question.Whereas the initial analysis stresses the structural commonality between phantasy and image-consciousness, characterizing phantasy as essentially a form of image-consciousness in which the moment of the physical image is lacking, Husserl's further analyses come with greater descriptive precision to focus on the way in which the privation that characterizes phantasy has the effect of making its image-object quite different from the image-object that occurs in image-consciousness. Because the image-object of phantasy is not borne by a physical object, it does not appear amidst actuality, does not appear on the scene of actual presence. The result is a difference in its appearance, and Husserl's analyses outline a series of specific differences: for example, the phantasy image appears with a certain schematic character, bordering on emptiness, its colors unsaturated, its shape ill-defined; the phantasy image also involves a high degree of discontinuity, changing, as Husserl says, in protean fashion, in starkest contrast to perception, but also in distinction from the image-object of image-consciousness, which is anchored in and borne by a physical object. Because of these and other specific differences exposed by the further analyses, Husserl comes finally to question the appropriateness of the structural parallel, putting into question, in particular, the duality initially traced in phantasy. Here is the question that he now comes to pose: "In phantasy is there really constituted an image-object through which the image-subject is intuited?" (*Hus.* 23: 55). By the time he reaches the middle of the 1904–1905 lecture course, Husserl confesses that he has serious doubts.

In a supplementary text dated 1905, Husserl's formulations of the question are more pointed: the question is whether the phantasy image refers beyond itself, whether the image-object of phantasy opens intuitively upon an image-subject, whether the act intentive of the phantasy image bears, in and of itself, another act in which what is imaged would be intended. Husserl expresses his suspicion that the image/ original structure characteristic of image-consciousness may have been simply imposed upon phantasy. Indeed, he declares at one point: "When I live in the phantasy, I notice no representational consciousness at all; I do not see an appearance before me and grasp it as representative of something else; rather I see the thing, the events, etc." (*Hus.* 23: 150).

Husserl returns to the question again and again, analyzing phantasy in ever greater detail, sometimes venturing general conclusions that make it sound as if the question were settled, but then launching new analyses in which the question is reopened and reoriented. Yet, even if one takes straightforwardly certain declarations in the manuscripts, for instance, in one dated Spring 1909 in which Husserl declares that apprehension in phantasy is to be essentially distinguished from the genuine apprehension of an image (*Hus.* 23: 276), even then one cannot but return to Husserl's own compelling example: "If the Berlin castle hovers before us in a phantasy image, then it is the castle in Berlin that is meant, that is the represented thing. But from it we distinguish the image hovering before us, which of course is not an actual thing and is not in Berlin."

The heterogeneity of the relevant texts is sufficient to justify regarding the outcome of these interrogations of phantasy in very different ways. One may regard them as effecting a reversal of Husserl's initial position, in which case one will go on to consider how phantasy is then to be analyzed once it has been detached from imaginality.[2] On the other hand, one might take the outcome to be fundamentally indecisive; one might conclude that, in particular, the question of the duality of the phantasy image remains undecided, that for all their descriptive power and rigor, utterly unprecedented, Husserl's analyses prove incapable of demonstrating once and for all whether the phantasy image merely hovers unifoldly before one's inner vision or whether, in and of itself, it refers beyond itself, opening intuitively upon something else, something imaged.

Taking the outcome in this latter way, one might then renew the interrogation in an effort to decide what Husserl left undecided. One

---

2. See, above, chap. 7, "Spacing Imagination," (especially section c).

might propose how the question could be decided and undertake to carry out an analysis capable of grounding a decision. Or, instead, one might raise and begin to develop another question, one that puts in question the undecided Husserlian question. For can one be assured that it is a question of decision, that *in principle* one *could* decide between the unifoldness and the duality of the phantasy image, that it is only a matter of developing a sufficiently powerful and rigorous analysis, one sufficient to decide finally in favor of one or the other alternative? What if, on the contrary, the phantasy image were both, both single and double, both an image hovering unifoldly before one's inner vision *and* an image opening beyond oneself and beyond itself upon something else, something imaged? Is this not what the Husserlian descriptions perhaps serve to show, despite their orientation toward deciding between these alternatives? Is not the undecidability that haunts the analyses perhaps only an index of an undecidability that belongs to phantasy itself, a duplicity within the very structure of phantasy: that an image present only to one's ownmost, solitary vision is *at the same time* an image of something beyond? The duplicity assembled by this "at the same time" borders of course on self-contradiction. But even if something like the formal law (as it is called) of non-contradiction could be made binding on concrete phenomenological description, it would have little force in this case: for who has ever supposed that there could be no contradiction in the sphere of phantasy?

(c)

A connection between phantasy and perception is proposed in a manuscript "Phantasie und Vergegenwärtigung," composed for the most part in 1905–1906, with some additions dating from 1909. In perception of an object, says Husserl, the side of the object that is turned away is intuitively represented (*vergegenwärtigt*) in phantasy. He notes that this phantasy does not merely occur next to the perception of the front of the object; rather, the phantasy intuition of the back side is unified with the perceptual intuition of the front side. Husserl adds: "This representation takes place in perception; it brings it about that the *entire* object is presumptively there" (*Hus.* 23: 212f.).

This is a remarkable proposal, remarkable both in what it accomplishes and in what, if sustained, it would disrupt. It provides a descriptively based account of the most notable characteristic of perception: that one always perceives the object as a whole, the object itself; that even though what is actually present to one's perceptual intuition is never more than a single face of the object, one profile, that profile is always perceived as a profile *of* the entire object, as a profile opening upon the object as a whole. Husserl's proposal is to account for this presumptive presentation of the whole by assigning to phantasy the representation of what is not actually present, the gathering, as it were, of the unseen sides, which in the full perceptual act would then be unified with the actually presented profile, making it a profile of the entire object by surrounding it with a horizon of unseen profiles. But then phantasy would be integral to perception; and the demand that all representation through images be excluded from perception, the demand that the critique of the image-theory sought to enforce, would have been violated. Once phantasy is admitted into perception, the rigorous differentiation that Husserl would otherwise maintain between perception and imagination will have broken down and the subordination of imagination to perception will have been interrupted.

Little wonder, then, that in the very context of this proposal regarding phantasy and perception Husserl added in 1909 a note aimed at sheltering perception from the encroachment of the image. The relevant part of the note reads: "The intention directed at the side turned away is not to be confused with the intention directed at a perceptual image or phantasy image of the side turned away" (*Hus.* 23: 212; cf. 656). But, to say the least, it would prove difficult to differentiate rigorously and decisively between a phantasy representation of the hidden side and a representation of that side through a phantasy image.

But this is not the connection that I want to pursue, at least not directly. Rather, I have traced the development of Husserl's analysis of phantasy, especially the transformation and the indecisiveness involved therein, in order now to mark a certain structural commonality between phantasy and perception, specifically, between the phantasy image and the image that, despite the critique, remains unexpelled from perception. In other words, I shall undertake to expose in perception, as Husserl unfolds his descriptive analysis of it beginning with the *Logical Investigations*, a duplicity that corresponds closely to that indicated by the undecidability of the analysis of phantasy.

Let me mark as economically as possible some of the primary distinctions articulated in Husserl's analysis of perception. First, there is the distinction between presentation (*Vorstellung*) and experience (*Erlebnis*), the distinction that subverts what Husserl brands in the Second Investigation as "one of the worst conceptual distortions known to philosophy" (*LU* II/1: 165). The distortion consists in defining the presentation of a content as its merely being experienced, thus in simply identifying presentation with experienced contents. What is at issue in this distinction is the intentional character of presentation, its character as presentation of an object, which is distinct from the sense-content belonging to one's stream of experience. Hence, correspondingly, there is a second distinction, that between object and psychic content. Husserl's formulation is decisive: "Perplexed by the confusion between object and psychic content, one overlooks that the objects of which we are 'conscious' are not simply there in consciousness as in a box, so that one can merely find them therein and grasp at them; but that they are first *constituted* as being what they are for us and as what they count as for us, in various forms of objective intention" (*LU* II/1: 165). Still more directly: "When, for example, we have a presentation or judgment about a horse, it is the horse, not our momentary sensations, that is presented and judged about" (*LU* II/1: 161). In these formulations a threefold schema is outlined: there is, first, the psychic content, the sensations immanent in consciousness; then, second, there is the objective intention, which somehow objectifies the content in such a way as to constitute the object, the third moment, which is to be rigorously distinguished from the psychic content.

In the Fifth Investigation Husserl elaborates this schema, analyzing more closely the relations between its three moments. Let me excerpt the passage that focuses perhaps most sharply on the differentiation of sense-content from the intentional object. Husserl draws the distinction as one between two kinds of contents, between intentional contents, those belonging to the object as intended, and what he calls truly immanent contents. Of the latter he writes:

> *Truly immanent contents*, which belong to the real make-up [*zum reellen Bestande*] of the intentional experiences, are *not intentional*: they build up the act, provide the necessary points of support [*Anhaltspunkte*] that make the intention possible, but they are not themselves intended, they are not the objects presented in the act. I do not see color-sensations but colored things; I do not hear tone-sensations but the singer's song, etc. (*LU* II/1: 374)

The intentional object, that *of* which one is conscious, that which is straightforwardly intended, does not itself really belong to consciousness; it is not there in consciousness as in a box, as were those images put forth by the image-theory in explanation of perception. What really belongs to consciousness are the non-intentional contents that provide, as Husserl says, the points of support for the intention, that is, the immanent sense-contents.

How is this immanent sense-content to be characterized? The passage just cited exemplifies the way that, in Husserl's text itself, such a characterization is produced, namely, by transferring to the sense-content the name of a component or property of the object. Thus, identifying colored things as what one actually sees, Husserl distinguishes them from what he then calls color-sensations. In a corresponding discussion in *Ideas* I there is a similar but more specific transfer. Referring to the non-intentional character of so-called sensory data (*Empfindungdaten*), Husserl illustrates by means of an analysis of the perception of a piece of white paper. In the components of the experience that are, as Husserl says, related (*bezogen*) to the paper's quality of whiteness, it is possible to discover, says Husserl, the sensory datum white. Husserl calls it even: this white (*dieses Weiss*)—writing the word without any qualifying modifications, without italics and without quotation marks, effacing the transfer, disguising the citation as such. Husserl calls it a "presentative" content (*"darstellender" Inhalt*), that is, a content that presents the appearing white that belongs to the paper; as such, the content is the bearer (*Träger*) of an intentionality (*Hus.* 3: 81).

The sense-content is, then, related to something such as a quality in the object, and it is presumably this relation that warrants the transfer of name, the unmarked citation. What is the character of the relation? Husserl designates it as a matter of presentation, but clearly he would have to distinguish such presentation from the sense that presentation usually has for him, a sense that involves the intention and that he has insisted on distinguishing from the mere experience of sense-content. Such presumably is the reason that in place of the usual *vorstellen* he uses a form of *darstellen*, writing it in fact between quotation marks.

Still another discussion of color, near the beginning of the Fifth Investigation, characterizes the relation quite succinctly: though the seen color does not exist as an experience, "there is in the experience a real component that *corresponds* to it" (*LU* II/1: 348f.). Thus writes

Husserl, italicizing the word *corresponds* (entspricht), focusing the entire discussion on this name for the relation between sense-content and objective content.

Hence, one may say—Husserl does say—that the sense-content is related to the objective content in such a way as to correspond to it and thus to present it. Add, finally, what is said in one other passage of *Ideas* I: Using, as example, the color of a tree, distinguishing this color from all real components of the perceptual experience, Husserl notes that, on the other hand, one can find in the experience "something like color" (*so etwas wie Farbe*), namely, the so-called sensory color (*Hus*. 3: 243). Here especially the appropriateness of the word *image* seems to be announced. Do not these characterizations indeed suffice to legitimate calling the sense-content an image, even if in a sense that remains relatively undetermined? Yet, one direction in which it can readily be determined is toward the psyche: again and again Husserl stresses that the sense-content is a real component of one's experience, indeed that there is—as he says—"no difference between the experienced . . . content and the experience itself" (*LU* II/1: 352). Let it be said, then, that the sense-content is an image that is one's own, an image present only in one's ownmost, solitary experience. Only in coming to bear an intentionality does the sense-content get objectified and come to refer beyond itself.

And yet, Husserl does not always ascribe such utter immanence to sense-contents. Consider one of the most striking examples, put forth at the heart of the analysis of intentionality in the Fifth Investigation:

> I see a thing, for example, this box, but I do not see my sensations. I continually see *one and the same box*, however *it* may be turned and tilted. I continually have the same "content of consciousness"—if I care to call the perceived object a content of consciousness. [But] with each turn I have a *new* content of consciousness, if, in a much more appropriate sense, I so designate the experienced content. Very different contents are therefore experienced, and yet the same object is perceived. Therefore, the experienced content is not, generally speaking, itself the perceived object. (*LU* II/1: 382)

And yet, as this very example shows unmistakably, the experienced content can be *of* the perceived object; indeed the experienced content will be *of* the perceived object in every case where, as here, it is identified with the faces, the profiles (*Abschattungen*), that the object presents to perceptual consciousness. Here the content, even if not yet a quality of the thing as such, is nonetheless not something utterly enclosed in consciousness; it is not simply a component in experience of the sort that could be, at most, only something like a quality. On the contrary, a profile always, in and of itself, refers beyond itself to that of which it is a profile; it opens intuitively upon the object. Almost as if it were a phantasy image opening upon that something beyond that is imaged.

But is it only that the example of the box is an inappropriate one? This would be a difficult supposition, considering that the point made by the example, namely, the identification of sense-content with the profiles offered to perception, is repeated and indeed emphasized in *Ideas* I (*Hus.* 3: 93–95). It is perhaps in view of this example and the identification it exemplifies that one ought to pose with utmost seriousness the question whether indeed one can discover reflectively "something like white" in one's experience and completely this side of anything objective, a white within that is yet not at all the white that one sees, a white quite distinct from the white of the paper at which one will be looking as one searches reflectively for this other, unseen white, a white that is, at most, my own image of the white I see before me, beyond me. Or is such a white only an empty double of the white I see, a double that a certain theoretical orientation would project within? As the image-theory projected into the alleged interiority of consciousness an image doubling the thing outside.

Let it be said, then, that there is duplicity in perception, that the perceptual image, present only in one's ownmost, solitary experience, is *at the same time* an image of the object, a profile through which the thing shows itself, thus an image that, in and of itself, refers beyond itself, an image of something beyond.

(d)

Despite the critique of the image-theory that Husserl appends to it, his analysis of perception is such that, in its very indecision, it retains an image at the heart of perception. Furthermore, that image proves irreducible to a mere content hermetically sealed off within consciousness; rather, its duplicity is such that, however much it remains one's own, it is at the same time an image of the object beyond. Thus, there remains within perception—as Husserl's analyses unfold it, indecisively—not just an image but, in and through that image, a reference to the object, a certain representational function, a representation by way of the image. Far from excluding all imaginal representation, perception would be sustained at its core by an operation of imagination. Such rigorous differentiation as would be required in order simply to subordinate imagination to perception proves unthinkable.

But what about the submission of imagination to intentionality as such? In particular, can such subordination be sustained in the case of that imaginal operation integral to perception? In other words, what about the perceptual intention itself, which would be, says Husserl, borne by the sense-content? Must something like an intention come to supplement the sense-content, granted the redetermination of that content as duplicitous image?

The intention is designated by Husserl as an act (*Akt*), though not without awareness of—and, it seems, some uneasiness over—the fact that the term was quite controversial at the time of the *Logical Investigations* (*LU* II/1: 344). Husserl is concerned also with the ambiguity of the term and takes care to exclude a number of its senses, such as that of activity (*Betätigung*), that are inappropriate to his analyses (*LU* II/1: 379). If one recalls the way in which a certain intentional act is described in the critique of the image-theory, namely, as the capacity through which something first comes to be constituted as an image, then one will anticipate a certain slippage that the act-character will undergo once the sense-content that bears the intentional act is identified as the duplicitous image.

In the foundational analyses in the Fifth Investigation, Husserl repeatedly characterizes the intentional act as one of *Auffassung*—let me say, with a double translation, *apprehension* and *interpretation*. The word is meant to describe the process in which a variety of different contents are apprehended, interpreted, as presenting one and the same object. Such a process is what Husserl wants to exemplify in the passage that I cited concerning the box that is turned and tilted so as to show varying profiles; in fact, the example works against Husserl's insistence that transcendence, the reference beyond, is entirely the accomplishment of the intentional act. Another example compares the intentive process to that of one who, first, hears a completely strange (or foreign: *fremd*) word merely as a sound-complex without any suspicion that it is a word and who, afterwards, now acquainted with its meaning, hears the word again, now understanding it, apprehending it as a word (*LU* II/1: 384). In the latter instance, he will have apprehended the word as designating a meaning and in the apprehension/interpretation will have referred beyond the mere sound-complex to the meaning. But, even granting that this example is only analogical, one cannot but wonder whether its comparison of the perceptual intention to the transition from sound-complex to meaning is not fundamentally misleading. For when, through the varying profiles of the box, one apprehends the object, it is a matter, not of an interpretive transition to a meaning, but rather of apprehending the thing itself, this particular sensible box as it is turned and tilted before one's very eyes.

But what is perhaps most decisive with regard to the character of the so-called intentional act, is the duplicitous character of the image that it would come to supplement, to objectify. For that image is not simply in consciousness as in a box, not simply enclosed in one's ownmost solitary experience, but rather in its duplicity is, at the same time, already an image of the object. What would be required would be neither an act of interpretation nor one of constitutive apprehension but, rather, an "act" more fitted to the duplicitous image, an act whose very character as such would be exposed to slippage precisely in its being fitted to the duplicitous image. What would be needed would be an "act" capable of resolving the duplicity of the image, of fixing it in the direction of the object, of making it decisively *of* the object and no longer just one's own. Such resolution would occur precisely insofar as the image comes to be set within a complex of horizons, not only the inner and outer horizons to which Husserl's late texts refer, but also horizons such as those by which something like an equipmental complex is determined, in the manner so aptly described by Heidegger. But horizons, for example, the inner horizon comprised of all the presently unseen profiles of the perceived thing, have precisely the character of being—in the broad sense—intuitively apprehended without, however, being actually present, without being actually displayed there before one's vision.

Thus would the so-called intentional act also be drawn toward imagination, which in its most classical determination is the capacity to make present something that also is, and remains, absent. Thus would intentionality be contaminated, as it were, by imagination. And thus would imagination, at the same time, be freed of its submission to intentionality.

9

The Truth of Tragedy

> "Ohne Musik wäre das Leben ein
> Irrthum."
>
> Nietzsche, *Götzen-Dämmerung*

Impossible.

That is what Nietzsche called it.

He called it an impossible book, called it such in a saying marked as repetition (*nochmals gesagt*), a saying also dated and oriented (*heute ist es mir ein unmögliches Buch*). It is more than fourteen years later, the *today* of this saying, which occurs in a kind of retrospective preface (entitled "*Versuch einer Selbstkritik*") written in 1886 for a new edition of *The Birth of Tragedy*.

An impossible book? Why impossible? How? For it had, after all, been written. What is to be understood by impossibility in this instance? How is impossibility to be thought within the purview of tragedy and its birth? How *can* impossibility be thought—especially considering the virtual inevitablity with which, as this formulation shows, the question doubles back upon itself? Is it possible, in particular, to think impossibility otherwise than in relation to contradiction? Even when it is a matter of particulars? Is it possible even in this case to extricate impossibility once and for all—or even for the briefest moment—from the force of what for a long time has been called the *law* of non-contradiction? Is it possible— in thinking impossibility—to elude the force that would, that has for a long time, enforced this law?

Can Nietzsche have wanted to say only that the book was improperly conceived, that it was of questionable birth, of dubious parentage? But then why *impossible* if it is only a matter of its being, as he indeed says,

badly written? Is it badly written only because of the formal heterogeneity of its language, of its logic, of its imagery? Is it only, as he says, that
the book is uneven in tempo, that it lacks the will to logical cleanliness,
that its imagery is frenzied and confused? Or does it betray another kind
of heterogeneity, the operation of an expropriation having to do with
what was to have been said? A heterogeneity, even, that would be—em-
ploying provisionally concepts that could not fail to be threatened precisely by such heterogeneity—essential or structural and not merely the
result of the failings of the author? An expropriation linked to tragedy
and its birth? An impropriety produced by the very truth of tragedy?

Is this why it is not just badly written but impossible? Is it a book that
cannot have been written, even though a certain inscription bearing the
title *The Birth of Tragedy* indeed took place? Is it precisely this inscription that remains questionable?

But not only in what it says, not only in the recoil of the content upon
the inscription. Equally questionable is the voice that speaks in the inscription. Nietzsche does not hesitate to say—fourteen years later—that
in "this questionable book" there spoke a strange voice, the voice of a
foreigner (*eine fremde Stimme*):

> What spoke here was a *strange* voice, the disciple of a still "un-
> known god," one who concealed himself for the time being under
> the scholar's hood. . . . What spoke here . . . was something like a
> mystical, almost maenadic soul that stammered with difficulty and
> willfully, as in a strange tongue, almost undecided whether it should
> communicate or conceal itself.[1]

It is as if a foreign voice spoke through the author, submitting him to
a certain phonic self-dispossession while at the same time concealing itself behind his voice, continuing to sound like his voice except for
the interruptions and the indecision. Hesitating, hovering, between self-
communication and self-concealment, concealing itself—though indecisively—in its very self-communication, the voice is one that *stammers*.
It is the voice of a maenadic soul translated—indecisively, with difficulty and willfully—into the speech of the scholar; its stammering, its
disordered and disordering stops and repetitions, testifies to its strange-

---

1. *Die Geburt der Tragödie*, in vol. III 1 of *Werke: Kritische Gesamtausgabe*, ed. Giorgio Colli
and Mazzino Montinari (Berlin: Walter de Gruyter, 1972), 8f. Subsequent references to this edition are given in the text by volume number and page number.

ness, its foreignness, and provokes the question of the linkage between this phonic configuration and *what* would be *said* by this complex of voices. Does the very thing to be said, the birth of tragedy, escape the mere voice of the author-scholar, requiring in its place—though concealed behind it—the strange voice of a maenadic reveler?

What is to be said is the way in which tragedy is born from music through the coupling, the crossing, of Apollinian and Dionysian, the way in which, though monstrously opposed, they eventually come to "appear coupled with each other and in this coupling finally generate the equally Dionysian and Apollinian artwork of Attic tragedy" (III 1: 21f.). What is to be said is the truth of tragedy, a truth that even in this simplest of declarations is already doubled: the voice of *The Birth of Tragedy* is to say both the truth about tragedy (the truth about the way in which it was—and necessarily is—born) *and* the truth that comes to be disclosed in and through tragedy, by the double mimesis enacted in it. In this doubling the space of a certain torsion—a certain possible dispossession—is opened: Can the same voice that declares the truth about tragedy (the voice of the scholar capable of retracing the birth of tragedy among the Greeks) also say the truth that is disclosed in and through tragedy? Can this double truth be said by a single voice, by one and the same voice? Or is another voice, a foreign one, required? Can *any* voice simply *say* what tragedy *shows*? What would be required in order to declare in speech the truth made manifest in tragedy? Could such a voice—or complex of voices—speak otherwise than by stammering?

Yet with tragedy it is, most decisively, not only a matter of saying, of speech. First of all, because of the link to acting, to deeds: to the enactment of the drama of course, its performance, but also deeds lying entirely outside the sphere of art, deeds of war, deeds belonging to the sphere of politics. Nietzsche underlines the relevant identity: "It is the people of the tragic mysteries that fights the battles against the Persians" (III 1: 128). What is the connection attested by this identity? Not only that the Greeks needed tragedy afterwards as a kind of potion by which to recover from the experience of war. For it is not as though, beforehand, they were innocent of the element of tragedy, the Dionysian. Quite the contrary—hence the force of the question: "Who would have supposed that precisely this people, after it had been deeply agitated through several generations by the strongest convulsions of the Dionysian daimon, should still have been capable of such a uniformly vigorous effusion of the simplest political feeling, the most natural patriotic instincts

[*Heimatsinstincte*], and original manly desire to fight?" (III 1: 128f.).
Was it perhaps precisely tragedy that renewed in them the manly desire
to fight? Was it the engagement with tragedy, with its truth, that enabled
the Greek warrior?

With tragedy it is a matter not only of words and deeds but also of
images. The images whose shining comes into play in tragedy are properly Apollinian. Simply as Apollinian, even prior to tragedy and their
shining within it, they bear decisively on truth: what shines forth in
Apollinian images as such is a "higher truth," a certain "perfection . . .
in contrast to the incompletely intelligible everyday world [*zu der lück-
enhaft verständlichen Tageswirklichkeit*]" (III 1: 23). In Apollinian images the things of everyday appear perfected, and the shining of this
perfection, of this truth, provides a certain release from the negativity of
the everyday, a certain relief from its fragmentariness. Apollo is the
healer: especially in the images by which art redoubles the Apollinian,
life is revealed in its higher truth, as in a transfiguring mirror. In the
Olympian gods the Greek gazes upon himself transformed, beholds
the everyday, but now completed and transfigured: "Existence under the
bright sunshine of such gods is regarded as desirable in itself" (III 1: 32).
Through the Apollinian, truth comes to shine, and its shining uplifts and
transforms. Or rather, *Apollinian* truth, a certain truth of the everyday, comes into play. For with Apollo's shining, truth will already have
been—at least—doubled. Apollinian truth is not only the truth *of* the
everyday but also stands in a certain opposition to an *other* truth, a
truth that would underlie the everyday rather than transfiguring it, a powerful truth that Apollinian truth serves indeed to cover over, to conceal.
This other truth Nietzsche finds expressed in the profoundly pes-
simistic words that the captured Silenus addressed to mankind through
King Midas:

> Oh, wretched ephemeral race, children of chance and misery, why
> do you compel me to tell you what it would be most expedient for
> you not to hear? What is best of all is utterly beyond your reach:
> not to be born, not to *be*, to be *nothing*. But the second best for you
> is—to die soon. (III 1: 31)

This Silenic truth proclaims the terror and horror of existence, which the
Greeks knew and before which, in order to be able to live at all, they had
to interpose their Olympian images: "It was in order to be able to live
that the Greeks had to create these gods from a most profound need" (III
1: 32). Apollinian art thus served not only to reveal a higher truth but

also to veil—for some time at least—this Silenic truth, which otherwise can only incapacitate life and provoke its negation. Nietzsche writes in his notebooks: "The world of the Greek gods is a fluttering veil, which covers [*verhüllte*] what is most frightful" (III 3: 77). That in the face of which Silenic truth is provoked and proclaimed, that which Apollinian art would cover with its fluttering veil, is the abyss underlying the every-day—or rather, not even underlying but rather, precisely as abyss, dis-rupting all underlying, dissolving all would-be grounds. Nietzsche calls it *the Dionysian*.[2]

It is decisive that Silenic truth is not the only truth possible in the face of the Dionysian, that truth before the Dionysian—or, on the temporal axis, *after* it, resulting from engagement with it—is not unique but is doubled. There is not only Silenic truth and its veiling by Apollinian truth. There is also an other, the truth of tragedy, which comes into play through a reorientation of the Apollinian by which the latter, rather than veiling the Silenic effect, is fused, coupled, crossed with the Dionysian.

One can also refer—though not unproblematically—to Dionysian truth. In effect Nietzsche himself does so in a passage in which he de-scribes how the Apollinian world was overwhelmed by the Dionysian:

The muses of the arts of "shining" ["*Schein*"] paled before an art that, in its frenzy [*Rausch*] spoke the truth. The wisdom of Silenus cried "Woe! woe!" to the serene Olympians. The individual, with all his limits and restraint, succumbed to the self-oblivion of the Dionysian states, forgetting the Apollinian precepts. *Excess* [Das Übermass] revealed itself as truth. (III 1: 37)

What is the linkage joining this truth as excess, Dionysian truth, to Silenic truth and to the truth of tragedy? How is it that the manifold dou-bles of truth are gathered through the birth of tragedy?

The linkage is determined, not simply by the engagement with the Dionysian, but in reference to the *return* from such engagement. This ori-entation is outlined in a series of remarkable passages near the end of sec-tion 7 of *The Birth of Tragedy*. Nietzsche writes:

The rapture of the Dionysian state with its annihilation of the ordinary bounds and limits of existence contains, while it lasts, a

---

2. Here it must suffice to recall Nietzsche's discourses on the Apollinian and the Dionysian only in broadest outline and only to the extent required for addressing what is at stake in the *truth* of tragedy. I have ventured a more extended discussion of the Apollinian and the Dionysian as well as of tragedy as such in *Crossings*.

lethargic element in which all personal experiences of the past become immersed. This chasm of oblivion separates the worlds of everyday reality and of Dionysian reality. But as soon as this everyday reality reenters consciousness it is experienced as such with disgust [*Ekel*]; an ascetic will-negating attunement [*Stimmung*] is the fruit of these states. (III 1: 52)

It is this attunement, produced in the return from engagement in the Dionysian, that provokes the proclamation of Silenic truth; it is this attunement, brought on in and by the return to the everyday, that gives Silenic truth its force, that gives it the force of truth. It is this attunement, too, that most decisively threatens Apollinian truth, that threatens to shatter it, to tear aside its veil, to withdraw its force. Referring to the "insight into the horrible truth," Nietzsche continues:

Now no comfort any longer avails. . . . Existence is negated along with its glittering reflection in the gods or in an immortal beyond. Conscious of the truth he has once seen, man now sees everywhere only the horror or absurdity of being. (III 1: 53)

This is precisely the juncture at which tragedy, the truth of tragedy, comes into play:

Here, where the danger to his will is greatest, *art* approaches as a saving sorceress, expert at healing. She alone knows how to turn these disgusting thoughts about the horror or absurdity of existence into representations with which one can live. These are the *sublime* as the artistic taming of the horrible and the *comic* as the artistic discharge of the disgust of the absurd. (III 1: 53)

The first of these artistic turnings, a turning from the horrible to the sublime, is what is achieved by tragedy. In tragedy the engagement with and the return from the Dionysian is carried out mimetically in such a way that the abyss is disclosed as sublime. In a later passage Nietzsche characterizes tragedy with the phrase "sublime ecstasy [*erhabene Entzückung*]" (III 1: 128), which, across a series of mediations thoroughly prepared by Nietzsche's discourse, merely says again: the Dionysian as sublime. Such is, then, the *truth of tragedy*: the Dionysian (disclosed) as sublime.[3] It is the truth about tragedy, the truth that ren-

---

3. In *Crossings* (especially chapter 3c) I have given a close analysis of the passages in *The Birth of Tragedy* addressed to the sublime and have undertaken to show how they converge in this determination. See also Michel Haar, *Nietzsche et la métaphysique* (Paris: Gallimard, 1993), chap. 8.

ders to an extent intelligible the coupling that the Greeks brought about between the monstrously opposed Apollinian and Dionysian as well as the force that this coupling, tragedy itself, proved to exercise in shaping Greek existence, not only in the sphere of art but also in that of politics, eroding even the very distinction between such spheres. This truth about tragedy, beginning with which the scholar can retrace the birth of tragedy among the Greeks, is also the truth disclosed in and through tragedy, the truth shown in the deed, or rather, in tragedy's peculiar configuration, its crossing, of enactment, speech, and music. It is the double truth of tragedy.

This truth is precisely what links tragedy to, for instance, deeds of war. Though the Dionysian as such—if it can be said that there *is* a Dionysian *as such*—is nonpolitical, its excess, its recurrent dissolution of all limits, violating every canon of political order, everything changes when Dionysian truth is taken up, taken over, into tragedy. Because tragedy has to do with the way one *returns* from engagement with the Dionysian, because it brings one back to the everyday in a way that, unlike Silenic truth, does not negate the everyday, tragedy has its distinctive political significance. Whereas "the Dionysian genius has no civic relations" (III 3: 230), tragedy serves to reinstall Dionysian man in the state, at least insofar as it counters the life-negating pessimism that otherwise results from exposure to the Dionysian. Thus it is that tragedy brings a renewal of the patriotic instincts, of the manly desire to fight, to defend one's life and all that belongs to it. Thus the identity that Nietzsche underlines: "It is the people of the tragic mysteries that fights the battles against the Persians" (III 1: 128).

But how does the truth of tragedy happen? What takes place in the disclosure of the Dionysian as sublime? Precisely a crossing of the Dionysian with the Apollinian: in tragedy the artistic Dionysian, as music, is projected into images, which are intrinsically Apollinian but which in tragedy are put in service to the Dionysian so as to effect a "visible symbolizing of music," so as to cast on the stage "the dream-world of a Dionysian rapture" (III 1: 91). What takes place is thus also a crossing of the respective truths: what is carried out mimetically is not only the exposure to Dionysian truth but also a distant shining forth of the Dionysian in its *higher truth*, in an Apollinian truth now put in service to the manifestation of the Dionysian. The Apollinian truth that takes place within tragedy—that is, the shining forth of the higher truth of the Dionysian, of the abysmal (here the monstrosity of the opposition is especially marked)—comes to take the place of Dionysian truth, or, more precisely, to reconstitute, recast, that truth as the truth of tragedy.

Yet tragedy is not simply a matter of disclosure but also is that supplement through which is overcome the attunement (*Stimmung*) otherwise brought on in and by the return from the Dionysian to the everyday, that will-negating disgust the outcome of which is Silenic truth. If one may assume that a particular attunement is to be overcome only through the production of another attunement that comes to displace and replace it, then it will be evident that through the very disclosure that tragedy effects it must also produce another attunement by which one would be delivered, as it were, from the negativity of Silenic attunement. In the notebooks from the time when Nietzsche was composing *The Birth of Tragedy* one reads: "Tragedy is the natural healing power against the Dionysian" (III 3: 69).

Tragedy has, then, the character of an *attuning disclosure*. It is a disclosure of the Dionysian in its higher truth, and this higher truth of the Dionysian lies precisely in its sublimity. But what precisely is that character of the Dionysian by disclosure of which it comes to shine forth as sublime? And what is the attunement that is drawn forth by this sublimity? An often-cited passage in *The Birth of Tragedy* gives a decisive indication regarding both Dionysian sublimity and tragic attunement. Let me extract some portions of it:

> We are forced to look into the terrors of the individual existence—yet we are not to become paralyzed [*erstarren*]: a metaphysical comfort tears us momentarily from the bustle of the changing figures. We are really for a brief moment primal being itself [*das Urwesen selbst*], feeling its raging desire for existence and joy in existence; the struggle, the pain, the destruction of appearances, now seems necessary to us, in connection with [*bei*] the excess of countless forms of existence that force and push one another into life.... We are pierced by the maddening sting of these pains just when we have become, as it were, one with the boundless primordial joy in existence.... (III 1: 105)

There is much to be questioned in this very remarkable passage. Nietzsche himself—fourteen years later—will put in question the very name that the passage gives to the attunement of tragedy. Posing the image of the tragic man of some future generation, posing the question of his need of metaphysical comfort (*metaphysischer Trost*), Nietzsche asks:

"Would it not be *necessary?*" and exclaims: "No, thrice no!" The problem with metaphysical comfort is precisely that it is metaphysical; or, more precisely, it is problematic precisely to the extent that it remains metaphysical. It is problematic insofar as, in coming to be comforted metaphysically, in ending up this way, one ends up "as romantics end, as *Christians.*" To such comfort Nietzsche opposes another: "No! You ought to learn the art of *this-worldly* comfort first; you ought to learn to laugh, my young friends!" This other comfort would even enable one perhaps someday "to send all metaphysical comforts to the devil—metaphysics in front" (III 1: 16). The question with which Nietzsche's "*Versuch einer Selbstkritik*" leaves us, the question that remains today, the question that no post-Heideggerian reading of *The Birth of Tragedy* can evade, is whether this dispatching of metaphysics is not already in force in *The Birth of Tragedy*, despite much that seems contrary to it, not least of all the name *metaphysical comfort.*[4] It is a matter of whether the determination of the attunement of tragedy that is achieved in *The Birth of Tragedy* effectively erases the *metaphysics* of *metaphysical comfort* and uncovers in Greek tragedy the production of an attunement that it is impossible to draw into the orbit of metaphysics, an impossibility that seems already to be projected in the opposition that *The Birth of Tragedy* outlines between Socratism and tragedy. One will also want to ask whether this very impossibility is not linked decisively to the impossiblity of this impossible book.

As with everything sublime, the sublime Dionysian—the Dionysian disclosed, in tragedy, as sublime—is marked by excess; yet not only in the sense of exceeding all limits or measure (*Übermass*), but also in the sense of abundance, profusion, exuberance (*Überfluss, Überschwang*). Yet what Nietzsche's text marks most persistently is a certain necessity that becomes manifest in and through the tragically disclosed excess: looking into the terror of existence, one also—indeed *with necessity*, in what is still called metaphysical comfort—feels the joy in existence. The passage cited marks the necessity as such: struggle, pain, the destruction

---

4. Even the passage from which I have drawn the above excerpt contains phrases that are highly problematic in this regard, for example, the reference to the world-will (*Weltwillen*), which I deliberately omitted from the excerpt. This reference indicates with utmost succinctness what it is that is preeminently at issue in this connection, namely, the extent to which *The Birth of Tragedy* is inscribed within the conceptuality of Schopenhauer's *The World as Will and Representation*. I have attempted to address this issue, which proves much more complex than usually supposed, in *Crossings*, especially chapter 3c.

of appearances now seems—that is, looks, shows itself as—*necessary in their connection* with the excess of existence, with the force of generation. In tragedy one is pierced by the sting of pain at the very same moment (*in demselben Augenblicke*) that one becomes the very feeling of joy in existence. The necessity connecting pain and joy is of such force that not even the slightest interval of time remains between the opposites it binds together. Neither is the joy that is felt at the very same moment as the sting of pain something sensed at a distance, something that might arouse desire and prompt a transition; rather, one becomes the very feeling of joy, one becomes it immediately in the very same moment that one is pierced by the sting of pain, one feels it with an immediacy, an absorption of self, that leaves no interval whatsoever between the sting of pain and the feeling of joy.

There is another very remarkable passage addressed to the connection of opposites that becomes manifest in its necessity in the tragic disclosure of the Dionysian. The passage occurs in the penultimate section of *The Birth of Tragedy* and is set amidst open invocations both of Wagner's *Ring* and of Heraclitus' fragment on the playing child. Play (*Spiel*) as such is brought forth seemingly to explicate what both was said earlier and is now repeated regarding the world as an aesthetic phenomenon; in effect, play is set forth as characterizing the tragically excessive—that is, the sublime—Dionysian, in which there is destruction within its very joy of creating, like "a playing child who places stones here and there and builds sand hills only to overthrow them again" (III 1: 149). And yet, Nietzsche stresses the difficulty of grasping Dionysian art; one might indeed suppose—though Nietzsche offers only the slightest hint—that, rather than simply providing a means by which to grasp the Dionysian conceptually, the concept of play works against any such grasp, operating at cross-purposes with the labor of the concept. Be this as it may, Nietzsche appeals to music as the only way by which to make the *Urphänomen* of Dionysian art understandable (*verständlich*), thus confirming again, though now within a different order, the kinship that binds tragedy and music. Here is the very brief excerpt that I want to draw from the passage:

> The joy aroused by the tragic myth has the same origin [*Heimat*] as the joyous sensation of dissonance in music. The Dionysian, with its primal joy experienced even in pain, is the common womb of music and tragic myth. (III 1: 148)

Born from the Dionysian, tragedy discloses it as sublime, as a play in which joy and pain are connected through a necessity different from that of the concept, a necessity that one could call, in the obsolete, etymological sense, ludicrous. In the tragically disclosed Dionysian, such opposites show themselves to be yoked together in their very opposition; what is disclosed is a dissonant play, and the attunement that *The Birth of Tragedy* still calls metaphysical comfort is precisely an attunement to this play. In tragedy, as in musical dissonance, everything comes down to this yoking together of opposites, a yoking together that prevents either from cancelling the other (that excludes, for example, the configuration typical in determinations of the sublime, that by which pain would prepare the way for and finally give way entirely to joy). They are yoked together in their very opposition, and being attuned to the dissonant play of this yoke is—Nietzsche draws the comparisons—like seeing more deeply than ever yet wishing one were blind, like having to see at the very moment when one also longs to transcend all seeing, like desiring to hear while at the same time longing to go beyond all hearing. It is a matter of a wavering attunement, of an attunement that would hover between them just as they are yoked together in their opposition. From this hovering one could perhaps begin to think the Dionysian or tragic imagination.

It would not be inappropriate to call this yoking together of opposites *monstrous* and to link it to the numerous monsters that bestride Nietzsche's impossible book. One could speak also of contradiction, of the sort of monstrous contradiction of which Nietzsche writes the following: "Contradiction, the bliss born of pain, spoke out from the heart of nature" (III 1: 37). These words immediately follow the characterization of Dionysian truth that was cited earlier and that concludes: "Excess revealed itself as truth." Indeed, the two statements form a single sentence, the word *contradiction* (*Widerspruch*) set in apposition to *truth*. What speaks out from the heart of nature, what becomes manifest in the sublime Dionysian, is contradiction, and thus one can say that the *truth of tragedy is contradiction*. And yet, the fundamental law that has been made to govern the discourse of philosophy virtually from its beginning is the so-called law of non-contradiction, which declares that contradiction is not to be said, that it cannot be said except at the cost of interrupting the very saying.

But the book Nietzsche would write, *The Birth of Tragedy, would say it*. It is the very truth of tragedy that keeps what Nietzsche writes at a distance, that at the same time draws his discourse into the distance, away from the discourses of philosophy, rendering it strange, foreign. Its voice cannot cease stammering. *The Birth of Tragedy* is an impossible book from the moment Nietzsche begins trying to write it.

The question left suspended by *The Birth of Tragedy*, by its impossibility, is whether and how a discourse on the truth of tragedy is possible. Also whether such a discourse, if it were possible, could extend across the various doublings of truth that Nietzsche's text broaches, gathering them so as to confirm the unity of the word itself. Could such a discourse declare what truth as such *means*, without in that very declaration siding with a certain double of truth and becoming foreign to others?

Leaving these questions suspended, let me conclude with two brief indications regarding them, indications as to how among the Greeks themselves there may already have been discourses on the truth of tragedy, discourses outside the sphere of tragic poetry, discourses akin—if still also foreign—to those of philosophy.

The first is marked by Nietzsche himself in the celebrations of Heraclitus that extend from *The Birth of Tragedy* and the manuscripts, notes, and lectures of that period up through Nietzsche's final works.[5] For what Nietzsche undertakes to show is that in his thinking Heraclitus sets out the very same phenomenon that the tragic poets set out in their dramas. Both in *Philosophy in the Tragic Age of the Greeks* and in the Basel lectures on the Preplatonic philosophers, Nietzsche's intent—at least a major intent, if not the only one—in reading the fragments is to indicate how in them the Dionysian comes to be thought cosmologically. Let me cite a single passage from the discussion of Heraclitus found in Nietzsche's lectures:

> At first, eternal becoming has something terrifying and uncanny about it; one could compare it to the sensation that someone feels who, in the middle of the ocean or during an earthquake, sees everything moving. It requires an astonishing strength to transform

---

5. In *Ecce Homo*, for example, Nietzsche calls himself "the first *tragic philosopher*": "Before me this transposition of the Dionysian into a philosophical pathos did not exist." But then he confesses that it may indeed have existed in the case of "Heraclitus, in whose proximity I feel altogether warmer and better than anywhere else." Heraclitus is the teacher of "a Dionysian philosophy . . . that under any circumstances I must acknowledge as more closely related to me than anything else thought to date." Nietzsche adds even: "The doctrine of the 'eternal recurrence,' that is, of the unconditional and infinitely repeated circular course of all things—this doctrine of Zarathustra could in the end have been taught already by Heraclitus" (VI 3: 311). On

this effect into its opposite, that of the sublime and of happy wonder. If everything is in becoming, then no predicate can adhere to a thing but rather must likewise be in the stream of becoming. Now, Heraclitus observed that opposite predicates are drawn toward one another . . . : they are as if tied together in a knot.⁶

Nietzsche adds a translation of fragment 88: "In the same is the living and the dead and the waking and the sleeping and the young and the old." It is this connection, precisely because of this connection of opposites, because of such dicta as—Nietzsche translates, in fact generalizes—"Everything forever has its opposite within itself," that Heraclitus was accused by Aristotle "of the highest crime before the tribunal of reason: to have sinned against the law of [non]contradiction" (III 2: 317). In this connection, in the knotting together of opposites, which was thought also as πόλεμος, Heraclitus thought and said the sublime Dionysian, the monstrous contradiction, that tragedy—through music, enactment, and poetic word—disclosed.⁷

The other Greek discourse to which I want to refer—ever so briefly—occurs in a Platonic dialogue. The question is whether in this dialogue something like the truth of tragedy is inscribed, despite an effacement in the history of philosophy that Nietzsche never ceased to link closely to what he calls Platonism, also despite the ancient quarrel between philosophy and poetry that never ceases to be enacted in the dialogues. What is at issue is a doubling, the distinction between the intelligible and the sensible that would double it in the form of the image. What is decisive is that it was not in fact Nietzsche—as the author, most notably, of *Twilight of the Idols*—who first called this doubling into question in

Nietzsche's discussion of Heraclitus in *Philosophy in the Tragic Age of the Greeks* and other texts of this period, see *Crossings*, 105–7.

6. *Die vorplatonischen Philosophen*, in vol. 19 of *Werke* (Leipzig: Alfred Kröner Verlag, 1913), 179.

7. In *Philosophy in the Tragic Age of the Greeks* Nietzsche broaches, though without developing it, a connection between the Dionysian, thought cosmologically as the knitting together of opposites, and the imagination: "While Heraclitus' imagination [*Imagination*] was gauging the ceaselessly moved cosmos, 'actuality,' with the eyes of a blissful spectator who is watching innumerable pairs of contestants wrestling in joyous combat under the care of stern judges, he was overcome by a still higher premonition [*Ahnung*]; he could no longer regard the contesting pairs and the judges separately from one another; the judges themselves seemed to be contesting and the contestants themselves to be judging—indeed, since he observed basically nothing but justice eternally holding sway, he dared proclaim: the strife of the many is itself justice! And as such: the one is the many" (III 2: 320f.).

a radical and uncompromising manner; on the contrary, it was Plato himself, as the author of the *Timaeus*, in the second of the three long discourses delivered by Timaeus in that dialogue. What Timaeus introduces is a third kind, adding it to the first kind (the intelligible) and the second kind (the sensible, which in being opposed to the first kind doubles it). The addition has the effect of disrupting the simple opposition between intelligible and sensible. And yet, the third kind—called, for instance, mother, nurse, receptacle, and finally, untranslatably, χώρα—is precisely what is required in order for things of the second kind to be possible, in order for there to be sensible, generated things. Only by virtue of the χώρα is it possible for such things to hold to being even though they are distinct from what truly is, even though they *are not.* Thus, the χώρα is thought—even if in a kind of bastard reckoning—as what allows sensible things both not to be and yet to be. Considered within the perspective of Nietzsche's impossible book, the χώρα can be said to make possible a certain yoking together of opposites, of opposites that one would call the most fundamental if such language could still remain intact here. What the χώρα makes possible is the yoking together of being and nonbeing, allowing both to remain determinative of the sensible, allowing contradiction, allowing the entire generated, sensible world to be, as it were, constituted by ontological contradiction. What the χώρα makes possible is something like the truth of tragedy, and one could perhaps say that in the *Timaeus* the truth of tragedy is thought not only cosmologically but also ontologically.

Thus might one begin to vindicate the claim voiced in the *Laws* regarding tragedy. Especially if one were to bring the discourse on the χώρα to bear also on the question of the πόλις, of its πολιτεία, then one might indeed confirm the Athenian's claim to compose a tragedy, not just *a* tragedy but the truest tragedy. Here are his words:

> Best of strangers, we ourselves, to the best of our power, are the makers of a tragedy that is at once most beautiful and best; at least, all of our πολιτεία is composed as mimesis of the most beautiful and best life, which, then, we assert to be actually the truest tragedy. (817b)

10

Mimesis and the End of Art

The Greek view of art as essentially mimetic remained effective throughout much of the history of metaphysics. Yet, at least by the time of Kant, of romanticism, and of German idealism, this classical concept seems to have lost much of its force and to have given way to an approach that focuses on the creativity of the artist, on the natural poetic genius, rather than on the talent for fashioning mimetic reproductions of nature. Thus Kant draws the contrast in the *Critique of Judgment*: "Everyone is agreed that genius is to be wholly opposed to the spirit of mimesis [thus I translate, back in the direction of Greek, Kant's word *Nachahmungsgeist*]."[1] In romanticism the corresponding contrast between genius and talent becomes virtually a commonplace.[2]

And yet, along with this devaluation of mimesis, there is also a doubling by which another, superior form of mimesis is both opposed to the devalued form and put forth as essential to art. Thus, with Kant, despite the opposition of genius to the spirit of mimesis, there occurs a certain reinstatement of mimesis: "art can only be called beautiful if we are conscious of it as art while yet it looks like nature [*als Natur aussieht*]."[3] Similarly, in discussing the role of classical models in art, Kant notes that they are to serve as "models not to be copied but to be imitated [thus I translate, in the spirit of English romanticism: *Muster nicht der Nach-*

---

1. I. Kant, *Kritik der Urteilskraft* (Hamburg: Felix Meiner, 1974), 161.
2. See John Spencer Hill, ed., *Imagination in Coleridge* (Totowa, NJ: Rowman and Littlefield, 1978), 133f.
3. *Kritik der Urteilskraft*, 159.

171

machung, sondern der Nachahmung]."[4] Coleridge is explicit regarding this hierarchical opposition within mimesis, this doubling of mimesis: "Now an *Imitation* differs from a copy in this, that it of necessity implies and demands *difference*—whereas a copy aims at *identity*."[5] In Schopenhauer the doubling is even more explicit: a false, concept-bound mimesis is rejected precisely in order to reinstate mimesis in its genuine form, as repetition (*Wiederholung*) of the eternal ideas apprehended through pure contemplation.[6]

But with Hegel it would seem to be otherwise. Almost at the beginning of the *Aesthetics* one finds an extended critique of the view of art as essentially mimetic. This critique one might easily take as definitively excluding mimesis from the Hegelian view of art, in which case Hegel's *Aesthetics* would, in this regard at least, constitute a decisive break with the history of metaphysics rather than a completion, rather than the moment in which the metaphysics of art is thought through to the end.

And yet—as I shall undertake to show—there is no such break. Not only does Hegel's critique of an impoverished form of mimesis come to be matched by a reinstatement of another, transformed mimesis, one so transformed that it goes unnamed as mimesis; but also, by reclaiming at a more profound level the Greek determination of art as essentially mimetic, Hegel thinks this determination, *the* metaphysical determination of art, through to its end. In the end, thinking the metaphysics of art through to its end, Hegel announces the end of art.

My concern is, then, with mimesis: with the word, with the concept, and with the thing itself. With the word—that is, with the Greek word that has been both transliterated into the modern European languages and translated into those languages, for instance, as *Nachahmung* and as *imitation*. With the concept—that is, with the meaning of the word, or, rather, the configuration of meaning corresponding to the history of the transliteration and translation of the word. With mimesis itself, with the thing itself—if indeed one can speak of the thing itself in the case of the operation that, reproducing the thing, setting alongside it an image, opens the very opposition by which the *itself* of the thing itself would be determined.

---

4. Ibid., 163.

5. *Imagination in Coleridge*, 91.

6. A. Schopenhauer, *Die Welt als Wille und Vorstellung* (Cotta-Verlag/Insel-Verlag), vol. 1, §§ 36, 52.

First, then, I shall want to consider how the concept of mimesis comes into play in the Greek determination of the essence of art. In this determination the word *mimesis* comes to be taken as that which says what art itself *is*. And yet, at the same time, it comes also to signify a certain reproduction that almost the entire history of metaphysics denounces as sham, as a mere phantom of genuine art, if not indeed of truth as such. From Plato to Nietzsche it will be said again and again: the poets lie.

The determination of mimesis as the essence of art is governed by metaphysics as it opens in the thought of Plato and Aristotle. And yet, it is not as though metaphysics is itself first determined and then simply brought to bear on the determination of mimesis; for the opening of metaphysics is itself inextricably bound up with mimesis, most notably by way of such oppositions as that between image and original. Precisely because a concept of mimesis will already have been in play in the formation of the very means, of the conceptual resources, by which it will then come to be determined, the concept of mimesis will never have been simply determined. It will never have been delimited once and for all beyond all possibility of slippage but will retain a certain indetermination, a certain play, outlining the space in which the reiterated determination of mimesis will be carried out, most notably the doublings in which an inferior mimesis is devalued and opposed to a superior form of mimesis.

It is just such slippage that will prove to be in play when Hegel, having excluded an impoverised concept of mimesis, recovers another mimesis at a more profound level. I shall want to show, then, that through this recovery Hegel thinks the Greek determination of art through to its end and that he does so precisely in thinking through the end of art, in announcing that art is at an end.

In the Afterword to "The Origin of the Work of Art" Heidegger discusses a series of passages from Hegel's *Aesthetics* in which the end of art is declared. He refers to the *Aesthetics* as "the most comprehensive reflection on art that the West possesses," explaining that its comprehensiveness derives, not (as one might suppose) from the wealth of material discussed, but from the metaphysical basis on which the reflection proceeds. Then Heidegger concludes: "A decision has not yet been made regarding Hegel's declaration, for behind this declaration there stands Western thought since the Greeks."[7] Heidegger's point is that Hegel's

---

7. M. Heidegger, *Holzwege*, vol. 5 of *Gesamtausgabe* (Frankfurt a.M.: Vittorio Klostermann, 1977), 68.

declaration of the end of art issues from the completion of the metaphysical determination of art originating with the Greeks. What has not yet been decided is whether Hegel's declaration is to remain in force; or whether there are means by which to rethink art outside the end announced by Hegel. Can mimesis, the essence of art, be reconstituted outside the closure of the metaphysics of art?

I shall deal, thus, with three themes: (1) the Greek determination of art as essentially mimetic; (2) Hegel's recovery of mimesis at a level that allows him to think the Greek determination of art through to that end at which the end of art can be declared; (3) the question of rethinking art outside the metaphysical end.

(a)

Let me begin by recalling the familiar scene in Book 10 of the *Republic* where Socrates, resuming what he calls "the old quarrel between philosophy and poetry" (607b), poses to Glaucon the question: What is mimesis? Taking the example of a couch, Socrates distinguishes between the couch itself, that is, the εἶδος, and the many couches that are fabricated by craftsmen. Then Socrates mentions another, a different sort of craftsman, one who "is not only able to make all implements but also makes everything that grows naturally from the earth." Socrates continues: "And he produces all animals—the others and himself too—and, in addition to that, produces earth and heaven and gods and everything in heaven and everything in Hades under the earth." Glaucon is amazed at this marvelous craftsman and even more so when told by Socrates that he, Glaucon, could make all these things. Socrates explains: "You could fabricate them quickly in many ways and most quickly, of course, if you were willing to take a mirror and carry it around everywhere." Glaucon answers: "Yes, appearances but not beings in truth" (596c–e).

Such appearances, such images cast in this craftsman's mirror, constitute a third order, the order of mimesis. The ordering is ontological: still further from the couch itself than the couches made by other craftsmen, the image produced by mimesis is an image only of the looks of a couch—of its φάντασμα, its phantom, if you will—not of its truth. Socrates concludes: "Therefore, mimesis is surely far from the truth" (598b). It is because of this remoteness from the truth and because of the corruptive power of the phantoms produced by mimesis that the poet must be banished from the philosophic city, at least as long as he is not able to give an apology for poetry:

> But as long as it is not able to make its apology, when we listen to it, we shall chant these words to ourselves as a countercharm, taking care against falling back again into this love, which is childish and belongs to the many. We are, at all events, aware that such poetry must not be taken seriously as a serious thing laying hold of truth, but that the man who hears it must be careful, fearing for the regime [πολιτεία] in himself, and must hold what we have said about poetry. (608a)

But then—most remarkably—having banished the poet, having posed in the discourse on mimesis the opposition between philosophy and poetry, having posed it as the opposition between truth and phantom, then the *Republic* itself ends in a way that tends to efface in deed that very opposition. Socrates tells a story, that of Er's visit to the underworld. It is a story not unlike those told by the poets, not unlike the story of Odysseus' visit to the dead, to the phantoms in Hades, the story told by Homer in Book 11 of the *Odyssey*. It is as though, in order to complete his struggle against the poets, Socrates had himself to become a kind of poet. It is as though, even after the philosophic denunciation of poetry, even after it is set outside the truth and the poet banished from the city—it is as though poetry continued to haunt philosophy, as though philosophy could never quite be done with the phantom of mimesis.

Aristotle's discussion of mimesis is quite different. It is set much more within predetermined limits, within a discourse on poetry as such that does not open so directly upon ontology and politics. Precisely for this reason Aristotle's discussion has been, from the point of view of art, the more effective, and indeed the *Poetics* has served as the paradigmatic statement, the classical formulation, of the mimetic character of art.

Let me review a few points of that formulation, taking it up at the level where the question is that of mimesis as such and not yet specifically of the form assumed by mimesis in tragedy. The first point pertains to a passage in which Aristotle asks about the origin of poetry. How is it, he asks, that there came to be poetry? He answers that it arose from natural causes; hence, what later thought will regard as the opposition between art and nature is thought by Aristotle as an opening within nature. Here is the passage in which he describes the first of the two natural origins of poetry:

Mimesis is natural to man from childhood, one of his advantages over the lower animals being this, that he is the most mimetic and learns at first by mimesis. (1448b2)

So, mimesis belongs naturally to man from childhood, and poetry grows out of the naturally mimetic activities. Aristotle notes that especially in childhood one learns by mimesis. But, if one can learn by mimesis, then mimesis must have a capacity to disclose things—that is, mimesis of something must serve to bring that thing into view in such a way that one comes to know it, that is, learns about it. One thinks, for example, of the way in which a child learns about things by drawing pictures of them; also of the way in which children learn about doing certain things by playing mimetically at doing them. This connection between mimesis and disclosure is of utmost importance; for it indicates that mimesis is not simply remote from the truth, that it does not merely produce phantoms that would mislead and hence corrupt the regime within the soul; but rather that it produces images of the truth, images opening disclosively upon things in such a way that one can, through mimesis, learn of those things.

Let me refer next to the passage in which Aristotle goes on to identify the second cause of poetry:

And it is also natural for all to delight in works of mimesis. This is shown by experience: Though the things themselves may be painful to see, we take delight in seeing the most perfect images [εἰκών] of them, the forms for example of obscene beasts and corpses. The reason is this. Learning things gives great pleasure not only to philosophers but also to the rest of mankind, however small their capacity for it. The reason that we enjoy seeing images is that one is at the same time learning and gathering what each thing is. . . . (1448b2-6)

The second cause of poetry is thus the delight, the pleasure, afforded by products of mimesis.[8] Yet, again, it is the connection with learning that is most significant, that is even the cause of the delight in imitation, the

---

8. In Aristotle's text it is not entirely clear whether the delight in mimesis is to be considered the second cause of poetry or whether it is to be taken together with the first-mentioned cause (that mimesis is natural) so that the second cause would then be the naturally possessed sense of harmony and rhythm of which Aristotle goes on to speak. This ambiguity is noted by the editor of the Loeb edition of the *Poetics*.

cause of the cause: one takes delight in seeing images because one learns by looking at them and learning is naturally a source of pleasure for all men. By looking at works of mimesis, one learns, with delight, about things that, if looked upon directly, would be painful to see. Both the delight and the learning are constituted in the difference between the image and the thing itself: instead of turning away in pain, one looks at the image, with delight, and learns of the thing. The difference, the remoteness of the image from the truth, is no longer just a source of deception but rather is the very condition of the possibility of a certain kind of learning.

Yet only of a certain kind of learning, one subject to a certain precondition. Thus, Aristotle continues:

> If one has not happened to see the thing before, one's pleasure is not due to the mimesis as such but to the technique or the color or some other cause. (1048b6)

This says: in order to be able to take delight in an image produced by mimesis, in order to be capable of that delight that arises in learning of the thing imaged, one must already have seen the thing itself. Otherwise, whatever delight one may take in the image has a different source, has no connection with learning. For—though Aristotle leaves it unsaid— one can learn through the image *only* if it is recognized *as* an image of the thing itself; and such recognition requires that somehow one has seen the thing itself already, in advance, that one has already caught a glimpse of those obscene beasts and corpses themselves, even if only in turning, in pain, away from them to their images. Poetry, arising in mimesis, would be subordinate to a prior vision of the truth.

The more radical import of this subordination is broached when, a bit further in the *Poetics*, Aristotle focuses on the difference between poet and historian:

> The difference between a historian and a poet is this, that one tells what happened and the other what might happen. Hence poetry is something more philosophic and serious than history, since its statements are of the nature rather of universals, whereas those of history are singulars. (1451b2–3)

The differentiation turns on the difference between the things addressed by historian and poet, respectively. Whereas the historian speaks of the singular, of what has happened, the poet refers mimetically to what might happen, to what is possible, to the universal. Unlike those things of which Herodotus tells in his history, the things of which the poet would bring forth images are not things that one can simply see, as the historian may have seen the events of which he tells. But, if these things of which the poet speaks are not to be seen as such, then poetic mimesis, bringing forth an image, would not simply allow one to see better—for instance, with delight rather than with pain—something that could also be seen without the intervention of mimesis. On the contrary, mimesis would make visible something that otherwise could not be seen at all, a thing itself withdrawn as such from sight.

Now the questions begin to accumulate, open questions, left open by Aristotle, opening the very space in which subsequent thinking about art will be played out.

What of the subordination of poetic mimesis to a prior vision of the truth? What of the requirement that one must have seen the thing itself in order to be able to recognize and to learn from the image? How is one to have seen the thing if the thing cannot as such be seen? Is the prior vision to be entrusted, as it were, to the mind's eye? Must art be preceded by an intellectual vision of the universal? Would this not amount to subordinating art to philosophy—at least in the sense that philosophy would always need to be called upon to give art its ratification, to demonstrate that the images produced by artistic mimesis are not deceptive phantoms but rather open upon the true things themselves? In this case philosophy and not poetry would be called upon to give the apology for poetry and to recall to the city those poets thus ratified.

But even if subordinate to a prior vision and subject thus to such philosophic ratification, poetry remains distinct. For the poet does not tell of what might happen in general, simply translating in his discourse a vision of universality, but rather tells, for example, the story of Odysseus, of Agamemnon, or of Oedipus. In a singular image the poet—somehow—constitutes a mimesis of the universal. Somehow, the poet lets the universal shine forth in the singular images evoked by his words or, in the case of the dramatic poet, brought upon the stage to voice those words and to enact what is bespoken.

For all that is said in the *Republic* about the remoteness of the artistic image from the truth, it is in another Platonic dialogue that this shining forth of truth in the image is named. In the course of the *Phaedrus*, which takes place not at the limit of the city but entirely outside, in the countryside, Socrates contrasts τὸ καλόν (the beautiful) with the other εἴδη that, according to the story he has just been telling, are gazed upon when the soul, prior to birth, follows in the train of the gods up through the heavens. Whereas subsequently, after embodiment, none of the other εἴδη can be seen by that sight provided through the body, the beautiful is an exception: "For the beautiful alone this has been ordained, to be the most shining-forth and the most lovely [ἐκφανέστατον εἶναι καὶ ἐρασμιώτατον]" (250d). Τὸ καλόν names, then, the shining forth of being, of what will be called the universal, its way of shining forth amidst the visible and the singular. If art is a matter of beauty, of bringing forth works that are beautiful, it is because the work of art is a privileged site for the shining forth of being amidst the visible and the singular.

Through the Platonic and Aristotelian discussions of mimesis, there is established a certain axiomatics that will remain in force throughout the history of metaphysics. This axiomatics is such as to assign to mimesis contrary values. These values may be taken as corresponding to the two standpoints from which the mimetic relation between the thing itself (i.e., the original) and its image may be considered. If one takes the standpoint of the original, then the image will represent a falling away, a derivativeness, a certain decline—in short, remoteness from truth, as in the discussions in Book 10 of the *Republic*. But if, on the other hand, one takes the standpoint of the image and looks to the original, then the image will have the positive value of being disclosive of the original.

It is an open question—and I shall leave it open—whether and how these two contrary valuations of mimesis come to be thought together in Greek thought. However this may be, they do come eventually, in the history of metaphysics, to be thought together, within a certain unity. Such thinking reaches its culmination in Hegel's *Aesthetics*, where such unity is thought as the end of art.

(b)

Let me turn now to Hegel's *Aesthetics*, focusing, first of all, on Hegel's extended critique of the view that would identify mimesis as the aim, the end, of art. In Hegel's text *mimesis*, the word, has been translated into *Nachahmung*; and the mimesis in question is oriented to nature. Both the translation and the orientation mark, if they do not indeed produce, such a divergence from the Greek determination that it is little wonder that when Hegel addresses *das Prinzip von der Nachahmung der Natur* his tone is utterly critical. Hegel's formulation of the principle marks the divergence even more clearly: "According to this view, *Nachahmung*, as facility in copying [*nachbilden*] natural forms just as they are, in a way that corresponds to them completely, is supposed to constitute the essential end [or: aim—*Zweck*] of art."[9]

The first of the three criticisms that Hegel offers of this view begins by indicating, still further, how impoverished the concept of mimesis here employed really is. This determination of art as mimetic involves a purely formal end, namely, that whatever exists in the world is to be made a second time, made over again. But such mere repetition, Hegel observes, is superfluous labor, for whatever might be displayed by such mimesis—flowers, natural scenes, animals—we possess already in our gardens or in the countryside beyond. And those originals will always be superior, for mimetic art can only produce one-sided deceptions, the mere *Schein der Wirklichkeit*—that is, the mere "look," a phantom of what truly is, not the reality of life but only a pretence of life. Hegel retells some stories about such deceptive copying: the story of the grapes painted by Zeuxis and declared a triumph of art because living doves pecked at them; and the story of Büttner's monkey, which ate away a picture of a beetle in Rösel's book *Amusements of Insects* but then was pardoned by its master because it had proved how excellent the pictures in the book really were. Hegel summarizes by way of a bizarre comparison: "In sum, however, it must be said that, by mere *Nachahmung*, art cannot stand in competition with nature, and, if it tries, it looks like a worm trying to crawl after an elephant" (52/43).

Despite the exotic examples, none of this is very far from what Socrates said of that marvelous craftsman who could make everything

---

9. G. W. F. Hegel, *Ästhetik*, ed. Friedrich Bassenge (West Berlin: Verlag das Europäische Buch, 1985), 1:51. English translation by T. M. Knox: *Hegel's Aesthetics: Lectures on Fine Art* (Oxford: Oxford University Press, 1975), 1:41. Subsequent references to this work (all to vol. 1) will be given by page number within the text, the first number referring to the German edition, the second to the English translation. This text is based on the second edition published in 1842 by Hegel's student H. G. Hotho, which, in turn, was a slightly revised version of the 1835 edition that Hotho put together on the basis of Hegel's notebook and several sets of student notes. Recently Hotho's editorial work—and indeed not only his failure to differentiate the various versions of the lectures, which Hegel presented four times in Berlin—has come under considerable criticism, most notably from Annemarie Gethmann-Siefert (see "Ästhetik oder Philosophie der Kunst: Die Nachschriften und Zeugnisse zu Hegels Berliner Vorlesungen," *Hegel-Studien* 26 [1991]: 92–110). In the present context it is important to note her observation, based on the relevant student notes still available, that Hegel's thesis concerning the end of art was considerably sharpened in the last version of the lectures (1828–29), corresponding to systematic changes that Hegel made in the relevant sections of the 1827 version of the *Encyclopedia*.

and whom one could imitate by carrying a mirror around everywhere; in particular, it is not far from what Socrates said about the images produced by such a third-order craftsman. And yet, in declaring such images remote from truth, Socrates was attentive to their power, their power to deceive and hence to corrupt; and it was because of this dangerous power of the products of mimesis that the poets had to be expelled from the philosophic city. For Hegel, on the other hand, there is no danger at this level. Hegel's examples illustrate deception exercised, not on human beings, but on monkeys and doves; and what for Socrates was a deceptive power capable even of corrupting the soul becomes with Hegel a matter of mere conjuring tricks, in which one might take a certain brief pleasure but by which one would not for long be deceived. This difference again indicates the divergence between such *Nachahmung* and mimesis, the impoverishment that mimesis has undergone in the translation. One might thus expect that a certain doubling is to come into play, a return of mimesis at a more profound level, in a more powerful form. But not yet.

Hegel proceeds to the second criticism: since the principle of *Nachahmung* is purely formal—prescribing simply that things be made over again, copied—no place is given in art for objective beauty. For if this principle is made the end of art, then there will be no question of the character of *what* is supposed to be copied, but only a demand for the correctness of the copy. As for the choice of objects and their beauty or ugliness, everything will depend on merely subjective taste; that is, even if art remains oriented to the beautiful, bound to produce copies only of beautiful objects, the decision regarding which objects are beautiful will be purely subjective.

Yet, even aside from the question of objectivity, this principle of *Nachahmung* of nature is not to be accepted, says Hegel, "at least in this general, wholly abstract form" (54/44). For though painting and sculpture represent objects that appear similar to natural ones, such is not at all the case with works of architecture or even with works of poetry insofar as they are not confined to mere description. This is, then, the crux of the third criticism: the principle is not universally applicable, if indeed it is applicable to any of the arts.

Hegel's conclusion, delimiting succinctly the form of mimesis thus brought under criticism, differentiates it decisively from the end of art: "The end [or: aim—*Zweck*] of art must therefore lie in something still other than the merely formal *Nachahmung* of what is present, which in every case can bring to birth only technical tricks but not works of art [*Kunststücke, nicht aber Kunstwerke*]" (55/45).

And yet, despite all the criticism, Hegel's formulations betray that his rejection of mimesis is qualified, is limited to mimesis "in this general, wholly abstract form," to mimesis as formal *Nachahmung* of what is merely present, of particular things in nature. Indeed, in the sentence immediately following the just cited conclusion he broaches the doubling thus prepared, the transition to what, though he will not name it as such, will prove to be another form of mimesis, one that is not a matter of mere form, that is not merely formal, one to which a certain content is essential. Here is the sentence that follows the conclusion: "Certainly it is an essential moment of a work of art to have a natural shape as its basis, because what it presents is presented in the form of an external and therefore also natural appearance." The work of art is thus to be conceived as a natural appearance that presents something else, as a natural appearance through which some content distinct from the work is presented. The word that I am translating as *present*, the word that names the more profound, more powerful form of mimesis is *darstellen*.

The question that arises at once is that of the content presented by the work of art. Hegel discusses various alternatives, for example, that the content is everything that has a place in the human spirit, an alternative whose inclusiveness makes it, in the end, no specification of content at all, only something purely formal; or, again, that it is a matter of a certain spiritual content by which moral improvement would be accomplished, art thus being reduced to a means to an end other than itself. Recalling the need to supersede the rigid oppositions especially characteristic of what he calls the modern moralistic view, Hegel asserts, finally, "that the vocation of art is to unveil the truth in the form of sensuous artistic configuration and to present the reconciled opposition, and so to have its end [*Endzweck*] in itself, in this very presentation and unveiling [*Darstellung und Enthüllen*]" (64/55). Art is sensuous presentation of the truth and as such remains, in a profound sense, mimetic.

Such is, then, in the most general terms, Hegel's redetermination of mimesis.

In order to gauge the profound import of this redetermination, it is necessary to consider the way in which it constitutes a recovery of the Greek determination of art as essentially mimetic; indeed, not only a recovery but a fulfillment of the Greek view, carrying it through to the end. Let me consider, then, three points: first, the way in which Hegel recovers the positive value assigned to mimesis by the axiomatics constituted in Greek thought; second, the way in which, beyond the negativity that led him to reject the impoverished concept of mimesis, he also recovers a negative value for mimesis as redetermined, a negative value that parallels up to a point at least that assigned by the ancient axiomatics; and third, the way in which Hegel thinks both values together, in a unity, precisely by thinking the end of art. In this thinking even the apparent polysemy of *end*—that it would mean aim, also fulfillment of the aim, as well as a certain termination—will be surmounted in the direction of unity.

The positive value is evident in Hegel's formulation of the redetermination. It is a matter of a mimesis that would consist in presenting the truth, unveiling it, disclosing it, just as those images of which Aristotle tells disclose the things themselves in such a way that one learns, with delight, of those things. Also, as with Aristotle, that which art sensuously presents, which it discloses, is the universal, even if thought concretely, not the particular things of nature that would be copied by that form of mimesis that Hegel has rejected.

Though Hegel himself passes quickly over the Platonic idea of the beautiful, criticizing its abstractness, insisting that it must now be thought more concretely (32/22), there is, in fact, a profound affinity between Hegel's discussions of beauty and that discussion that I have recalled from the *Phaedrus* as expressing, in contrast to the *Republic*, the positive value accorded to art. From the very outset Hegel's *Aesthetics* is oriented to the idea of beauty, essentially to the idea of artistic beauty; and the beauty of art is taken to lie in its sensuously presenting (the word is, again, *darstellen*) the most comprehensive truths of spirit (19/7). Hegel addresses an objection that might be raised concerning the worthiness of art, thus determined, to be treated philosophically. The objection is aimed at the character of art as *shining* and as *deception* (*Schein und Täuschung*—I merely transliterate the German *Schein*, in hopes of retaining something of its broad range of meanings: shine, look, appearance, semblance, illusion). Hegel's response is that the objection would be justified if shining could be considered something that, in principle, ought not to be. But, he continues:

Shining itself is essential to essence. Truth would not be truth if it did not shine and appear [*scheinen und erscheinen*], if it were not truth *for* someone, *for* itself as well as for spirit in general too. (19/8)

Art presents sensuously the truth, the truth of spirit. But it belongs to the essence of spirit to be for itself, to be not only essence but also actual appearance, to appear to itself. Thus, the appearing, the shining, that is characteristic of art has its justification in the very essence of truth, in the very determination of spirit as for itself. Or, rather, the shining has its full justification in the determination of spirit as in and for itself (*an und für sich*), for it is as such that the shining has its proper *a priori*, the prior vision of truth that Aristotle required for mimesis; for as in itself spirit is always already implicitly what it comes to be explicitly, for itself, namely, self-present. Not only does the shining of art have its justification, but indeed it constitutes the very beauty of the work of art: when, later in the *Aesthetics*, Hegel develops a rigorous determination of beauty, he defines it as "the sensuous shining of the idea" (117/111). Virtually a translation of Plato: τὸ καλόν as the shining forth of the ideas, as the idea that most shines forth, τὸ ἐκφανέστατον.

Still further in the *Aesthetics*, when he comes to discuss specifically the beauty of art, Hegel—in a move comparable to the classical form of art—illustrates artistic shining, i.e., beauty, by referring to the human body and to the privilege of the eye. Let me cite some excerpts from this remarkable passage:

> But if we ask in which particular organ the whole soul appears as soul, we will at once name the eye; for in the eye the soul is concentrated and the soul does not merely see through it but is also seen in it. . . . It is to be asserted of art that it has to convert every shape in all points of its visible surface into an eye, which is the seat of the soul and brings the spirit into appearance. . . . So, art makes every one of its productions into a thousand-eyed Argus, whereby the inner soul and spirit is seen at every point. And it is not only the bodily form, the look of the eyes, the countenance and posture, but also actions and events, speech and tones of voice, and the series of their course through all conditions of appearance that art has everywhere to make into an eye, in which the free soul is revealed in its inner infinity. (155–56/153–54)

Art would bring spirit to shine forth in pure transparency, in a transparency as pure as that of the eye, or, rather, in as pure a transparency as is possible in a presentation that is sensuous. And yet, one cannot but wonder about this limit. Especially since Hegel, having posed the objection that art involves shining *and deception*, has proceeded to vindicate the shining of art but has said nothing directly regarding the charge of deception.

Let me turn, then, to the second point, the negative value of mimesis, which in the ancient axiomatics was constituted primarily by the deceptive and corruptive power of art. For Hegel, on the other hand, the negative value lies in the inadequacy of art with respect to the higher phases of the content to be presented. Hegel outlines this negativity in the following passage near the beginning of the *Aesthetics*, just after the vindication of shining:

> But while, on the one hand, we give this high position to art, it is, on the other hand, just as necessary to remember that neither in content nor in form is art the highest and absolute mode of bringing to consciousness the true interests of the spirit. For precisely on account of its form, art is limited to a specific content. Only one sphere and stage of truth is capable of being presented in the element of art. In order to be a genuine content for art, such truth must in virtue of its own determination be able to go forth into [the sphere of] sense and remain adequate to itself there. This is the case, for example, with the gods of Greece. On the other hand, there is a deeper comprehension of truth which is no longer so akin and friendly to sense as to be capable of being taken up and expressed in this medium. (21/9–10)

That deeper comprehension of truth belongs to those two forms that supersede art, namely, religion, in which the content is linked to the inwardness of the subject; and philosophy, in which the same content comes to have the form, not of representation (*Vorstellung*), as in religion, but of conceptual thought. Hegel is outspoken about the subordination of art to philosophy, about the authority of philosophy, from which art, he says, must receive its genuine ratification.

And yet, that ratification cannot but also declare that art, however much it may let truth shine forth, falls short of the truth as it has now come to be comprehended. The end of art, its aim, falls short of the intrinsically highest end, namely, the self-presentation of spirit in its true form and content. Because art falls short of that end, as it is now comprehended, art is at an end.

Hence the third point: precisely by thinking art in reference to its end, the sensuous presentation of spirit, Hegel thinks together the positive and the negative values to be attributed to art—that is, he thinks the axiomatics of mimesis in its unity. But, in turn, to think thus the end of art is also to be led to declare that art is at an end. Hegel's *Aesthetics* abounds in such declarations.

Art is now at an end. Hegel declares that it "no longer fills our highest needs . . . , no longer affords that satisfaction of spiritual needs that earlier ages and nations sought in it and found in it alone" (21–22/10). He continues: "In all these respects art, considered in its highest destination, is and remains for us a thing of the past" (22/11). Not that art will now simply cease to be; not that there will no longer be artists producing works of art. Hegel says: "We may well hope that art will always rise higher and come to perfection." And yet, as he continues, "the form of art has ceased to be the supreme need of the spirit. . . . We bow the knee no longer" (110/103). Art is at an end precisely in the sense that it is *aufgehoben*; and the polysemy of ends is submitted to the complex unity of *Aufheben*.

And yet, this *Aufhebung* of art was prepared long ago, prepared by art itself, by the very limitation of its end in comparison with the highest end of spirit. Art is not only now at an end but was already at an end with the end of classical Greek art. For in Greek art, the classical form of art, the human body counts as the natural shape of spirit; the presentation of spirit that is thus given, most notably in Greek sculpture, is the most adequate presentation that art can achieve. In Hegel's words:

> The classical form of art has attained the pinnacle of what illustration [*Versinnlichung*] by art could achieve, and if there is something defective in it, the defect is just art itself and the restrictedness of the sphere of art. (85/79)

When romantic art, attentive to the inwardness of self-consciousness, cancels the undivided unity achieved by classical art, it becomes, Hegel says, "the self-transcendence of art but within its own sphere and in the form of art itself" (87/80).

And yet, if one refers to the individual arts, the self-transcendence will prove not to have waited for the accomplishment of the classical art of the Greeks. For in poetry the very last remaining sensuous element, sound, becomes merely a sign of an idea; and thus poetry is not dependent on external sensuous material for its realization, as are the other arts. Or, rather, poetry is precisely in the movement of passing over from such dependence into freedom from the sensuous—that is, poetry too is as such the self-transcendence of art: "Yet, precisely, at this highest stage, art now transcends itself, in that it forsakes the element of a reconciled embodiment of the spirit in sensuous form and passes over from the poetry of representation to the prose of thought" (89/94). But there has always been poetry, just as there has been, at least for a long time, stern denunciation of art, of its claim to present the truth; Hegel mentions the Jews, the Mohammedans, Plato, and the Reformation (110/103).

Not only now is art at an end. Not only with the end of classical Greek art was it at an end. Art was always already at an end.

(c)

According to the determination that is in play from Plato to Hegel, mimesis is a matter of imaginal presentation, of presentation in and through an image. In mimesis something is presented, made present, brought to presence, while also remaining to a degree withdrawn, absent, never being quite captured in the image. Through its presence the image makes present an original while also, by its very character as an image, leaving the original withdrawn, keeping open the difference. Mimesis, thus determined, aims at making present; it is governed by a certain demand for presence, even though the very structure of mimesis is such as to preclude the possibility of full presence. Correspondingly, the ancient axiomatics of mimesis is governed by a privileging of presence: the positive value of mimesis lies in its capacity to present, to bring the original to presence; its negative value derives from its incapacity to bring that original fully to presence, from the necessity of leaving the original also withdrawn, to some extent concealed.

The privileging of presence operative in this axiomatics is not merely a gratuitous presupposition; it is not an unmotivated assumption with which one can simply dispense with impunity. On the contrary, the Platonic discussions show unmistakably that the demand for presence, the privileging of it, is linked to a certain need, a need that one might even venture to call ethical, namely, the need for vigilance in the face of the possibility of deception and of the corruption that can be spawned by deception. It is because of the deceptive and corruptive power of the mimetic phantoms that one must safeguard the regime within oneself; it is thus that Socrates and Glaucon require the poets to deliver an apology before the tribunal of philosophy with its demand for presence.

And yet, from the side of the poets, this is a demand that is improper, not to say unjust. For the axiomatics that philosophy brings to bear upon mimesis serves only to disguise an instability within the very concept of mimesis. The instability lies in the conflict between two moments constitutive of the philosophical concept of mimesis: on the one hand, mimesis is subject to the demand for presence, is determined by an orientation to full presence; yet, on the other hand, its very structure, the difference between image and original, precludes the possibility of full presence. A mimetic presentation that succeeded in bringing the original fully to presence would thereby—by an essential, structural necessity—have ceased to be a mimetic presentation. The instability is thus a tendency to self-effacement, self-annulment.

It is precisely this tendency, inherent in the very determination of mimesis, that allows Hegel to reinscribe mimesis within the logic of *Aufhebung*. Passing over that power of deception and corruption that marked the negative value of mimesis in the ancient axiomatics, Hegel regards the negativity of mimetic presentation as merely its incompleteness, its inadequacy for presenting its content; he regards it, in short, as a determinate negation, which, even if harboring deception and the possibility of corruption, is to be overturned into revelation and perfection. Thus, it is by releasing the tendency to self-effacement inherent in the very concept of mimesis that Hegel comes to declare the end of art. Thus it is too that he settles the old quarrel between philosophy and poetry, indeed so decisively that it hardly matters anymore whether the poets remain in exile or return to the city.

Under the reign of the demand for presence, mimesis cannot but be effaced and art declared to be at an end, the very determination of end, the unity of its senses, being governed by the logic of *Aufhebung*.

And yet, one might venture with justification a break with that logic. One might venture to set the demand for presence out of action so as to reconstitute and rethink mimesis within the field thus opened. One might so venture in the interest of justice to art, in behalf of art itself, art proper, which one would then want to distinguish from the improper determination brought to bear upon it in the history of metaphysics. But also one might so venture still in the name of philosophy, justifying the break by appeal to the necessity of *questioning* the privilege of presence. Even though neither the venture nor its justification will be able to escape the continual risk of falling back into the very system that would be suspended.

Traces of such a rethinking of mimesis can be found in the work of Nietzsche and of Heidegger. In *The Birth of Tragedy*, for instance, where with the familiar double gesture Nietzsche dismisses the determination of art as mere imitation of nature only to restore to art a more profound sense of mimesis as supplement. Most notable is Nietzsche's determination of Dionysian art—hence also, of tragedy—as involving a form of mimesis in which no images are operative, a form of mimesis which is thus such as to preclude the demand for presence. With Heidegger, on the other hand, one finds only the negative gesture, the dismissal of mimesis as presentation of natural things or of universals. And yet, despite Heidegger's silence regarding any reconstitution of mimesis beyond these determinations, one could read the entire analysis in "The Origin of the Work of Art" as elaborating a mimetic relation between the work of art and the truth (redetermined as strife of world and earth) that would be set into the work, that would be constituted only in being set into the work, that would thus not precede its mimesis.[10]

If one can gather these traces into a rethinking of mimesis outside the privilege of presence, one will disrupt the unity of end enforced by the Hegelian *Aufhebung*. Then a decision will have been made regarding Hegel's declaration that art is at an end. Then one will have to think differently the end of art, to think it from difference, to think its relation to the limit of presence, to that which, delimiting presence, remains itself withheld, concealed.

And yet, one will need—perhaps more than ever—to recall the Socratic warnings about the deceptive and corruptive power of the phantoms produced by art. One will need to renew—at the limit—the old quarrel between philosophy and poetry. Without reinvoking the demand for presence, one will need nonetheless to resume Socratic vigilance, to learn the vigilance of questioning at the limit, at the end.

---

10. I take the liberty of referring to the analyses given in *Crossings* and in *Echoes: After Heidegger* (Bloomington: Indiana University Press, 1990), chap. 7.

11

The Place of Wonder

(a)

" . . . a peculiar *return to beginnings*,
a turning toward what
already determines it."

*Phenomenology and the
Return to Beginnings*

How is one to recall a way gone? How summon again that thinking, those times, that nothing less than time itself—threatening every *itself*, even that of thinking itself—has withdrawn? How revive from mere traces all the distress of perplexity, the passion of questioning, the attentiveness of reading, the cautious ecstasy of writing, the patience of waiting for what was hoped would come, for the words that might both open and seal a certain way?

Is there a tense—or can one be invented—in which it becomes possible to tell of another time without depriving it of its intensity and reducing it to a vague shadow of the present?

How is one, then, to retrace a way coming from another time? Only by remembrance. Only by thinking back along the way toward its beginning. Such rememorative thinking has nothing to do with representation: it does not aim at reproducing the way, at producing a duplicate, a present double of a past original (which could never simply be withheld and protected from the duplicity of reproduction). Rather, in remembrance one sets out to think what determined the way and extended its fortune.

In remembrance one turns back to the beginning that will always have sustained thinking in its fortune, even rememorative thinking itself.

One will want, perhaps first of all, to remember thoughtfully what was bespoken in the word by which the beginning of philosophy was named in the beginning of philosophy, the word by which, even if always with a certain reference back to the Greek beginning, it has never ceased to be named. Both Plato and Aristotle call the beginning of philosophy: θαυμάζειν. Both Hegel and Heidegger repeat the name, even if in order to mark a certain distance from the Greek beginning.

Remembrance will trace more openly an exceeding of philosophy that philosophy itself already broached in its beginning: the return to the beginning, the move back from philosophy to the ἀρχή that precedes it and first makes it possible, the regression across the limit of philosophy to the ἀρχή from which it would first be delimited. Remembrance cannot but unfold as archaic thinking; and in archaic thinking remembrance will always already have commenced. In turning toward the ἀρχή, remembrance will always have been determined also by it. When one comes to pose a question of the beginning, that beginning will already, long since, have been in play, depriving the question of its privilege. One will not have been able to begin without being engaged in the beginning, engaged by it; and when one comes to question it, one only returns differently to it, interrogatively, turning toward what already determines the question.

Remembrance will translate the beginning. Into the stable, well-established English translation of θαυμάζειν it will undertake to translate what is bespoken in the decisive discourses on θαυμάζειν, in those discourses that at the limit of philosophy turn back to name its ἀρχή. The structure of such translation is quite different from that in which a Greek word is merely transliterated or reinscribed in English; it is different, too, from that in which an English cognate of a Latin translation is activated. For *wonder* offers a certain resistance to the translation, that is, it brings its own semantic force into play in a kind of oblique resistance that skews the translation, yet in such a way as to promise a translation in which those ancient discourses may be opened beyond themselves. It is a matter of bringing the semantic force of *wonder* to supplement what is sounded in those discourses, echoing them in another tongue, making them resound in the sounding of *wonder*.

What are some of the things that sound in *wonder*?

There sounds amazement in the face of extraordinary occurrences, the rapture into which one is drawn in beholding mysterious or magical events that appear to bespeak the unknown or to portend what is to come. As in the case of Macbeth, whose letter to his wife tells of his wondrous encounter with the three witches. Hailed by them not only as Thane of Cawdor but also as king to be, he burned with desire to question them further about their more than mortal knowledge. Yet, charged by him to reveal the origin and intent of their prophecy, the witches vanish:

> When I burned in desire to question them further,
> They made themselves air, into which they vanished.
> Whiles I stood rapt in the wonder of it, . . .
>
> (*Macbeth* I, v, 4–6)

Its sound is not very different from that of its Anglo-Saxon ancestor *wundor*: a wondrous thing, a portent, something outside the usual course of nature, like the tracks of the dragon pursued in *Beowulf*, like the dragon itself or the strange creatures (*wundra*) that assaulted Beowulf in the deep (*Beowulf* 840, 1509). Transliterating the Latin, opening *wonder* to its history, one says: monster.

There sounds too the wonder of a vision in which one comes to see the world anew, in which it opens as if for the first time so as to disclose something wondrous. As when Miranda exclaims:

> O, wonder!
> How many goodly creatures are there here!
> How beauteous mankind is! O brave new world
> That has such people in't!
>
> (*The Tempest* V, i, 181–84)

Wonder, as in the face of a young child suddenly beholding something for the first time.

(b)

" . . . putting an end to wonder."

Spacings—of Reason
and Imagination

The Aristotelian discourse on wonder occurs within a discussion of the knowledge (ἐπιστήμη) that is most archontic (ἀρχικωτάτη), that is, most royal, most suited to rule. Both the knowledge thus determined and the treatise to which the discussion belongs will later be designated by the word *metaphysics*. Such knowledge is said to consist in speculation (θεωρητική) regarding first beginnings and causes (τῶν πρώτων ἀρχῶν καὶ αἰτιῶν). Aristotle's concern is to show that such speculation is not a matter of production (ποιητική), that philosophy is not pursued in order to produce something. This is shown by consideration of the first philosophers, by turning to the beginning of philosophy, to that beginning from which philosophy proceeded in its beginning. In the turn Aristotle thus doubles the beginning: "It is through wonder that men now begin and first began to philosophize" (*Mtp.* I, 982b12–13).[1] Hence, wonder is identified as the beginning of philosophy both in the beginning and now. All begin from wonder (ἀπὸ τοῦ θαυμάζειν) (*Mtp.* I, 983a12–13) both in the past and in the present. Only as regards the operation of this beginning in the future does Aristotle remain—initially—silent.

Aristotle outlines a progression through which wonder moves: from perplexities regarding things close at hand to perplexities about the genesis of all that is. Thus, wonder would function as beginning not only in the beginning of speculation but throughout its entire course up to the point at which it would finally open upon the whole of what is.

How does wonder function as a beginning throughout the course of speculation? It functions by bringing about an awareness of ignorance: "Now he who wonders and is perplexed considers himself ignorant" (*Mtp.* I, 982b12–13). Wonder is like the sting of the gadfly, driving men out of their pretense to know, setting them adrift in their ignorance, as if paralyzed by a stingray. It is in order to escape the ignorance made manifest through wonder that men pursue philosophy, the aim of which is thus simply knowledge and not production. Thus, it is by making ignorance manifest, by bringing about perplexity, that wonder incites the pursuit of knowledge and functions as the beginning of philosophy.

Aristotle adds that myth, too, can incite the pursuit of knowledge, that the lover of myth (ὁ φιλόμυθος) is in a sense a philosopher. But this is only because myth is composed of wonders (ἐκ θαυμασίων). Philosophy can begin from μῦθος only because the wonders in the μῦθος incite one to pursue knowledge. And yet—one cannot but notice—the wonders within μῦθος (for instance, the wonder of Er's return from the underworld, the wonder of his (re)embodiment) are not quite the same

---

1. In *Mtp.* V 1 Aristotle enumerates the various senses of ἀρχή and concludes: "It is common to all beginnings [κοινὸν τῶν ἀρχῶν] to be the first [thing] from which something either is or comes to be or becomes known" (1013a18–19).

as that kind to which Aristotle's text seems otherwise to refer, a wonder in alliance with perplexity (ἀπορία), a wonder linked more to λόγος than to μῦθος.

Yet, wonder is only the beginning, inciting men in the beginning and now. Wonder does not belong to the future toward which the pursuit of knowledge moves. Rather, that pursuit, Aristotle insists, must lead to the opposite (εἰς τοὐναντίον) of that with which inquiry began (983a12). He repeats that all begin by wondering that things are as they are. But now—most remarkably—he presents wonder not only as making ignorance manifest but also as essentially linked to, even constituted by, ignorance: the incommensurability of the diagonal of a square seems wonderful (θαυμαστόν . . . δοκεῖ) to everyone who has not beheld the cause thereof. One ends, he says, with the opposite and the better: the opposite not only of ignorance but also of wonder. Thus, in the end knowledge is opposed, as the better, to wonder. Though it is through wonder that one comes to pursue knowledge, that pursuit has the effect finally of dissolving wonder. In the end there would be no place for wonder in knowledge, no place for a knowledge to which wonder would be essential and not merely an incitement. In the end there would be only knowledge, beyond the wonder of perplexity, beyond the wonders that compose μῦθος. Philosophy would achieve its end by putting an end to wonder.

Hegel renews the Aristotelian discourse on wonder. One such renewal occurs in the philosophy of subjective spirit, specifically, in that part of the psychology devoted to intuition (*Anschauung*). In displacing wonder from metaphysics to psychology Hegel only carries out the displacement that Aristotle has fully prepared by linking wonder to ignorance and opposing it in the end to the knowledge in which it would finally have been dissolved. Hegel puts an end to wonder still more decisively by assimilating wonder to intuition. Thus, it is in a discussion in which Hegel is concerned to explain how intuition is only the beginning of knowledge (*der Beginn des Erkennens*) that he recalls and confirms the Aristotelian discourse:

Aristotle refers to its [intuition's] place when he says that all knowledge begins from *wonder* [Verwunderung]. Initially, the object is still loaded with the form of the irrational, and it is because it is within this that subjective reason as intuition has the certainty, though only the *indeterminate certainty*, of finding itself again, that its subject matter inspires it with wonder and awe. *Philosophical* thought, however, has to raise itself above the standpoint of wonder.[2]

With Hegel it is a matter of putting an end to wonder as soon as knowledge progresses beyond intuition. That end, that aim, that function, that Aristotle granted to wonder as the beginning of philosophy is now virtually withdrawn from it, even in confirming the Aristotelian statement that all knowledge has its beginning in wonder. For it is no longer wonder but the power of negativity that drives the advance of knowledge. Wonder belongs neither to the future nor to the present of philosophy but only to its past. And even if, like every past, it is retained in the depth of the present and the future, it is not retained *as wonder.*

Another discussion of wonder is found in the *Aesthetics.*[3] Referring again to Aristotle, Hegel broadens the context by declaring wonder to be the beginning from which art, religion, and philosophy arise; all the forms of absolute knowledge are thus said to have begun from wonder, even though their determination as absolute prescribes that they will— now, in the future perfect—have surpassed wonder. In the case of art, in particular, wonder is said to come into play in the origination of the symbolic form of art, the least developed form of art, a form that, strictly speaking, constitutes only preart (*Vorkunst*) and not yet art as such. Hegel locates wonder in the interval between a *not yet* and a *no longer.* One who does not yet wonder lives still in obtuseness and stupidity, bound to the immediate individual existence of objects, not yet free. On the other hand, one who no longer wonders has broken with such externality and has become clear about it, transforming the objects and their existence into a spiritual and self-conscious insight into them. Wonder occurs in the interval where one has already separated oneself from the most immediate, purely practical relation to nature, that of desire, where one thus stands back and seeks in things something universal, implicit (*Ansichseiendes*), and permanent. At this stage things remain other, an other in which one strives to find oneself again. One is conscious of them as external, natural things, and yet one has a certain awareness, a presentiment (*Ahnung*), of something higher, something spiritual. The contradiction between nature and spirit thus

---

2. *Enzyklopädie der philosophischen Wissenschaften.* Dritter Teil: Die Philosophie des Geistes. *Werke* (Frankfurt a.M.: Suhrkamp, 1970), 10:255. The passage cited occurs in the Zusatz to §449.
3. *Ästhetik,* 1:309–10.

embodied in natural things renders them both attractive and repulsive. It is this feeling of the contradiction along with the urge to resolve it that generates wonder. Within this interval of wonder art has the form of symbol. When developed independently and in its proper form, it has also the character of sublimity.[4]

But only within the interval. When the classical form of art, art proper, comes upon the scene, then the symbol, the sublime, and wonder itself will have been surpassed. In the presence of Greek sculpture there will no longer have been any wonder in play.

In the future perfect of philosophy and of art, hardly a trace of wonder is still to be found. And yet, even a trace may make one hesitant to join in putting an end to wonder. Or rather, it may prompt a reversal in which one would submit the end to wonder, bringing wonder to bear upon that very end that would have alleged to bring it to an end. Now, opening wonder to the future.

(c)

" . . . provoked by the mixing-up
of opposites. . . . "

Being and Logos

The Platonic discourse on wonder occurs in the *Theaetetus*. This is the only Platonic dialogue that is doubly written: it is authored not only by Plato but also, except for the introductory conversation, by Euclides of Megara. One function of the introductory conversation is to betray the double authorship: Euclides relates to Terpsion that he had once gone to Athens and heard from Socrates himself an account of the latter's conversation with Theaetetus; Euclides goes on to tell that, upon returning to Megara, he wrote down some reminders of the conversation and that subsequently as he recalled things he wrote them down, checking with Socrates on subsequent visits to Athens so as to fill out what he could not remember. He concludes: "So nearly the whole discourse has been written by me" (*Theaet.* 142d). Euclides shows Terpsion the resulting book (βιβλίον) and explains how he composed it, transforming it from a dialogue narrated by Socrates into one directly

---

4. Ibid., 1:298.

presented. That transformation will not only, as Euclides says, have eliminated the tedious repetition of such phrases as "and I said"; it will also have eliminated whatever Socrates may have reported about the conversation other than the actual speeches. Thus, Euclides' book, doubling the Socratic narrative, is different from it (and not only by virtue of the difference between speech and writing). Euclides' book is also different from Plato's, though only by virtue of the addition of the introductory conversation. As for the conversation between Socrates and Theaetetus, its inscription is one and the same in both books. In the dialogue the inscription is framed as doubly authored.

The entire dialogue can be read as a discourse on wonder, gathered around a single passage in which wonder is identified as the beginning of philosophy. The entire dialogue is framed by occurrences of forms of the word, both in the final speech by Socrates and at the outset, in the response to Euclides' opening question about Terpsion's arrival from the country: Terpsion explains that he arrived some time ago and that he has been wondering (ἐθαύμαζον) that he could not find Euclides in the marketplace. A brief report on his recent whereabouts leads up to Euclides' account of his authorship of the book from which will be read the conversation between Socrates and Theaetetus. Euclides tells of going down to the harbor (εἰς λιμένα καταβαίνων); as in the opening speech of the *Republic* Socrates had told of going down to Piraeus (κατέβην . . . εἰς Πειραιᾶ), the harbor of Athens; as Odysseus had told of how he "went down [κατέβην] to Hades to inquire about the return of myself and my friends" (*Odyssey* 23.252–53). There Euclides met Theaetetus, wounded and suffering from dysentery, being carried from the army camp at Corinth to Athens. A little later Euclides will tell of how he accompanied Theaetetus part of the way from Megara to Athens, as far as Erineos, situated on the Cephisus River, also said to have been the place where Persephone was snatched away by Hades.[5]

When Euclides reports that Theaetetus has been praised for his conduct in the battle, Terpsion responds that it would have been more to be wondered (θαυμαστότερον) had he not so conducted himself. Euclides reports his own wonder: as he was returning from Erineos, having accompanied Theaetetus, he recalled and wondered (ἐθαύμασα) at Socrates, at how prophetically (μαντικῶς) the latter had spoken of Theaetetus. Socrates,

---

5. See *The Being of the Beautiful: Plato's Theaetetus, Sophist, and Statesman*, translated and with commentary by Seth Benardete (Chicago: University of Chicago Press, 1984), I. 184.

says Euclides, had met Theaetetus a little before his own death and on the basis of conversation with the young Theaetetus had expressed great admiration for the lad. The conversation is the one that Euclides goes on to report having written down in the book, which is now to be read to Euclides and Terpsion by another, unnamed boy.

Theaetetus proves to be a double of Socrates, closely resembling him in appearance (with his snub nose and protruding eyes), just as the young Socrates (mentioned at 147c–d), who remains silent throughout, is his double in λόγος. Telling Socrates of Theaetetus just before the lad arrives on the scene, Theodorus praises him as being wonderfully fine (θαυμαστῶς εὖ), as one who advances in learning as a stream of olive oil flows without a sound; one wonders (θαυμάσαι) that someone of his age conducts himself in such fashion. Thus is wonder gathered around Theaetetus. Before he ever appears in the dialogue, one knows that he is wondrous.

And yet, as the book in which the conversation is inscribed is being read, Theaetetus is dying. The inscribed conversation takes place not only under the shadow of the impending death of Theaetetus but also under that of the death of Socrates. Euclides has reported that the conversation took place a little before Socrates' death; indeed the conversation ends with Socrates' telling that he must go to the porch of the king to meet the indictment drawn up by Meletus. Thus, as regards its dramatic date, the *Theaetetus*—or, more precisely, the conversation inscribed in it between Socrates and Theaetetus—is the first in that series of dialogues that lead up to the death of Socrates.

Nonetheless, these shadows of death serve to accentuate the opposite, the expectancy of birth and the flowering of youth that inform the conversation between Socrates and Theaetetus. The conversation brings back the dying Theaetetus, brings him back in the vigor of his youth. It also brings on the scene a young Socrates, who silently doubles a Socrates brought back from his death. In the conversation as read to Euclides and Terpsion, both Socrates and Theaetetus, thus brought back from death, are reborn in a conversation devoted largely to birth, especially to the birth of philosophy.

For the question that Socrates asks Theaetetus, "What is knowledge [ἐπιστήμη]?" it suffices neither merely to number (ἀριθμῆσαι) the various forms, to collect them in an enumeration of types, nor to divide, as Theodorus and Theaetetus had divided the numbers into square and oblong. He must, rather, says Socrates, try to address the many knowledges with one discourse (λόγος). Or rather, Theaetetus must try to give birth to such a discourse; for, as Socrates tells him in response to his plea of incapacity, "you're suffering labor pains, on account of your not being empty but pregnant" (148e). Socrates, the midwife ready to assist him, thus launches on his own discourse describing his peculiar art. It is a wonderful art that this son of a midwife practices, also an art over which the Socratic daimon exercises a certain authority. The greatest thing (μέγιστον) in this art is that it can test whether the thought of a young man is giving birth to an image and a lie (εἴδωλον καὶ ψεῦδος) or to something fruitful and true (γόνιμόν τε καὶ ἀληθές). Socrates declares that those who associate with him and receive the benefits of his art make wonderful (θαυμαστόν) progress. Many of these, he observes, thinking they alone are responsible and even despising him, have departed earlier than they should have, only to suffer abortion or to rear badly what Socrates had midwifed. Recognizing their foolishness, they have often returned to Socrates, begging for renewed association and doing wondrous (θαυμαστά) things; whereupon, says Socrates, "the daimon that comes to me checks me from associating with some and allows me to associate with some" (151a).

Theaetetus is quickly delivered: he declares that knowledge is nothing else than perception or sensing (αἴσθησις).

Socrates sets to work determining whether the declaration is fruitful or only a wind-egg. He refers indeed to the wind, applying to it the maxim of Protagoras that man is the measure of all things, observing thus that the same wind may be cold to one person and not cold to another. He continues: sensing is always the sensing of something that is (τοῦ ὄντος), of something existent that appears (φαίνεται) to sensing. Because, according to Theaetetus, sensing is knowledge, it cannot be false. The consequence can be foreseen: such sensing as knowledge, such sense-knowledge, must be knowledge of things that truly are, knowledge of them in their truth. Yet—most remarkably—Socrates foregoes saying that the wind is in truth both cold and not cold, invoking the Graces instead of declaring openly such mixing of opposites, invoking the Graces and then charging Protagoras with having put forth enigmas while reserving the truth for his pupils.

Theaetetus' response is most telling: "How, then, are you saying this, Socrates?" (152d). The response may of course be taken as a request that Socrates explain what his reference to Protagoras' esoteric teaching only suggests. Yet, it may also be taken to refer back to the consequence that Socrates left unsaid; for what Socrates goes on to say in the uncommon discourse that immediately follows is precisely how one says the mixing (κρᾶσις) of opposites. Again it is a matter of birth, of a birth attested to by a great line of philosophers and poets (including Protagoras, Heraclitus, Empedocles, Epicharmus, Homer and excluding only one philosopher, Parmenides): the birth of all things from flow and motion. Thus it is that nothing is one itself by itself (ἕν . . . αὐτὸ καθ᾽ αὐτό). Socrates continues: "But if you address it as large, it will also appear small, and if heavy, light . . ." (152d). It is not as though the opposites simply appear mixed with one another such that something is then said, for example, to be both large and small. Such is precisely the kind of saying that Socrates has left unsaid. Rather, the mixing of opposites comes to light precisely in and through discourse: if you *address* it as large, it will also appear small. Even its appearing small cannot, given the flow of all things, be independent of discourse and of the determinacy (the being one itself by itself) that discourse puts into effect. It is in discourse that the determinate opposition is constituted, and thus it is only in relation to discourse that the mixing of opposites can become manifest as such.

Extending the discussion, Socrates remarks finally to Theaetetus: "We're being compelled somehow to say recklessly some wondrous and laughable things [θαυμαστά τε καὶ γελοῖα], as Protagoras would say and everyone who tries to say the same as he does" (154b). What is wondrous and laughable is (to say) that one cannot say the same, that there is no same to be said, or rather, that sameness (being one itself by itself) belongs only to saying. And yet, for that reason the mixing-up of opposites in discourse is even more wondrous. As in the paradigm that Socrates offers in response to Theaetetus' query: the six dice that are more than four and less than twelve—that, therefore, not only are both more and less but also can become more without being increased. Theaetutus' response is now itself mixed, both affirming and denying the mixing that Socrates has posed. When Socrates goes on to elaborate the conflict, Theaetetus finally responds by confessing his wonder: "Yes indeed, by the gods, Socrates, I wonder exceedingly [ὑπερφυῶς . . . θαυμάζω] as to what these things are, and sometimes in looking at them I get truly dizzy" (155c). Thus is Theaetetus wonderstruck by what must and yet cannot be said in reference to the mixing-up of opposites. Thus is his wonder provoked by the mixing-up of opposites. One can imagine even the look of wonder on his Socratic face; one can imagine even that in the account that Euclides heard Socrates give of the conversation there may well have been reference to the appearance of wonder in the protruding eyes of Theaetetus; but Euclides' manner of composing his book (double-authored with Plato) subordinates everything to discourse, lets things appear only in relation to discourse, thus enacting precisely what it says.

Socrates remarks that Theodorus' guess about Theaetetus' nature—that it is philosophic—is not a bad one, since the pathos of wonder (τὸ πάθος, τὸ θαυμάζειν) is very much that of a philosopher: "for nothing else is the beginning [ἀρχή] of philosophy than this, and, seemingly, whoever said that Iris was the offspring of Thaumas made a not bad genealogy" (155d). One who said this was of course Hesiod: according to his genealogy Thaumas married Electra, and among their offspring was Iris (*Theogony* 265–66). If one takes the names for what they say, then one may say: The rainbow (Iris) is the offspring of wonder (Thaumas) and shining (Electra). Furthermore, both Thaumas and Electra are linked genealogically to Ocean and Tethys;[6] earlier in the conversation, in that uncommon discourse in which Socrates marshalled the great line of philosophers and poets, Homer's saying "Ocean and mother Tethys, the genesis of the gods" is interpreted as saying that everything is the offspring of flowing and motion (152e). Hence, in the beginning there is flowing and motion; and then, born therefrom, if not directly, there is wonder and shining (that is, appearing to sense). There is, as in Theaetetus, the wonder provoked by the appearance of a mixing-up of opposites. The offspring of Thaumas (wonder) is the rainbow and philosophy. Not only this, but also the determination of wonder as the beginning of philosophy is presented as confirmation of the genealogy by which the rainbow is the offspring of wonder.

What does philosophy have to do with the rainbow? Iris is a messenger of the gods to men, and it is this vocation that is evoked in the *Cratylus*: "Iris [Ἶρις] also seems to have received her name from εἴρειν [to speak], because she is a messenger" (*Crat.* 408b). Both philosophy and the rainbow have to do with discourse; for instance, with the discursive distinction between the different colors that blend into one another in the shining rainbow that joins heaven and earth.

Homer speaks of "rainbows that the son of Chronos has set in the clouds, a portent for man" (*Iliad* 11.27–28). A portent (τέρας) is a sign, a marvel, something wonderful that serves as an omen; it may be even some wondrous creature, a monster (Latin: *monstrum*). As in Theaetetus (and perhaps in every philosophic nature) there is a bit of monstros-

---

6. Ibid., I. 107.

ity: for it is Theaetetus' nature to wonder exceedingly (ὑπερφυῶς); it is his nature to exceed nature.

Yet, the rainbow is not merely a sign sent from heaven to earth but rather is such that in being sent it spans and thus discloses in its openness the very space across which it is sent, that between earth and sky, between the abode of mortals and that reserved for immortal gods. As philosophy, beginning in the discourse of wonder, opens the space between that which appears to sense and that which is said (that is, set forth in and through discourse).

The opening of philosophy is traced perhaps most directly in a discussion between Socrates and Glaucon in Book 7 of the *Republic*.[7] Socrates focuses on those sensings that are such as to provoke thought (νόησις), calling them those that at once (ἅμα) go over to the opposite. Again it is a matter of such mixing-up of opposites as is shown in the *Theaetetus* to provoke wonder and thus the beginning of philosophy. Now the example is that of three fingers: the index finger, which appears large in relation to the smallest finger but which appears small in relation to the middle finger, so that in the index finger there is a mixing-up of large and small. What is required is an opening in which the mixture can be sorted out. Here is the discussion of that sorting:

> "Therefore," I said, "it's likely that in such cases a soul, summoning calculation [λογισμός] and intellection [νόησις], first tries to determine whether each of the things reported to it is one or two."
> "Of course."
> "If it appears to be two, won't each of the two appear to be different and to be one?"
> "Yes."
> "Then, if each is one and both two, the soul will think the two as separate. For it would not think the inseparable as two but as one."
> "Right."
> "But sight, too, saw large and small, we say, not separated, however, but mixed up together. Isn't that so?"
> "Yes."
> "In order to clear this up the intellect was compelled to see large and small, too, not mixed up together but distinguished, doing the opposite of what the sight did." (*Rep.* 524b–c)

---

7. I have discussed this passage in detail and in context in *Being and Logos: The Way of Platonic Dialogue*, 2nd ed. (Atlantic Highlands: Humanities Press, 1986), 428–31.

Thus, it is a matter of a distinguishing that separates the mixture into distinct "ones," taking what *large* says and what *small* says, taking each by itself, taking each as being itself one by itself. And then, it is a matter of posing—or rather, of already having posed and now only enforcing—these "ones" (the large and the small) in their distinctness (each being itself one by itself) over against the mixture; it is a matter of spacing, of letting a space open between these "ones" and the mixing-up of opposites that appears to sense.

Socrates says: "And it was thus that we called the one intelligible [νοητόν] and the other visible [ὁρατόν]" (524c). Thus philosophy opens. Thus it begins in the Platonic beginning. Provoked by the mixing-up of opposites, philosophy begins from wonder.

(d)

"Nothing escapes the play . . . , the
play of indeterminate dyads."

The Gathering of Reason

Not only in the beginning but also now, in the end, in the future perfect, wonder will have remained the beginning.

Thus one returns to wonder in the end, returns again finally to the beginning, putting the end to wonder, or rather, letting the end be provocative, letting it provoke wonder, or rather—one suspects—reawaken wonder from its metaphysical slumber.

For the end is that which has been called the end of metaphysics. No doubt a great deal of caution is required if this phrase is to be used in a rigorous discourse. One must distinguish the relevant sense of end from others that have been posed for—and by—metaphysics: most notably, that by which the end would consist in a gathering of metaphysics into its fulfillment; and, all too symmetrically opposed to this, the sense that would make of the end of metaphysics its mere termination. In every case one must be attentive also to the slippage to which the sense of end is exposed in the end of metaphysics, since it is within metaphysics that the sense(s) of end (to say nothing of the sense(s) of sense) will have been determined. One must also hold in a certain suspension the assumption of homogeneity that would otherwise be put in play by discourse on the end of metaphysics—that is, one will need to leave the name suspended between singular and plural. Nonetheless, whatever the extent of the pluralizing heterogeneity, the Platonic beginning remains decisive. Metaphysics—whether singular, plural, or both—will always have begun with the opening between intelligible and sensible. Even if this beginning remains largely unrecalled, metaphysics circulates within the space thus opened; and insofar as it assumes that space, taking the opening for granted, it is authorized to put an end to wonder. For wonder, provoked by the mixing-up of opposites, is what first draws one into the opening. It is as such that wonder is the beginning of philosophy.

But what is wonder? The question comes too late. For when one comes to ask the philosophical question "What is . . . ?" ("τί ἐστι . . . ?"), one moves already within the opening and wonder has already come into play in prompting that opening. The operation of wonder belongs to the very condition of the question "What is wonder?"; and one will never be able simply to disengage that question from the wonder about which it would ask. One will never be able to interrogate wonder philosophically except by way of a questioning that the operation of wonder will already have determined. To say nothing of all the means that philosophy would bring into play in response to the question, in declaring wonder to be, for instance, a passion of the soul, in assimilating it, for instance, to intuition.

The end of metaphysics inhibits the question even more. For this end brings, in Nietzsche's formula, the final inversion of Platonism, the inversion which constitutes the final possibility of metaphysics, the possibility which announces the exhaustion of all possibilities of circulating within the space of the Platonic opening. Once—in Nietzsche's phrase—the true world finally becomes a fable, once what was called the intelligible drifts away further and further and finally without limit, rendering the space of metaphysics unlimited, or rather, reducing it again to the plane of sense, then the very resources that would enable the question are themselves put into question, set adrift. And yet, one is then drawn back to the place of wonder, to the place where, in a discourse addressed to the mixing-up within what came to be called the sensible, wonder was in the beginning provoked.

Let it, then, be said: the end of metaphysics brings a return to wonder, prompts a return of wonder.

Yet, the provocation of wonder at the end, of a wonder that would be the beginning of a thinking at the limit of metaphysics, would not be quite the same as in the beginning. One would of course be drawn back toward the discursively articulated mixing-up of sensible opposites. And yet, precisely because the discourse in relation to which the mixing-up would appear to sense is nothing other than the discourse fashioned and empowered by the history of metaphysics, that discourse cannot but effect the double separation, that between opposites and that between the mixed-up sensible opposites and the distinct intelligible opposites. It is a discourse that *means* something, a discourse that in its very operation is taken to mean something, to exceed what appears to sense, to open the difference between meaning and sense, between two different senses of sense. Even if in the end of metaphysics meaning is set utterly adrift, language does not cease to mark the difference that two millenia of shaping and theorizing have taught it to mark. Inasmuch as one continues to speak the language of metaphysics—is there any other?—one continues to exceed the plane of sense, opening the difference that is bespoken by the ambiguity in the word *sense*, the gigantic difference within *sense*.

What now cannot but provoke wonder is the γιγαντομαχία into which one is thus drawn. For the end of metaphysics brings a double effacement of that which would be opposed to the sensible (that is, to what has been called the sensible). On the one hand, the intelligible is effaced as original, as independent of its sensible imagings and as governing such imagings. Now there will be no preventing its becoming in turn an image, if not in a simple reversal then at least in a perhaps unlimited chain of pairs, related as image/original without any final anchoring in an original as such that would be itself immune to the play of imaging. On the other hand, the intelligible is effaced as meaning, or, more precisely, as pre-established meaning such as would antedate discourse, as a transcendental signified that would precede and govern from without the play of signifiers.

However much meaningful discourse drives one beyond sense, the intelligible can no longer be released from the play of discourse and sense and posited over against that play, aloof from it. The dyads cannot be submitted to final determination by reference to a term that would no longer be itself determined by dyadic linkage. Thus would wonder be provoked at the end of metaphysics: wonder at the play of the indeterminately dyadic, wonder at the gigantic opening within the word *sense*.

One could also call it poetic wonder, provided *poetic* is either diverted toward what Jacques Derrida calls *invention* or referred back to the ποίησις that Heidegger sought to preserve in advance of its determination as production (*Herstellung*). It is a matter of wonder at the power of the sense image to bring forth its original and of discourse to bring forth meaning, to bring forth in the double (one would have said, at least, almost contradictory) sense of both first giving place to (letting take place) *and yet* uncovering as already there (not simply produced). It is a matter of wonder at a bringing-forth that is both inaugural and memorial—like remembrance. One could call it a wonder of imagination.

(e)

" . . . to *hover* between heaven and
earth, . . . "

Delimitations

Can wonder be provoked still more archaically? Can it be provoked by what one might call still—even in the end of metaphysics—the ἀρχή: neither an intelligible nor *the* intelligible nor even the beginning of the intelligible, but rather the opening, the openness, within which sense could be exceeded and dyads brought into play? Such wonder would be in place before one could come to address something *as* something, for instance, to address as large what then would appear small, such that a mixing of opposites would become manifest, provoking the wonder at the beginning of philosophy. Archaic wonder would also be in place before discourse could exceed sense and broach the opening, setting in play the dyads that, even in the end of metaphysics, still would provoke wonder. Such archaic wonder would be, not just the beginning of philosophy (in its beginning or in its end and transmutation), but rather a beginning that would precede philosophy, a turning toward the beginning in which the very space of philosophy would open. The place of such wonder would be the very unfolding of place as such, the spacing of the ἀρχή, archaic spacing.

Heidegger attests to a wonder that, like such archaic wonder, would not simply stand at the beginning of philosophy. Referring to a wonder that, instead, would sustain and in a sense govern philosophy throughout, he writes: "To say that philosophy arises from wonder means [*heisst*]: it *is* essentially something wondrous and becomes more wondrous the more it becomes what it is."[8]

---

8. *Grundfragen der Philosophie: Ausgewählte 'Probleme' der 'Logik', GA* 45: 163.

In *What Is Philosophy?* Heidegger refers to the πάθος of wonder (*Erstaunen*) and translates πάθος as *Stimmung* or *dis-position*, proposing thereby to avoid understanding it in the modern psychological sense. Wonder (θαυμάζειν) he then characterizes as a stepping back in the face of beings ("Wir treten gleichsam zurück vor dem Seienden"), a stepping back that becomes attentive to beings, that they *are* and that they are *so* and not otherwise. Thus to step back is at once to be also transported to and bound by that before which one has stepped back. Wonder is, hence, the "dis-position in which and for which the Being of beings opens up."[9]

In the lecture course of 1937–38 *Basic Questions of Philosophy*, Heidegger discusses wonder at much greater length. Again he regards wonder as *Stimmung*, taking the latter as a displacement (*Versetzung*) by which one is brought into a fundamental relation to beings as such. Wonder (θαυμάζειν—now Heidegger writes it: *das Er-staunen*) is the fundamental attunement (*Grundstimmung*) that—at least for the Greeks—was the origin of philosophy. Heidegger carefully distinguishes wonder from a variety of related forms of attunement: surprise (*Sichwundern, Verwundern*), in which one is struck by something out of the ordinary; admiration (*Bewundern*), in which one frees oneself, sets oneself over against, the extraordinary thing or event by which one is struck; astonishment (*Staunen, Bestaunen*), in which one is thrown back by the extraordinary. Wonder, Heidegger insists, is essentially different from these forms; for in all three of them there is a determinate individual thing, something extraordinary, that is set off, contrasted, with the things of ordinary experience. In wonder, on the other hand, "the most ordinary becomes itself the most extraordinary" (*GA* 45: 166). Everything becomes extraordinary (*GA* 45: 174), and one is displaced into the utter unfamiliarity of the familiar, into an inverted world.[10] Yet, what is most ordinary is simply that which is, beings; and what is extraordinary about them is that they *are*. Wonder, says Heidegger, brings the most ordinary

---

9. *Was Ist Das—Die Philosophie?* (Pfullingen: Günther Neske, 1956), 26.

10. This formulation comes from Eugen Fink: "What breaks out in wonder . . . is an unfamiliarity of the familiar. . . . In wonder the world is inverted [*verkehrt sich die Welt*]" (*Einleitung in die Philosophie*, ed. Franz-A. Schwartz [Würzburg: Königshausen & Neumann, 1985], 19). Klaus Held has also taken up these discussions and described differently the transformation that the world undergoes in wonder: for the wonderer the world comes forth as though emerging for him for the first time, as though it were completely new and utterly surprising. In its reflective moment, Held adds, wonder lets one experience oneself as though one were a newborn child. (See "Fundamental Moods and Heidegger's Critique of Contemporary Culture," in *Reading Heidegger: Commemorations*, ed. J. Sallis [Bloomington: Indiana University Press, 1993], esp. 298–300).

forth in such a way that it announces its extraordinariness, shines forth as extraordinary. Wonder attends to the outbreak of the extraordinariness of the ordinary. Wonder, says Heidegger, opens to what is "uniquely wondrous, namely: the whole as the whole, the whole as being [*als das Seiende*], beings as a whole [*das Seiende im Ganzen*], *that* they *are what* they *are*; beings *as* beings, *ens qua ens*, τὸ ὄν ᾗ ὄν." He adds: "What is named here by the *as*, the *qua*, the ᾗ, is the 'between' thrown open in wonder, the open space . . . in which beings as such come into play, namely, as the beings *they* are, into the *play of their Being* [Spiel seines Seins]" (*GA* 45: 168–69).

In a sense, then, Heidegger ventures to say what wonder is: not, however, by submitting it to the philosophical question of *what* it *is*, but rather by situating it, delimiting its place, with respect to the very shining forth of the *is*, by bringing out its attunement to the very opening of the *as* of beings *as* beings. Thus, in spite of all that he says of wonder, Heidegger can also insist that such wondrous displacement withdraws as such from explanation, from analysis of the sort that would resolve it into various components. If one can in a sense say what wonder is, one can do so only through a *Wiederholung*, only by "a reproject [*Rückentwurf*] of the simplicity [*Einfachheit*] and strangeness *of that displacement* of man into beings as such, which takes place [*sich ereignet*] as wonder, which remains just as incomprehensible as the beginning [*Anfang*] to which it is bound" (*GA* 45: 171).

One could think archaic wonder only in the return to it, only in a certain doubling back to its place as that of the opening of beings as such. It is a matter, then, of how the opening is to be thought, or, more precisely, a matter of that *from which* the opening is to be thought, a matter of that from which the spacing of the ἀρχή would take place. No doubt it is to be thought, as Heidegger insists, from beings *as* beings. Then one may, extending the project of fundamental ontology, undertake to think the space in which beings come into the play of their Being—that is, to think what would be called *Temporalität, Lichtung, Ereignis*, to think (the) beyond (of) Being (ἐπέκεινα τῆς οὐσίας), as did also Plato. Or one may insist on pairing such a project with another, with one that would be attentive to the eruption of questioning from out of beings as a whole; a project that in adhering to beings *as* beings would in the end be no project at all but rather a return to thrownness, a *Wiederholung* of the thrownness of the project (as in metontology, to recall the most striking title that Heidegger gave it).

And yet, beings as beings always also—from the beginning, before every beginning—*appear to sense*; the opening is always also an opening within what one can call (twisting it free of the metaphysical opposition): *the sensible*. Is archaic spacing not, then, to be thought from the sensible? Is it not in the opening from and within the sensible that archaic wonder has its place? *From and within* the sensible—a spacing that would trace within the sensible the opening from the sensible, the opening in which the sensible would be exceeded, either in the metaphysical opposition of intelligible to sensible or in the play of indeterminate dyads that commences in the end of metaphysics. From and within the sensible—just as the word *sense*, which comes to be divided from itself (divided into two different senses of sense—an abysmal division, presupposing itself), is nonetheless divided within itself, enclosing the gigantic space in which both imaging and discourse have their place.

One would return, then, to a wonder placed at an opening from and within the sensible, an opening that in a sense—in *sense* itself, if there could be sense *itself*—would precede even the play of beings in their Being, a foreplay, a prelude, as with Wordsworth:

> As if awakened, summoned, roused, constrained,
> I looked for universal things; perused
> The common countenance of earth and sky.
>   ("The Prelude," 3: 105-7)

One would return, then, to a wonder whose place would be to hover, like a dove, between heaven and earth, open to the wondrous shining of the rainbow that joins earth and sky even while setting them apart. Then one might abandon oneself to the wondrous sights and sounds of earth and sky and, in Emerson's sense, draw a new circle, a circle that would open upon everything that could be said or that could appear to sense:

> The one thing which we seek with insatiable desire, is to forget ourselves, to be surprised out of our propriety, to lose our sempiternal memory, and to do something without knowing how or why; in short, to draw a new circle. Nothing great was ever achieved without enthusiasm. The way of life is wonderful: it is by abandonment.[11]

---

11. "Circles," in *The Essays of Ralph Waldo Emerson* (Cambridge: Harvard University Press, 1987), 190.

Index

313558